SEX AND DEATH ON THE WESTERN EMIGRANT TRAIL

SEX AND DEATH ON THE WESTERN EMIGRANT TRAIL

The Biology of Three American Tragedies

Donald K. Grayson

The University of Utah Press | Salt Lake City

The Defiance House Man colophon is a registered trademark of the University of Utah Press. It is based on a four-foot-tall Ancient Puebloan pictograph (late PIII) near Glen Canyon, Utah.

Library of Congress Cataloging-in-Publication Data

Names: Grayson, Donald K., author.
Title: Sex and death on the western emigrant trail : the biology of three American tragedies / Donald K. Grayson.
Description: Salt Lake City : University of Utah Press, [2017] | Includes bibliographical references and index.
Identifiers: LCCN 2017037702 (print) | LCCN 2017041871 (ebook) | ISBN 9781607816027 () | ISBN 9781607816010 | ISBN 9781607816010?q(pbk.)
Subjects: LCSH: Overland journeys to the Pacific. | Donner Party. | James G. Willie Emigrating Company. | Edward Martin Emigrating Company. | Biometry. | Mortality—Sex differences. | Mortality—Statistics. | Disaster victims—West (U.S.) | Mormon pioneers—United States—History—19th century. | Mormon handcart companies.
Classification: LCC F593 (ebook) | LCC F593 .G74 2017 (print) | DDC 978/.02—dc23
LC record available at https://lccn.loc.gov/2017037702

Printed and bound in the U.S.A.

For Heidi,
whose ancestors made the overland journey
to Oregon in 1844, guided by Joseph Walker

Fliegt heim, ihr Raben!
Raunt es eurem Herren,
was hier am Rhein ihr gehört!
  —Götterdämmerung

Fly home, you ravens,
and tell your Master
what you have learned
on the Rhine today.
  —Götterdämmerung

CONTENTS

LIST OF ILLUSTRATIONS

LIST OF TABLES

ACKNOWLEDGMENTS

Many thanks to all the friends and colleagues who have made insightful comments on various aspects of my work in this area over the years—in particular, Kristine M. Bovy, Lyndia Carter, Dan Eisenberg, Lee Ann Kreutzer, David B. Madsen, Evelyn Seelinger, and Gary Topping. Thanks as well to Mike Caputi and Marcos Llobera for critical technical help and to Ken Hickman for his photographic skills (Figure 3.3). My initial work on the handcart companies was done with the support of the History Department Library, Church of Jesus Christ of Latter-day Saints, and especially Melvin L. Bashore, then senior librarian. Very special thanks to Reba Rauch of the University of Utah Press for her help at every stage of this project and for her support of everyone interested in the Desert West; to Diane Bush for her heroic editing efforts; to Heidi Lennstrom for her insightful reading of two drafts of this manuscript; and to Will Bagley and Dennis O'Rourke, whose critical comments on this work are deeply appreciated.

1

AN INTRODUCTION TO SEX, DEATH, AND DISASTER

"Never take no cutofs and hury along as fast as you can," advised 13-year-old Virginia Reed after her ordeal as a member of the Donner Party had finally ended.[1] She and the rest of her family survived, but 39 others were not so fortunate.

Virtually all Americans have heard of the Donner Party. They are famous not simply because so many of them lost their lives but because most who died were cannibalized. Those who participated in the cannibalism—and that probably includes all who survived—were at first horrified by what they were doing. Not surprisingly, people safe at home were scandalized by this behavior. The Donner Party has had immediate name recognition ever since.

This might be the most famous group of mid-19th-century overland emigrants to lose many of its members to severe cold and starvation on its way west, but it is not the only one. Exactly 10 years after the Donner Party's troubles, two large groups sponsored by the Church of Jesus Christ of Latter-day Saints (LDS, the Mormon Church) ran into very similar difficulties, and many of their members died as well. These people were following a well-traveled path, but they were doing it in a novel way—transporting their goods, and often their children, in handcarts they pushed and pulled some 1,300 miles from Iowa City, Iowa, to Salt Lake City, Utah.

There are many reasons why these two handcart companies may not be nearly as well known as the Donner Party. A smaller proportion of them died, most of them were impoverished European emigrants who had chosen to join what was then a controversial religion, and the Mormon Church did not wish the full facts of the tragedy to be generally known.[2] In addition, the handcarters did not resort to cannibalism.

The histories of these groups have been told by different peoples in different ways.[3] Although I will summarize some necessary history here, my goals are not historical. Instead, I hope to show that the patterns of who lived and who died in these three groups of very unfortunate travelers can be explained by human biology. I argue that three prime factors—age, sex, and family ties—can explain not only the general patterns of mortality and survivorship in these groups but also such relatively minor matters as who attempted to escape on their own and who did not. Not all of what follows will be fun reading, but what happened to these people helps get at the core of who and what we all are.

SOME PERSONAL BACKGROUND

One of the most frequent questions I have been asked by those who are familiar with my studies of the relationship between human biology and mortality in nineteenth-century emigrant groups is how I became interested in this topic in the first place. Since I have been asked this question so often, I answer it here.

I am an archaeologist who studies the ways people interact with their environments, and how their impacts on those environments, in turn, change the lives of the people themselves. I have also done a good deal of fieldwork in remote places. The crews that help with this work almost always include men and women, often in similar numbers. Far more often than not things go well, but on occasion things go wrong. Over the years, these rare experiences of things gone wrong add up.

I began to realize that there are patterns to the responses that people make in these settings. Get a truck stuck or blow a tire or two in the middle of nowhere, and it is generally the men who rush to fix the problem while the women watch. But if the problem can't be fixed and you are stuck for substantial amounts of time, it is the men who take it the worst. They tend to become crabby, sullen, and annoyed. The women often react far more productively, primarily by taking everything in stride. This is not true of all the men or women with whom I have worked and gotten stuck, but it is true of the majority of them. It is as if the men excel at things that require strength, risk, and short-term aggressive behavior while the women excel at things that provide longer-term cohesiveness.

These are hardly novel insights. The popular literature on the differences between American men and women is full of such observations, and, as I will discuss in Chapter 3, important scientific literature exists in this area as well. My field experience did, however, make me wonder how men and women react when they are stuck enough to have their very existence threatened. Once I began to wonder about that, I decided to read accounts of groups of men and women in those kinds of situations. Because I work in the deserts of western North America, my reading focused on classic accounts of those who ran into serious trouble in the areas I know so well.

I began with *Death Valley in '49*, written by William Lewis Manly and published in 1894.[4] This classic tale concerns a small group of men, women, and children who decided, in the face of good advice to the contrary, to take a shortcut across southern Nevada to reach California. They ended up in one of the driest places on earth, though since they arrived there in winter, they did not have to contend with the debilitating heat that Death Valley can offer. Two of the men in the group—William Lewis Manly and John Haney Rogers—volunteered to walk out, find help, and return. In their book on the routes that the emigrants followed, LeRoy and Jean Johnson tell us that the trip from Bennetts Well in Death Valley (the Bennetts were one of the families in the stranded group) to Rancho San Francisco in southern California covered 270 miles and took twenty-six days.[5] The two men returned with pack animals and supplies and led those who had waited to safety. The only member of this group who died—Richard Culverwell—had left early. Those who waited survived and arrived at Rancho San Francisco on March 7, 1850.

I read this tale, and the Johnsons' retelling of it, as a result of my observation that, in my field projects that had gone awry, men tended to provide the muscle and took the physical risks, while women tended to provide the psychic glue that helped hold the group together. I expected to see that the same thing happened in Death Valley in 1849, but the story as Manly told it was relatively uninformative on this score. Two of the men did take the biggest risk—walking 270 miles to reach help and then returning to rescue their friends—but no evidence one way or the other showed that the men and women involved provided different amounts of psychic glue during the trip.

What struck me as I read about the experiences of these particular forty-niners was that while my thoughts—about men and risk on the one hand and women and psychic glue on the other—were not likely to be of particular value above and beyond my reading some interesting history, a thread here was worth pursuing.

I knew enough about human biology to know that when emigrant groups consisting of males and females of differing ages got into such serious trouble that numbers of them died, death should strike preferentially at the males and at the old and young, with family membership also playing a role in determining who survived and who died. I started reading *Death Valley in '49* as an amateur historian, but after I finished, I decided that these kinds of episodes merited more rigorous analysis and that much could be learned if we approached significant pieces of the story of western emigration not as history but as biology. I report the results of that analysis here.

SEX AND GENDER

In their discussion of the two published accounts that Manly wrote of his Death Valley experience, the Johnsons note that certain things changed between the earliest serialized account in 1888 and the 1894 book. For instance, in the first version, when referring to the trail taken across the Mojave Desert, Manly wrote, "the ground was very soft and light as snuff." In the second version, the trail was now composed of "dirt finer than the finest flour." This change, the Johnsons infer, reflects "a decidedly feminine touch."[6] They conclude, from this and other evidence, that a woman assisted Manly in writing the 1894 book.

In this, the Johnsons inferred the sex of Manly's hidden editor from the behavior of that editor. This is the difference between gender and sex. *Gender* refers to behaviors considered appropriate to males and females in a given society—analogies to snuff or flour, perhaps, in the nineteenth century. *Sex* refers to the biological status—whether male or female—of the people involved.

I observe this for a number of reasons. First, the word *gender* is often used in place of *sex*, as if the term *sex* is somehow embarrassing or offensive and is to be avoided at all costs. Thus, one can read about the gender of birds in scientific articles, when all that is meant is that the birds are either male or female, which is sex. Take, for instance, an article whose first sentence reads "gender determinations can be performed in sexually monomorphic birds through surgical examination."[7] Translated, the authors mean that when faced with birds of the same species that look identical to one another, one can tell whether they are girl birds or boy birds by looking inside them. This is sex, not gender.

Second, a number of people have criticized me for using the term *sex* rather than *gender* in my writings and lectures on sex and death. I have even had the titles of my talks changed, without permission, by those who thought they knew better. *Gender*, these people somehow believe, is the proper term.

In fact, it is and it isn't. Among other things, what I explore here is the relationship between a person's sex—male or female—and the chances that that person will live or die in certain challenging situations. What is fully worthy of exploration is the degree to which a person's sex influences their behavior. In Chapters 3 and 7, I discuss certain aspects of the relationships between sex and behavior, insofar as those relationships are relevant to surviving challenges of the sort I explore here. It is, though, clear that many aspects of a person's behavior are determined by their sex. Some of those behaviors—for instance, the propensity to take life-threatening risks, as Manly and Rogers did—in turn play a role in determining whether one lives or dies in such settings. But the distribution of body fat also plays a role in who lives and who dies, and this distribution is determined by sex, not gender.

Those members of Plains Indian groups called berdaches by Europeans provide a clear example of the difference. These men "donned the clothing of women, did women's work, and sometimes lived homosexually with another man. As berdaches, they were accepted by their societies and even allowed, like women, to carry scalps in the victory dance on the return of a successful war party."[8] Biologically these people were male, but their gender was female. That is the difference.

Finally, I note that my earlier work in this realm has been criticized for conflating sex and gender, as if I didn't know the difference. I have been accused of "decontextualizing" people in both time and space and ignoring the cultural determinants of human behavior.[9] I return to this issue in the last chapter, after we have seen the powerful influence of sex, age, and family ties in determining who lives and who dies in certain kinds of disaster settings. Many of the behaviors relevant to survivorship did, in fact, differ by sex—that is, they were gendered behaviors. Insofar as those gendered behaviors are determined by an individual's sex—as Wendy Wood, Alice Eagly, Shelley Taylor, and many others have argued[10]—then the best and most convenient term to use for this complex of critical attributes is *sex*. That is the term I use throughout this book.

THE STATISTICAL ANALYSES

Much of the work presented here is based on the statistical analysis of the data that I discuss. My goal in writing this book, however, is not to make my work available to statisticians, demographers, and biologists, all of whom are familiar with the techniques I have used. In the main text, I describe, as simply as I can, the results of those analyses. Details may be found in the chapter endnotes, where those interested in such things can consult them. However, in the body of the text, I routinely refer to statistical *significance*, and I need to make the meaning of that word clear.

Certain kinds of statistical techniques provide results that can be evaluated in terms of how likely it is that those results, or results even more extreme, could be due to chance. This likelihood is expressed as a probability, cleverly abbreviated "p." The concept involved can be explained with a simple example.

Let's say that you have agreed to go out to dinner every Saturday night with a friend and flip a coin to see who pays. The first night, you pick heads and lose. The probability of this happening is 1/2, or 0.50. No big deal. The next week, you do it again, and the same thing happens. The probability of this happening twice in a row by chance is 1/2 (the probability the first time around) times 1/2 (the probability the second time around), or 0.25. That is, one time in four, two tails will show up in a row. No big deal. The same thing happens again the third week. The probability of this happening by chance is $1/2 \times 1/2 \times 1/2$, or 1/8, or 0.125. That is, this outcome will happen by chance 12.5 times in 100. You feel unlucky, but that is all you feel. Next week, though, it happens again, and then again the following week and the week after that. You have now lost six times is a row, an outcome that will happen by chance only 1.6 times in 100 ($1/64 = 0.016$). This probability is so low that you become convinced that you are being cheated.

Some statistical tests provide probability values just like this one. That is, they tell you the exact probability that a given outcome can occur by chance. Usually, though, the probability values associated with statistical procedures tell you how often a given outcome, or an outcome even more extreme, can happen by chance. For instance, if you apply one of these statistical tests and get a result that is associated with a probability value of 0.08, you have learned that the result you got, or a result even more extreme, can happen by chance 8 times out of 100.

Scientists are often willing to accept as "real"—not due to chance—anything that can occur by chance no more than 5 times in 100 (p = 0.05 or less). I have used that probability level in what follows. When I say that some outcome is statistically significant, or simply significant, I mean that it is associated with a probability value of 0.05 or less. The values themselves are given in the chapter notes, allowing you to agree or disagree with my decisions to accept or reject any given outcome.[11]

A COMMENT ON WHAT HAS BEEN DONE BEFORE

Somewhat more technical versions of my earlier analyses of the Donner Party and Willie Handcart Company have been published in scholarly journals.[12] In this volume, I have redone these analyses and added new ones in order to explore issues I have not explored before. In some cases, the conclusions I have reached differ from my earlier ones. These differences are the result of newly available information on the members of the Donner Party and the Willie Handcart Company. The exploration of the Martin Handcart Company found in Chapter 6 is entirely new.

WHAT FOLLOWS

In the next chapter, I provide a brief historical outline of overland emigration to western North America. I do this because it is easy to be unaware of how untraveled the trail to California was when the Donner Party gave it a try. Both this chapter and later ones are full of quotations from diaries and other 19th-century sources. In providing these, I have not followed the custom of indicating original misspellings by inserting [*sic*] after each one. James Clyman's comment that he learned a "lisson on the charcter of the grissly Baare" (Chapter 2) would lose a lot if it instead said that he learned a "lisson [*sic*] on the charcter [*sic*] of the grissly [*sic*] Baare [*sic*]." I have left all of these quotations alone, though I have indicated correct spellings where I thought the meaning might otherwise be lost.

In Chapter 3, I change direction entirely and explore the implications that our knowledge of human biology has for understanding who might live and die in situations marked by extreme cold and famine. The later chapters contain the heart of the book—my analyses of three emigrant groups that got themselves into situations so horrible that it is now hard to imagine how bad it must have been. These were real people in real trouble, and I have tried to convey that even while using the outcome of their ordeals to extract biological lessons that are of general value.

CHAPTER 1 NOTES

1. Stewart 1960:287; Morgan 1963:287.
2. Bigler 1998:118.
3. For the Donner Party, see Stewart 1960; King 1994, 1998; Johnson 1996, 2011a, 2011b; McLaughlin 2007; Rarick 2009; and Brown 2009. The best general discussions of the handcart companies are provided by Hafen and Hafen 1992; Roberts 2008; and Bagley 2009. See also Carter 1995; Allphin 2012; Olsen and Allphin 2013; and, for the Willie and Martin Handcart Companies, Olsen 2006.
4. Manly 1977.
5. Johnson and Johnson 1987.
6. Ibid., 12–13.
7. Longmire et al. 1993.
8. Driver 1969:441.
9. Novak and Dixon 2011:7.
10. See, for instance, Brown 1970; Udry 1994; Taylor et al. 2000; Wood and Eagly 2002, 2012; and Becker and Eagly 2004.
11. There is a substantial debate over the use of p-values in scientific research. Many statisticians are appropriately wary of them because of their high potential to mislead the incautious (e.g., Nuzzo 2014; Wasserstein and Lazar 2016). Nonetheless, p-values continue in extremely common use—see, for instance, any recent issue of *Science* or the *Proceedings of the National Academy of Sciences*. I trust that my usage of these values has circumvented at least some of the traps they may provide—most notably, by examining the same issues across three different human groups.
12. Grayson 1991, 1994a, 1996.

2

"A GREAT LAMENTATION
ABOUT THE COLD"

A Brief History of the Donner Party Disaster

"The most direct route, for the California emigrants, would be to leave the Oregon route, about two hundred miles east from Fort Hall; thence bearing west southwest, to the Salt lake; and thence continuing down to the bay of St. Francisco."[1]

So reads the first substantial guidebook meant to help overland emigrants make the trek from what was then the United States to the Far West. Written by Lansford W. Hastings, *The Emigrants' Guide to Oregon and California* appeared in the spring of 1845. It was so successful that, by 1857, it had been reprinted five times with only minor revisions.[2]

Today, Hastings's recommendation for "the most direct route" to California can seem impressively insightful. After all, Interstate 80 follows part of this route—from Fort Bridger in southwestern Wyoming, about where Hastings meant when he said "two hundred miles east from Fort Hall," all the way to San Francisco. The road distance is about 810 miles. It is an easy two-day drive and can be done in one.

But Hastings, while a visionary of sorts, was not omniscient. At the time he suggested his most direct route, he had not even been in the area through which the route passed. This was unfortunate for the group that has come to be known as the Donner Party, since this is the way they went.

To understand what happened to the Donner Party and why, it is essential to realize how novel it was to cross the Great Plains to California by wagon in 1846. Not only was California still Mexican Territory when the members of the Donner Party began their trip, but there was no lengthy history of getting wagons to the rich central valleys of California this way.

THE BIDWELL-BARTLESON PARTY: 1841

This is not to say that it had not been tried, but the first attempt had occurred only five years earlier, and it was not a great success.

In May 1841, a group of 34 people now known as the Bidwell-Bartleson Party left Independence, Missouri, as part of a larger assemblage of travelers—some 890 in all—heading for various western destinations and including a group of Jesuit missionaries under the direction of Father Pierre-Jean de Smet. As far as Soda Springs, on the Bear River in what is now southern Idaho (Figure 2.1), they were led by the missionaries' guide, the experienced mountain man Thomas "Broken Hand" Fitzpatrick (the nickname comes from an 1836 hunting accident).[3] At the time, historian Will Bagley has noted, Fitzpatrick "was on his way to becoming the most renowned wagon-train pilot of all time."[4]

On August 11, the groups split from one another. The missionaries and Oregon-bound emigrants headed north toward Fort Hall, on the Snake River, while the Bidwell-Bartleson Party—34 people and nine ox- and mule-drawn wagons—headed south along the Bear River toward Great Salt Lake. Four members of the California-bound group went to Fort Hall as well, hoping to hire a guide to get them to the Sierra Nevada or, failing that, to the Humboldt River. As Bidwell later put it, albeit with some exaggeration, "we knew only that California lay to the west."[5]

No guide was available at Fort Hall, but the men did receive some guidance. They were told to travel to the west side of Great Salt Lake and that it was essential to go neither too far north nor too far south. Too far north, and they would end up in rugged, broken country and might "become bewildered and perish."[6] Too far south, and they would find themselves in a waterless country without grass for their animals (and might become bewildered and perish). Once west of Great Salt Lake, they should continue west to the Humboldt River and follow it down toward California. This was the sparse information they were able to share when, a few days later, they rejoined the rest of their group.

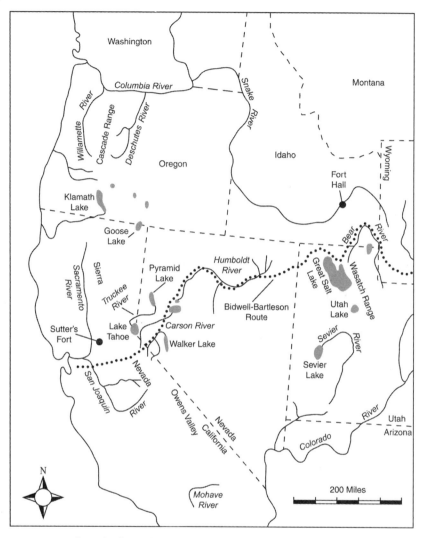

FIGURE 2.1. The Bidwell-Bartleson Party route across the Great Basin (after Nunis 1991).

What they did was extraordinary. They headed to the base of the mountains that flank Great Salt Lake on the north, then followed these mountains around to the west side of the lake.[7] They passed by what John Charles Frémont was soon to name Pilot Peak and, by heading west, found the Humboldt on September 24. This they followed to its sink and then, after moving south and then up the Walker River, crossed the Sierra Nevada, following the Stanislaus River to the San Joaquin Valley and safety. They reached the first white settlements on November 4. They had come close to starvation, but by eating crows, coyotes, and anything else they could find, all 34 survived, including Benjamin and Nancy Kelsey's baby daughter, Ann, six months old at the start of the trip.

But while the people made it, their wagons did not. They abandoned the first on September 12. Realizing they were moving too slowly, they abandoned the rest on September 16, eight days before they reached the Humboldt. Other goods were left along the way, and by the time they reached the San Joaquin Valley, little was left. So ended the first attempt to take wagons across the plains and over the Sierra Nevada to California.

THE CHILES-WALKER PARTY: 1843

No wagons made the attempt in 1842, but, remarkably enough, several former members of the Bidwell-Bartleson Party traveled east during the summer of that year. These included John Bartleson himself, who returned to Missouri, and his friend Joseph B. Chiles. Chiles returned because he had left his children back east (his wife died in 1837) and because he hoped to establish a sawmill in what is now Sonoma County, California. While he did not bring his family across until 1848, he intended to bring back mill equipment in 1843. He had also agreed to bring back the daughters of one of his California friends, George Yount.[8]

Chiles's group headed west from Independence at the end of May 1843 and reached Fort Laramie on July 17. Not far west of there, they met Joseph Walker, who, for $300, agreed to guide them to California. They could not possibly have done better. There is a reason that Walker Lake, Walker River, and Walker Pass are named after him.

In 1833, Walker had explored Great Salt Lake, crossed west to the Humboldt River, followed it to the Carson River, then went up and over the mountains to California. In the following year, he returned east via what we now call Walker Pass and Owens Valley.[9] Soon he even helped Frémont, the Pathfinder, find the path.[10] Walker was, as Ferol Egan put it, "the best of a vanishing breed."[11]

It has been suggested that Chiles was lucky to find Walker out here, but this seems unlikely. Walker's nephew Frank McClellan was in the party, and

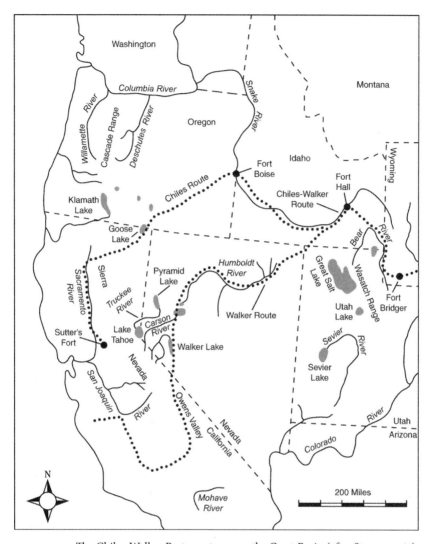

FIGURE 2.2. The Chiles-Walker Party route across the Great Basin (after Stewart 1962).

the Chiles and Walker families had been neighbors in Missouri.[12] No matter how the arrangement came about, Walker was now to lead them through.

Low on supplies, the party reached Fort Hall on September 12, only to find that little in the way of provisions could be obtained (Figure 2.2). As a result, they decided to split the group in two. Walker would guide most of the group—16 men, four women, and five children, along with either three or six wagons—directly to California. Chiles, with 13 men on horseback, would ride further north on the Snake River to resupply at Fort Boise and then make his way to California. There he would resupply, cross the Sierra Nevada, and meet Walker at the Humboldt Sink.

The plan almost worked, but they misjudged the amount of time it would take Chiles to do his part. It was mid-November by the time he and his men reached Sutter's Fort, where Sacramento now stands, and the snow in the Sierra Nevada would not allow any direct crossing to the east. This was fortunate, since by the time Chiles's group reached Sutter's Fort, Walker was long gone from the agreed-upon meeting place.

Walker left Fort Hall on September 16, the same day that Chiles left, and followed something quite close to what soon became the standard wagon trail to the Humboldt Sink. For a few days, he guided his group west along the Snake River. He then cut over to the Raft River, then to Goose Creek and Thousand Springs Valley, which in turn took the group to the Humboldt River. This they followed to the Humboldt Sink, arriving there on October 22. Walker waited here for over a week for Chiles to meet them. Finally, about November 1, he gave up.

Although low on food and knowing it was dangerously late in the year, the group did have Walker and his knowledge of the country. He led them south past Walker Lake and into Owens Valley. The mules gave out near Owens Lake, and the wagons had to be abandoned and the mill machinery cached. With that done, they continued south, then, on December 3, crossed the Sierra Nevada the way Walker had come east in 1834—that is, by Walker Pass—and descended into the San Joaquin Valley. Shortly after the new year, they, but not their wagons and goods, were in the California settlements.[13]

THE STEPHENS-TOWNSEND-MURPHY PARTY, 1844

Two attempts had now been made to get emigrants and their wagons directly to California from the east. All 72 people who had made the journey arrived safely, but the closest any wagons had come was Owens Valley. As baseball fans like to say, there's always next season.

Next season did, in fact, see substantial emigration westward. The very first overland emigration to the West Coast was to Oregon, in 1840, led by Joel Walker, Joseph Walker's brother. From that year through 1843, about

1,100 emigrants had made the overland passage to the West Coast. Of these, all but the 72 we have followed went to Oregon. In 1844, some 1,530 people are known to have made the trip, about 38 percent more than had gone during the preceding four years. Again, though, Oregon continued to be the prime target; only about 50 emigrants tried to get to Mexican California by traveling across the plains.[14]

These 50 belonged to the Stephens-Townsend-Murphy Party, led by frontier blacksmith and former fur trader Elisha Stephens.[15] The group also included the remarkable Caleb Greenwood and two of his sons. Greenwood, an experienced frontiersman who claimed to be 81 at the time, had been hired to guide them as far as the Rockies, and this he did without major incident.

The group left from Council Bluffs, on the western edge of Iowa Territory, around May 18 and followed the north bank of the Platte River to reach Fort Laramie around June 20. From here, they took, with one major exception, the standard route to Fort Hall (Figure 2.3).

After crossing South Pass and reaching the Big Sandy River, the "normal" thing to do would have been to head southwest to Fort Bridger, then northwest to Fort Hall. Greenwood, though, was not the only experienced mountain man in the party. Isaac Hitchcock was also with them, and he suggested that they head straight west from the Big Sandy, thus avoiding both the drop south and the return north, excluding, as a result, Fort Bridger. This they did, and although it wasn't easy, it worked. This route would later become known as the Greenwood or Sublette Cutoff, but it is Hitchcock to whom the credit would seem to belong.

After negotiating the cutoff, the party headed north to Fort Hall, arriving around August 10. They had begun the trip as part of a much larger contingent.[16] Many of these people, however, were headed for Oregon. The number that continued along the Oregon Trail toward California by the Raft River–Goose Creek–Humboldt River route was much smaller: the 50 or so people I previously mentioned, along with 11 ox-drawn wagons.

From the Raft River to the Humboldt Sink, they were without a knowledgeable guide. They did, however, have the trail that Walker had left the preceding year, and this got them to the Humboldt Sink around October 1. From the sink, Walker went south, but the Stephens group did not follow that route. Instead, they stayed at the sink for about a week, allowing their animals to recover and deciding what to do next.

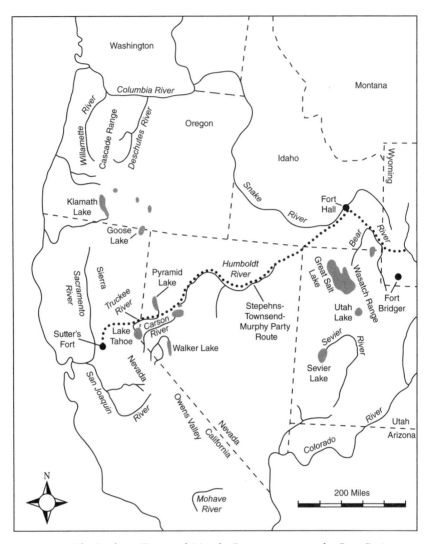

FIGURE 2.3. The Stephens-Townsend-Murphy Party route across the Great Basin (after Stewart 1962).

While there, and to their great fortune, they met one of the most famous nineteenth-century Northern Paiute Indians, a man whose name comes down to us as Truckee and for whom the California town of Truckee, the Truckee River, and Truckee Lake (later called Donner Lake) were named. Truckee was also the father of Chief Winnemucca, who would play a major role in later white-Indian relationships in the region and was the grand-father of Sarah Winnemucca Hopkins, a tireless supporter of her people's rights whom we will encounter later.

Communicating with Greenwood by signs and diagrams, Truckee explained that a river flowed from the mountains some 50 or 60 miles to the west. This information led the emigrants west across the waterless expanse that lay between the Humboldt Sink and the Truckee River, a stretch that soon became known as the Forty-Mile Desert. After finding the Truckee, they followed it up into the Sierra Nevada until, around November 14, they reached its junction with what would become known as Donner Creek. Here the river headed south toward its source in Lake Tahoe, while the creek headed west toward its source in what is now called Donner Lake.

Two possibilities were obvious at this point. They could follow the Truckee River south or they could follow Donner Creek west. In the end, they did both. One group—two women and four men on horseback—followed the Truckee to Lake Tahoe, becoming the first whites known to have reached the shores of this lake. After moving to the west side of the lake, they crossed the Sierra summit, hit the headwaters of the American River, and followed it down to Sutter's Fort, which they reached safely on December 10.

Those who remained with the wagons followed Donner Creek west-ward. By the time they reached Donner Lake, it had become clear that their oxen were in no shape to bring all the wagons through. As a result, six wag-ons were left at the lake. Three young men, including 18-year-old Moses Schallenberger, stayed behind to guard them.

On about November 27 and 28, these three men built a cabin just east of Donner Lake and settled in for what they clearly believed would not be long. "I did not suppose," Schallenberger later said, "that the snow would at any time be more than two feet deep, nor that it would be on the ground continually."[17] He was wrong on both counts. Soon after the cabin was built, it was nearly buried in white.

The group that went ahead was also in for a surprise. By dint of heroic effort, they took their five wagons over the summit and then camped on the South Fork of the Yuba River. Here they bore the brunt of the same storm that began to cover the Donner Lake cabin. Several feet of snow later, the wagons were stranded. It was no longer possible to continue as they had been doing, and the group decided to split yet again.

Although no detailed account exists of what happened next, the general outline, as reconstructed by historian George Stewart, is clear enough.[18] After building one or more cabins and slaughtering many of the oxen for meat, 17 men left their fellow travelers and the remaining wagons behind and headed down toward Sutter's Fort. They arrived on December 13, finding that the horse-mounted party of six had come in a few days before.

The plan was for the men to secure help and return immediately. Instead, and for reasons that are not clear, the 21 men who had made it out ended up riding south on January 1 as part of a ragged army assembled by Sutter in a failed attempt to put down an insurrection against Mexican governor Manuel Micheltorena. They did not begin to return until February, and it was not until late February that plans were made to extract those stuck along the Yuba. It took until March 1 to bring this group to safety, the wagons left behind.

By mid-December, the three men who had remained at Donner Lake had recognized the severity of their situation and decided to snowshoe out. Two of them made it, but Schallenberger's severe cramps forced him to turn back. He survived the rest of the winter in his cabin, eating foxes that he caught with traps that Elisha Stephens left behind. In late February, a rescuer arrived and led him out on snowshoes. He arrived in the Sacramento Valley on the same day as the Yuba River contingent.

Schallenberger later recalled that his life at Donner Lake was "more miserable than I can describe."[19] Things were not much better at the Yuba River camp, where Isabella Patterson and her two children lived on rawhide for two weeks. Ultimately, the wagons did get through, brought down in July of that year. By that time, however, most of the goods they had held were gone, apparently taken by Indians.

Although they had an extraordinarily hard time of it, all the people had once again made it through. In fact, while the Stephens-Townsend-Murphy Party started out with about 50 members, it ended up with two more than that. Ellen Independence Murphy and Elisabeth Yuba Murphy were born along the way—the former near Independence Rock in Wyoming, the latter along the Yuba River. In addition, the group had pioneered what became one of the prime variants of the California Trail: west from Humboldt Lake across the Forty-Mile Desert to the Truckee, up the Truckee to Donner Lake, then across the summit and down. They even brought their wagons across. These were major accomplishments. How they managed all that, however, was not what they had in mind when they began.

EXTRAVAGANT TALES: 1845

During the spring and summer of 1845, Col. Stephen Watts Kearny and some 300 soldiers rode the trail west to South Pass and back, providing a military presence for emigrants who took to the plains that year. One of the most curious travel narratives ever to issue from the overland emigration resulted from the pen of one of Kearny's officers, Lt. Col. Philip St. George Cooke. Cooke had a remarkable and important military career, but, as the great western historian Hubert Howe Bancroft later observed, his *Scenes and Adventures in the Army; Or, Romance of Military Life* (1859) "brims over with philosophical reflections to the entire exclusion of useful information."[20] When Cooke took one of his occasional breaks from pondering the deeper meaning of things, it was often to note the number of emigrants now on the trail. "Endless," he observed, "seemed the progression of wagons."[21]

In fact, 1845, with its roughly 2,800 overland emigrants, exceeded the total for all previous years.[22] The 600 or so wagons involved must have seemed endless to everyone who saw them, especially the Indians. Nearly all of these people were headed to Oregon, but there were those in California who wished it were otherwise. In fact, some think that Sutter sent Caleb Greenwood east to Fort Hall to convince as many emigrants as he could that California, not Oregon, was the easy and rewarding destination.[23]

The emigrants who arrived at Fort Hall in early August of that year were met by Greenwood, along with three of his sons. Several accounts describe what he told them, all so similar that the gist is clear. Joel Palmer, unmoved by what he heard, reported that "the most extravagant tales were related respecting the dangers that awaited a trip to Oregon, and of the difficulties and trials to be surmounted. The perils of the way were so magnified as to make us suppose that the journey to Oregon [was] almost impossible."[24] The river crossings, Greenwood asserted, were so dangerous that no company made it through without loss of life and no one had ever gotten more than 15 or 20 head of cattle all the way there. Perhaps even worse, "three or four tribes of Indians . . . had combined for the purpose of preventing our passage through their country, and should we attempt it, we would be compelled to contend with these hostile tribes."[25] Should they make it through that gauntlet, they would starve to death anyway, since they would never get to the far-off Cascade Mountains before winter.

Benjamin Franklin Bonney, whose father was swayed by Greenwood, later reported that the old guide had said that the rivers of California were full of salmon, that the road there was marked by "an easy grade," and that "crossing the mountains would not be difficult."[26] Sarah Ide recalled that her family had been told that "plenty of good grass" could be found along the way.[27]

Palmer was completely right about Greenwood being "well stocked with falsehoods,"[28] but many of those who listened found the old mountaineer compelling. Indeed, Sarah Ide's father, William, was one of them, even though "Oregon" was painted in large black letters on the back curtain of one of his wagons. In the end, some 35 wagons joined the 15 that had initially set out for California, and Greenwood was on his way.

For all the lies that Greenwood told about the trail to Oregon, he made good on his promise to lead people and their wagons to California. Taking the Raft River–Goose Creek–Thousand Spring Valley route to the Humboldt, they reached the Humboldt Sink in late September. From there, they did what the Stephens-Townsend-Murphy Party had done the year before. They headed west across the Forty-Mile Desert, up the Truckee River to the Sierra Nevada, then up and over the summit to Sutter's Fort. The wagons did not arrive all at once, but by the end of October, all of them were in.

For the first time, both people and wagons had made it to California together. It had not been easy—many cattle were lost on the Forty-Mile Desert and getting wagons over the summit was torturous—but the trail to Oregon wasn't easy either, as Palmer and the others found out. Indeed, while Greenwood was successfully leading his group to California, trapper and guide Stephen Meek convinced a group of over 1,000 emigrants headed for Oregon to leave the established trail near Fort Boise and follow him east into the heart of the Oregon desert. Six weeks of starvation and death ensued, until the survivors were finally rescued and brought to The Dalles in October. For this group, Greenwood's falsehoods had come true.[29]

LANSFORD W. HASTINGS

While Greenwood was at Fort Hall seeking people to follow him along the Humboldt, another group headed for California that year was still back at Independence. They did not get underway until August 15. This was foolishly late, but Lansford W. Hastings had bragged in the newspaper of his "thorough knowledge of both the route and the method of traveling." He was sure he could get them through in three months even if they left as late as August 1.[30] And now, here they were, Hastings and nine other men, leaving for California and starting out two weeks later than a date that made little sense to begin with.

This was not Hastings's first trip west. In 1842, the Ohio-born lawyer became one of the earliest Euro-Americans to head overland to Oregon. He stayed until the spring of 1843, when he led a group of unhappy emigrants south to California. California held him only until the fall of that year, when he boarded a ship and headed back east via Mexico and New Orleans. By March of 1844, he was in Missouri, some 25 years old (his exact date of birth is not known) and well traveled. Soon he was at work on what has become one of the most famous of overland guidebooks.[31]

The *Emigrants' Guide to Oregon and California* appeared in the spring of 1845, its publication supported by funds that Hastings had raised by giving temperance lectures in the Midwest (he was, the story goes, later reunited with his partner in this venture when they unexpectedly met in a California bar). The combination of the book, Hastings's subsequent activities in 1846, and the fate of the Donner Party ultimately destroyed any chance that he would be remembered in a positive light.

The book itself is some 150 pages of information on Oregon and California, the routes that might be taken to get there, and preparing for the trip. Some of that information was accurate, some not ("the Baron Munchausen of travelers in these countries," diarist Jesse Quinn Thornton was to call him[32]), but the overriding significance of the book is that it is a blatant piece of propaganda for California.

Hastings did describe parts of Oregon in glowing terms—the Willamette Valley, he said, was "very beautiful and productive . . . admirably suited to agricultural, and grazing purposes."[33] California, though, earned his deepest praise:

> There is no country, in the known world, possessing a soil so fertile and productive, with such varied and inexhaustible resources, and a climate of such mildness, uniformity and salubrity; nor is there a country, in my opinion, now known, which is so eminently calculated, by nature herself, in all respects, to promote the unbounded happiness and prosperity, of civilized and enlightened man.[34]

Given the superior attributes of California, it was fortunate, Hastings also observed, that getting there was so much easier than getting to Oregon: "From Fort Hall to the Pacific, by the Oregon route, a distance of about eight hundred miles, there is but one continued succession of high mountains, stupendous cliffs, and deep, frightful caverns, with an occasional limited valley."[35]

On the other hand, the route from Fort Hall to the Sacramento Valley

lies through alternate plains, prairies and valleys, and over hills, amid lofty mountains; thence down the great valley of the Sacramento, to the bay of St. Francisco, a distance from Fort Hall, of nine hundred miles. . . . Wagons can be as readily taken from Fort Hall to the bay of St. Francisco, as they can, from the States to Fort Hall.[36]

It is not clear whether Hastings began to write his *Guide* in California or waited until he was back east. No matter where the book was begun, however, it was written and published well before people had made it across the Sierra Nevada with their wagons. Hastings's statement about the ease of getting wagons over the Sierra Nevada and into California was a lie. In fact, when he made this statement, he had not even been over the route himself. In 1842, he had traveled overland to Oregon, not California; when he did go to California, he traveled through Oregon west of the Cascades and the Sierra Nevada. When he returned east in 1844, it had been via boat and Mexico, not via the Sierra Nevada.

After Hastings's book appeared, he gave lectures and wrote letters to newspapers to encourage people to go to California. And now, in August 1845, he was about to make his first overland attempt to reach that region. Of course, his book was largely aimed at those traveling by wagon, and he was going by horseback, but it was close enough.

Hastings had promised a trip of three months. In fact, it took over four, during which time the group twice ran out of provisions—once between Fort Bridger and Fort Hall (where, lacking money as well as food, they had to count on the good graces of fort personnel) and once while crossing the Sierra Nevada. The route they took was very much the same as Greenwood had taken earlier that year: Raft River–Humboldt River–Sierra Nevada. All involved made it safely, Hastings and some of his companions arriving at

Sutter's Fort on December 25, the rest arriving the next day. As Sutter later noted, "if they arrived one day later they would have been cut of[f] by the immense quantity of Snow."[37]

While they made it, they still had not taken what Hastings himself said was "the most direct route," the one that went "west southwest, to the Salt Lake; and thence continuing down to the bay of St. Francisco." It is not known how Hastings had initially learned of a possible route via Great Salt Lake, but in October, while he and his group moved toward Fort Hall, Frémont and his men were blazing just such a route.

Now on his third exploring expedition and traveling toward California, Frémont and his men had made their way to the south end of Great Salt Lake, camping, on October 25, 1845, in the north end of Skull Valley. They spent several days there deciding how best to continue. Frémont reported that not even Joseph Walker, who was with them, was sure what to do.[38] In the end, they decided to take the direct route, straight across the Bonneville Salt Flats, using as their target "the peak-shaped mountain"[39] that seemed to mark the far edge of the desert some 50 to 60 miles away.

Frémont sent four men, including Kit Carson, ahead. If they found water, they were to signal their success with a fire and the rest would follow. The plan worked, as Frémont's plans often did, and the men continued west from there. He was to name "the friendly mountain" Pilot Peak.[40]

Frémont reached Sutter's Fort on December 10 and left four days later, 11 days before Hastings showed up. Both men were, however, at Sutter's Fort for a few days in January and again in March. There is no proof that they actually met, but it seems highly likely that they did and that Hastings's subsequent actions were, in part, determined by this meeting.[41] Even if they didn't meet, Hastings would surely have learned about Frémont's accomplishment in other ways. As Frémont soon noted, "some time afterward, when our crossing of the desert became known, an emigrant caravan was taken by this route, which then became known as *The Hastings Cut-off*."[42]

Hastings's plan for the year was similar to Greenwood's a year earlier. He would head east in the spring, intercept emigrants who might otherwise go to Oregon, and lead them to California. Now, armed with the information Frémont's travels had provided, he aimed to do that by "the most direct route" touted in his book. He hadn't been over that route, but that problem could be solved. He would simply go east by the track that Frémont left across the salt flats.

THE HASTINGS CUTOFF

A small crowd of people traveling east from California that season had agreed to meet at Johnson's Ranch, north of Sutter's Fort on California's Bear River. By April 21, 1846, they were all there: 19 men, three women, three children, and about 150 horses and mules.[43] It was this group that Hastings and his assistant, James Hudspeth, joined.

It is hard to imagine a more interesting group of travelers, which, in addition to Hastings and Hudspeth, included Caleb Greenwood and two of his sons and, in a great stroke of fortune for historians, James L. Clyman, former trapper, accomplished explorer, and engaging diarist.

From a time and place full of remarkable people, Clyman emerges as one of the most remarkable of them all.[44] Born in Virginia in 1792, he spent much of the time between 1823 and 1827 as a fur trapper in and around the Rocky Mountains. Along with Jedediah Smith, Thomas Fitzpatrick and others, his travels through South Pass in 1824 helped make that spot the standard crossing of the Rockies. On his way east after this trip, he became separated from his companions and nearly all of his belongings and walked some 600 miles from the Sweetwater River to Fort Leavenworth. He was at the first fur trappers' rendezvous, on July 1, 1825; he was part of the first group of whites to circumnavigate Great Salt Lake, in 1826. He wrote poetry, quoted Shakespeare, and wondered about the meaning of infinity. He even sewed Jedediah Smith's ear on after a grizzly had tried to remove his head shortly before that South Pass crossing in 1824 ("this gave us a lisson on the charcter of the grissly Baare which we did not forget").[45]

All of these and later events Clyman recorded in his diary or in his reminiscences. He did not have much of a formal education, but he could read and write (often phonetically), was smart, had a sense of humor and proportion, and he observed.

Clyman went east in 1827, his western trapping days over. In 1832, he served in the Black Hawk War, a member of the same company as Abraham Lincoln and James Frazier Reed, a man we shall meet again shortly. Largely, though, he made his living as a farmer and businessman.

In 1844, he turned west once again, this time to Oregon by the Oregon Trail. He spent that winter and spring in the Willamette Valley ("four months rain," he reported on February 22, 1845, so things haven't changed that much[46]), and then headed to California in June. By April, he had done what he wanted to do and was now traveling east again along with Hastings and the others.

The group left Johnson's Ranch on April 23 and headed over the Sierra Nevada. As usual, the trip was challenging (there was still snow in the mountains), but at least the challenges were of a routine sort, though Clyman was deeply upset by the death of his beloved spaniel, Lucky, on May 9 ("to his sad disappointment and my sorrow he scalded himself almost instantly to death" in a hot spring; "I felt more for his loss than any other animal I ever lost in my life"[47]). By May 16, however, it had become clear that they had far too many animals to feed that early in the season, and so they decided to split the group in two. Exactly who went where is not fully clear, but the division meant that Clyman's group consisted of some eight or nine people, including Hastings, Hudspeth, and a family of four emigrants dissatisfied with both Oregon and California. Greenwood and his sons went with the others.

The Clyman-Hastings group continued to follow the Humboldt River upstream until, on May 21, they intersected the trail that Frémont's men had left on their way to California from Great Salt Lake. They had to decide whether to follow the way Frémont's men had come or simply continue up the Humboldt along the main trail (as Greenwood's contingent would do). Hastings wanted to go Frémont's way.

"Mr Hastings our pilot," Clyman recorded, "was anxious to try this rout but my beleef is that it [is] verry little nearer and not so good a road as that by fort Hall."[48] After "long consultation and many arguments," they acceded to Hastings's wishes and opted for the novel route.

To reach the Humboldt, Frémont's men had gone through Secret Pass, between the Ruby Mountains and the East Humboldt Range. Clyman and Hastings did the same thing in reverse, entering Ruby Valley on May 23. Hastings would have realized at this point that Secret Pass would be difficult for wagons, but he may have also noticed the same thing in Ruby Valley that Clyman did: that "several small streams fall into this vally and run off to the S & S W and no doubt fall into marys river."[49]

Actually, these streams do not run into Mary's River—thanks to Frémont, now called the Humboldt River—at all. Instead, they dead-end in Ruby Valley. Neither Hastings nor Clyman could have known this without following the streams down, something they did not do. The significance of this will soon become clear.

When Frémont headed west over the salt flats, he aimed for Pilot Peak, correctly assuming that it marked the end of the waterless desert. On May 27, the Clyman-Hastings party stood at the foot of that same peak but looking east and facing "a boundless salt plain without vegitatiom except here and there a cliff of bare rocks standing like monumental pillars to commemorate the distinction of this portion of the Earth."[50] They set out on the morning of the 28th, going as fast as they dared and for as long as they could. They camped that night in the Grayback Hills, having made, Clyman estimated, 40 miles and without seeing grass or water. Clyman was impressed:

> this is the [most] desolate country perhaps on the whole globe there not being one spear of vegitation [*sic*] and of course no kind of animal can subsist and it is not yet assertaind to what extent this immince salt plain can be south of whare we [are now].[51]

They did not find water until the next day, at Redlum Springs in northern Skull Valley. They had traveled over 80 miles from the base of Pilot Peak;[52] they and their animals had gone 30 hours without water. Because they were mounted on horses, though, the hard times were over. As if to mark the occasion, on May 30, "long before day was visibele a small Bird of the mocking bird kind was heard to cheer us with his many noted Song."[53]

The Wasatch Range brought them to the Weber River, which Clyman knew well, then to the Bear River, and then to an empty Fort Bridger. On June 8, the little group broke up. Clyman headed east; Hastings and Hudspeth went north to work the trail in search of emigrants who could be persuaded to follow them back to California.

Exactly where Hastings went during the next few weeks is not known, but what he did is clear enough. He rode the trails seeking converts. By July 7, he had reached the Sweetwater just east of South Pass, the furthest east he was to go. It was here that he met a sole rider, Wales B. Bonney, returning from Oregon. When they parted, Bonney carried an open letter to the emigrants in which Hastings reported that he had found a better way to California, by Salt Lake (just as it said in the book), and that he would wait for them at Fort Bridger to give them details and guide them through.

That year, about as many people headed west as the year before, some 2,700. This time, however, more than half of them would end up in California. Most of them started out in that direction, and there is little doubt that Hastings's *Guide* had a good deal to do with that. As Charles Stanton, who was soon to travel Hastings's route with the Donner Party, wrote to his brother before leaving, "If you have never seen Hastings Oregon & California get it and read it.—You will then see some of the inducements which led me to this step."[54]

DECISIONS MADE

At the same time the influential author was waiting at Fort Bridger to guide people west, two other people were heading east who knew Hastings's route as well as he did and who thought very little of it.

After crossing the salt flats with Frémont, Joseph Walker had spent the winter in California, involved in hostilities with Mexico. In May 1846, he began the trip back east. By July, he was at Fort Bridger, providing his thoughts on routes west to anyone who asked. Andrew J. Grayson, for instance, "consulted Capt. Walker, who happened to be at Fort Bridger, and well acquainted with both routes, and also a man whom I could believe; so I took his advice and went the old Trail."[55]

In Grayson's case, the old trail led to Oregon, but it was different for Edwin Bryant. Bryant was a gifted journalist (and a cousin of the poet William Cullen Bryant) who was determined to go to California and write a book about his experiences. On July 10, while still along the Sweetwater, Bryant had encountered Wales Bonney and the Hastings letter, along with its announcement of a shorter route to California via Great Salt Lake. At Fort Bridger a week later, Bryant met Walker, a man he accurately described as "much celebrated for his explorations and knowledge of the North American continent, between the frontier settlements of the United States and Pacific."[56] The great explorer, Bryant carefully observed, "spoke discouragingly of the new route via the southern end of the Great Salt Lake"[57] and estimated that the waterless stretch across the salt flats had to be 75 miles.

Bryant was not deterred by the news: he opted for Great Salt Lake. But Bryant was a single man traveling with eight other men, all on mules. He knew that Walker's information was far more important to those behind him and coming in wagons. And so, before he headed west from Fort Bridger on July 20 with Hudspeth as his guide, he left behind a series of letters for friends who were on their way. In those letters, he advised them "not to take the route, but to keep on the old trail, via Fort Hall."[58]

One of these letters was addressed to a key member of the Donner Party, James Frazier Reed. Much has been made of the fact that Reed never received that letter, the reason for which appears to be that those who ran Fort Bridger (Jim Bridger and Louis Vasquez) had little reason to pass along information that might ultimately convince emigrants to take the Greenwood Cutoff and thus drive them out of business.[59] In any case, Reed did not need Bryant's letter to learn about Hastings's route. That is because the other person heading east that summer with firsthand knowledge of that route was James Clyman himself.

As he made his way east, Clyman continued to travel with a small group of companions. At times that group split in two, so it is not exactly clear with whom he traveled. What is clear, though, is that one or more of these people detested California and that one of them may have been Clyman. Even though he was to settle in California after it became part of the United States, he had yet to take much of a liking to the place. "I immagine," he wrote in August 1845, "that but few americans would like the county or the people or any thing they may find at first sight unless it be the fine fat Beef which is used and wasted here in the greatest profusion."[60]

Between June 26 and 28, diary after diary records emigrants encountering Clyman's party in the vicinity of Fort Laramie, and it may well have been his negative feelings that are registered in these documents. "Met two Companies returning from California," Virgil Pringle reported on June 26, referring to the two detachments of Clyman's group. They were, he said, "dissatisfied with the country."[61] The next day, California-bound George McKinstry reported receiving "a verry bad account of California" from the same group.[62] On and on it goes: "The Californian affirmed," Thornton tells us, "that the country was wholly destitute of timber, and that wheat could not be raised in sufficient quantities for bread."[63] To Heinrich Lienhard, Clyman's party described California as something akin to "a desert waste inhabited by hordes of dark, naked savages."[64] Edwin Bryant's informant presented California as "scarcely habitable" and felt that "the population there must necessarily perish for want of food"; that "there was not a man in the country, now that he had left it, who was not as thoroughly steeped in villany as the most hardened graduate of the penitentiary."[65]

Clyman's diary is silent on all but one of these interchanges, but the one he does record shows that he was not enthusiastic about California. In his diary entry for June 27, made at Fort Laramie, Clyman reported that he met an old acquaintance, former Missouri governor Lilburn W. Boggs. We will meet Boggs again in Chapter 5, since his treatment of Mormon settlers was to play an indirect role in producing the handcart tragedies of 1856, but Boggs and a fellow Missourian, Judge James Morin, were now bound for California. They camped together that night, and whatever Clyman said about California could not have been positive, since "during our long conversation I changed the purposes of Govornor and the Judge for next morning they both told me they inte[n]ded to go to Oregon."[66]

Fifteen years later, Clyman filled in more of the details of this meeting, pointing out that members of the Donner Party, including James Reed—whom Clyman knew from the Black Hawk War days—were also there. "Mr. Reed," he recalled in 1871,

> was enquiring about the route. I told him to "take the regular wagon track, and never leave it—it is barely possible to get through if you follow it—and it may be impossible if you don't." Reed replied, "There is a nigher route, and it is of no use to take so much of a roundabout course." I admitted the fact, but told him about the great desert and the roughness of the Sierras, and that a straight route might turn out to be impracticable.[67]

There is no question that the cumulative effect of the negative comments of Walker and Clyman dissuaded many from following Hastings and at least some from going to California. But by the time Hastings and Hudspeth were done at Fort Bridger, they had convinced some 70 wagons of emigrants, as well as the Bryant party, to follow them along what has ever since been called the Hastings Cutoff. And that number does not include the Donner Party, which came later. Clyman had not been convincing enough.

THE DONNER PARTY
LEAVING HOME

On April 15, 1846, James Clyman was lost. He was trying to reach Johnson's Ranch and the gathering of those heading east from California that spring, but he had little idea of where the ranch was. He had directions from a "dutchman," but they so confused him that he thought he had ended the day further from his goal than when he had started out. "I advise all travelers hereafter to be carefull and allways take their Ideas of the rout in preferance to follow the directions of a dutchman for he will confus all the small Ideas you ever had in place of giving you any new ones."[68]

On the same day, in Springfield, Illinois, some 2,000 miles to the east, a larger group of people began their trip knowing exactly where they were and exactly how to get to their immediate destination: Independence, Missouri. Eliza Donner later put the number of travelers leaving together at 32. This would have included her parents, George and Tamzene Donner, and their four children;[69] George's brother Jacob, his wife Elizabeth, and their seven children; and their friends Margaret and James Frazier Reed, with their four children and Margret's ailing mother, Sarah Keyes. The families had three wagons apiece as well as livestock. Ten people had been hired on to help them: five by the Donners, another five by the Reeds.

Of the nine wagons that left that day, one has gathered a good deal of attention: the Reeds' "Pioneer Palace," as daughter Virginia Reed later called it. This wagon may have been larger than most, but it was certainly made with a greater eye toward comfort than usual. There was a single side entrance, like that of a stagecoach; the inside held high-backed sprung seats and a small stove and a second story for beds. Rather than being drawn by three yoke of oxen, as were Reed's other wagons, this one was drawn by four yoke.[70] All this because 70-year-old Sarah Keyes was ill when the trip began—"consumption" was the diagnosis—but could not be talked out of going. She was traveling either to see her son, Robert, then in Oregon, or because she would not leave her daughter, or both. Her daughter, Margret, was not well either, the victim of frequent and severe migraines. The comforts of the Pioneer Palace were also meant for her. The supposed restorative character of the California climate was one motive driving Reed west—just as it was for many others—but he had suffered business setbacks that would have provided substantial motivation as well.[71]

The Pioneer Palace has attracted attention not because of its novel interior but because its great size, the argument goes, would slow the Donner Party down significantly and lead, first, to resentment against James Reed and, second, to delays on the trail that were ultimately of fatal import.

Kristin Johnson has argued that there is little to support the suggestion that the Pioneer Palace was outlandishly large and nothing to support the argument that it caused delays any more severe than those caused by any other wagon.[72] There is incontrovertible archaeological evidence, based on tracks uncovered by Bruce Hawkins and David Madsen in the salt flats of Utah's western Bonneville Basin, that a larger-than-normal wagon was there at the right time to have been a Donner Party wagon.[73] Since these are just tracks, though, it is not possible to be sure that it was the Pioneer Palace that made them. Certainly, other than the Reeds, no one traveling in or with the Donner Party seems to have mentioned it. Most importantly, as we shall see, there is no reason to think that anything would have been different had the Pioneer Palace never left Springfield.

FROM INDEPENDENCE TO DISASTER

On May 12, Clyman was moving up the Humboldt River, reporting himself to be "in one of the most Steril Barren countys I ever traversed."[74] On the same day, the Donner and Reed families were just leaving Independence, making four miles that day.[75]

Many people, influenced by movies and novels, think of wagon trains as well-organized affairs—groups of people bound tightly together for their common good, under tight central direction, and sticking closely to one another until journey's end. The truth is far more human and far less pleasant.

Not all people traveled west in organized trains; some simply headed out more or less on their own. Indeed, at least one of the families that ultimately joined the Donner Party did just that. Most joined organized trains, but even these tended to be composed of people who just happened to end up together.[76] They elected a leader and established rules but could do little to enforce those rules, and the resultant trains were marked by squabbles, dissension, and interpersonal hostility. Individual families frequently came and went; leaders were chosen, then quit or were fired; families who got in trouble could and would be left on their own. Wagon trains were fluid affairs. The flocks of geese that flew overhead had more coherence.

The Donner and Reed families joined their train on May 19, a week west of Independence. This group had elected William H. Russell as leader on May 11. Former Missouri governor Lilburn Boggs was a member, as were many of the families that eventually joined the Donners and Reeds in following the Hastings Cutoff. The Eddy and Keseberg families, for instance, were also members of this group.

When Russell was elected, the train included 63 wagons and 178 adults. In typical fashion, the number had changed significantly by the time the Donners and Reeds joined: there were now 48 wagons and 148 adults. Edwin Bryant reported their arrival warmly: "We were joined to-day by nine wagons from Illinois, belonging to Mr. Reed and the Messrs. Donner, highly respectable and intelligent gentlemen, with interesting families. They were received into the company by a unanimous vote."[77]

Not long after, the Pioneer Palace lost a significant part of its reason for being. On May 29, Sarah Keyes died near what is now Manhattan, Kansas. "We miss her verry much," Virginia Reed was soon to write about her grandmother.[78] When Clyman saw the grave and headstone on July 15, it caused him to reflect that "all ages and all sects are found to undertake this long tedious and even dangerous Journy for some unknown object never to be realized even by those the most fortunate."[79]

Otherwise, the Donner-Reed group had a routine go of it up to Fort Laramie, which they reached on June 27. "My family affairs go on smoothly," James Reed wrote to his father-in-law on June 16, and by now, Tamzene Donner was convinced that, unless something went wrong, "the trouble is all in getting started."[80]

One of the Donners' hired men, Hiram Miller, kept a diary from the time he left Springfield to the time he decided to leave the Donners' employ in early July. The diary is terse, recording dates, distances traveled, places reached, and not much else. When Bryant, for instance, reports that Russell became ill and then, on June 19, resigned as captain to be replaced by Boggs, Miller reports only that they camped on the Platte. But Miller does tell us that on June 27, the Donners and Reeds "Crossed Over to fort Lairome and Camped."[81] And Clyman tells us that it was on this day that his trip east intersected with the Donner-Reed trip west and that it was here—at Fort Laramie—that he stayed up late but failed to convince Reed to avoid Lansford Hastings's "nigher route."

Miller, it turns out, was lucky. He did not have to deal with the consequences of any decision to take the wagons across some nigher route. Bryant—whose diary also intersects the others at Fort Laramie on June 27— had tired of the slow pace of his wagon train and decided to trade his wagon for mules. Not only did Russell join him—and thus leave the wagon train he had captained for over a month—but Bryant convinced Miller to join them as well. As a result, on July 3, James Reed took over the Miller diary while Miller, Bryant, and seven others sped ahead.

The Donners and Reeds would have to choose their route at one of two places. The first was on the Little Sandy River, where the Greenwood Cutoff went straight but the route to Fort Bridger swung left. The other was at Fort Bridger itself. Here, both the "old" road to Oregon and the standard trail to California went north, but the nigher route went southwest.

It is fairly clear from Clyman's comments that the Reeds and Donners had chosen the nigher way by the time they reached Fort Laramie. It could not have done much to change their mind when they encountered Wales Bonney, and Hastings's letter, on July 12 near Independence Rock. The Miller-Reed diary says nothing of the event, but Bonney carried Virginia Reed's July 12 letter east to her cousin Mary Keyes,[82] so they must have received Hastings's news.

The decision became firmer still when they reached the Little Sandy on July 19, where they camped with a large contingent of emigrants headed for both California and Oregon, and then, on the 20th, headed south toward Fort Bridger. Indeed, the group had now become coherent enough that it was on this day—July 20—that George Donner was elected captain. The name "Donner Party" stems largely from this event, and it was as the Donner Party that they rolled into Fort Bridger on July 27 (Figure 2.4).

In 1871, Reed observed that letters warning him away from Hastings's route had been left for him at Fort Bridger. These letters, he said, were not passed on to him because Louis Vasquez knew that the new route would be good for business. These things appear to be true, but it is also true that the letters could not have told him much, if anything, more than Clyman had, and Reed had already rejected that information. For instance, Clyman had found the country along the Humboldt to be one of the most sterile and barren regions he had ever seen, and he surely conveyed this to Reed. Yet on July 31, just before leaving Fort Bridger, Reed sent another letter east. "Mr. Bridger," he wrote, "informs me that the route we design to take, is a fine level road, with plenty of water and grass," with the exception of a 40-mile waterless stretch west of Great Salt Lake.[83] Given that he had rejected Clyman's opinion, it is hard to believe that any letter Bryant or anyone else left for him would have made much of a difference.

Hastings and Hudspeth had left Fort Bridger on July 20, exactly a week before the Donner Party arrived. With them went the 40 or so wagons of the Harlan-Young Party and the Bryant-Russell mule-mounted group, although the latter soon chose a different route.[84] When the Donner Party

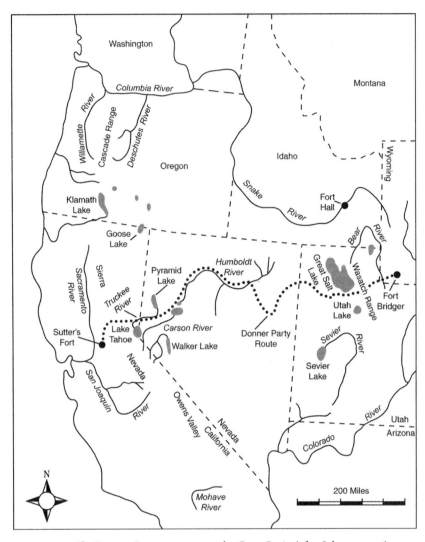

FIGURE 2.4. The Donner Party route across the Great Basin (after Johnson 1996).

arrived at Fort Bridger, there is no indication that any of them were concerned by the fact that their guides were well ahead. Indeed, they remained
there for four days, not leaving until July 31.

There was no reason they should have been concerned since they were
not the only group to follow in Hastings's tracks after he had left. In fact,
Heinrich Lienhard's group left the day before the Donner Party arrived.

It would have been reasonable to assume that they would be following a trail that Hastings was then busy cutting, insofar as any cutting was needed. And so the group, now nearing its full size, left the fort on July 31, following Hastings's trail—"The Cut off rout by the south of the Salt Lake," as Reed referred to it in his diary.[85]

All went well until August 6, when they reached the first crossing of the Weber River, about where Henefer, Utah, stands today. Hastings, Hudspeth, and the 70 or so wagons they led had gone straight down this canyon. Ultimately they made it, but this was not the route that Hastings initially had in mind, and he remained convinced there was a better way. Accordingly, he returned to the first crossing of the Weber and left a note visible to all. In that note, he requested that later parties simply remain in camp until he could return to show them the right way through.

The Donner Party did as they were told. They stopped, while Reed and two others rode ahead to find Hastings. In retrospect, it is too bad they did this. On August 3, Lienhard's group had encountered Hastings on his way to leave the message the Donner Party would find three days later. Hastings also told them that there was a better way and how to find it and then kept going. They spent August 4 trying to figure out what he meant but gave up. On the 5th, they went straight down the Weber and got their wagons through "with comparatively little difficulty."[86] The Donner Party, meanwhile, was about to pull in up above.

It is not fully clear when the Donner Party reached its final size, since Reed's diary does not record the event. But sometime between about August 7 and August 16, the Graves family, with their teamster John Snyder, added themselves to the roster. With this addition, the group reached its maximum size of 87 people, 23 wagons, and an unknown but large number of livestock (Table 2.1).

Reed and his two companions—Charles Stanton and William Pike—caught up with Hastings south of Great Salt Lake. By the time they reached him, he said he was committed to those with him and did not feel he could return the entire way. Instead, he returned far enough with Reed to point out the way, Stanton and Pike following behind on worn horses. Reed then followed this route back the best he could, blazing his way as he went. He reached camp on August 10. The next day, the group moved out.

It proved to be extraordinarily difficult. There was no road. In fact, there were hardly any openings, and the men—the survivors made it clear

TABLE 2.1. Members of the Donner Party (after K. Johnson in Novak and Dixon 2011).

Name	Sex	Survived?	Age	Family size
Antonio	Male	No	23	1
Breen, Edward	Male	Yes	13	9
Breen, Isabelle	Female	Yes	1	9
Breen, James	Male	Yes	5	9
Breen, John	Male	Yes	14	9
Breen, Margaret	Female	Yes	40	9
Breen, Patrick	Male	Yes	51	9
Breen, Patrick, Jr.	Male	Yes	9	9
Breen, Peter	Male	Yes	3	9
Breen, Simon	Male	Yes	7	9
Burger, Charles	Male	No	30	1
Denton, John	Male	No	28	1
Dolan, Patrick	Male	No	35	1
Donner, Elitha	Female	Yes	14	16
Donner, Eliza	Female	Yes	3	16
Donner, Elizabeth	Female	No	40	16
Donner, Frances	Female	Yes	6	16
Donner, George	Male	No	62	16
Donner, George, Jr.	Male	Yes	10	16
Donner, Georgia	Female	Yes	4	16
Donner, Isaac	Male	No	6	16
Donner, Jacob	Male	No	56	16
Donner, Leanna	Female	Yes	11	16
Donner, Lewis	Male	No	4	16
Donner, Mary	Female	Yes	7	16
Donner, Samuel	Male	No	1	16
Donner, Solomon Hook	Male	Yes	14	16
Donner, Tamzene	Female	No	45	16
Donner, William Hook	Male	No	12	16
Eddy, Eleanor	Female	No	25	4
Eddy, James	Male	No	3	4
Eddy, Margaret	Female	No	1	4
Eddy, William	Male	Yes	29	4
Elliot, Milford	Male	No	28	1
Fosdick, Jay	Male	No	23	12
Fosdick, Sarah	Female	Yes	21	12
Foster, George	Male	No	2	13
Foster, Sarah	Female	Yes	19	13
Foster, William	Male	Yes	31	13
Graves, Eleanor	Female	Yes	14	12
Graves, Elizabeth	Female	No	1	12
Graves, Elizabeth Cooper	Female	No	46	12
Graves, Franklin	Male	No	57	12
Graves, Franklin, Jr.	Male	No	5	12

TABLE 2.1. (*continued*)

Name	Sex	Survived?	Age	Family size
Graves, Jonathan	Male	Yes	7	12
Graves, Lovina	Female	Yes	12	12
Graves, Mary Ann	Female	Yes	20	12
Graves, Nancy	Female	Yes	8	12
Graves, William	Male	Yes	17	12
Halloran, Luke	Male	No	25	1
Hardcoop, Mr.	Male	No	60	1
Herron, Walter	Male	Yes	27	1
James, Noah	Male	Yes	16	1
Keseberg, Ada	Female	No	2	4
Keseberg, Louis	Male	Yes	32	4
Keseberg, Louis, Jr.	Male	No	2 mos.	4
Keseberg, Philippine	Female	Yes	23	4
McCutchan, Amanda	Female	Yes	25	3
McCutchan, Harriet	Female	No	1	3
McCutchan, William	Male	Yes	30	3
Murphy, John	Male	No	16	13
Murphy, Lemuel	Male	No	13	13
Murphy, Levinah	Female	No	36	13
Murphy, Mary	Female	Yes	14	13
Murphy, Simon	Male	Yes	8	13
Murphy, William	Male	Yes	10	13
Pike, Catherine	Female	No	1	13
Pike, Harriet	Female	Yes	18	13
Pike, Naomi	Female	Yes	2	13
Pike, William	Male	No	32	13
Reed, James	Male	Yes	45	6
Reed, James, Jr.	Male	Yes	5	6
Reed, Margret	Female	Yes	32	6
Reed, Martha (Patty)	Female	Yes	8	6
Reed, Thomas	Male	Yes	3	6
Reed, Virginia	Female	Yes	13	6
Reinhardt, Joseph	Male	No	30	1
Shoemaker, Samuel	Male	No	25	1
Smith, James	Male	No	25	1
Snyder, John	Male	No	25	1
Spitzer, Augustus	Male	No	30	1
Stanton, Charles	Male	No	35	1
Trudeau, Jean-Baptiste	Male	Yes	16	1
Williams, Baylis	Male	No	25	2
Williams, Eliza	Female	Yes	31	2
Wolfinger, Jacob	Male	No	?	2
Wolfinger, Dorothea	Female	Yes	29	2

that the men did the heavy work—quite literally cut their way through the Wasatch Range. They finally emerged from what is now called Emigration Canyon on August 22. On August 24, when they reached Great Salt Lake, Reed jotted in his diary "18 days to gett 30 miles."[87]

The group had done its job well. When the Mormons reached Great Salt Lake the next year, they followed the path cut by the Donner Party (see Chapter 5). But for the Donner Party itself, the cost was high. Lienhard's small group of wagons had left Fort Bridger July 26, five days before the Donners left. When Hastings told them not to go down the Weber, they did it anyway. They passed the Oquirrh Mountains, south of Great Salt Lake, on August 8. The Donner Party, on the other hand, obeyed Hastings's instructions carefully. They reached the Oquirrhs on August 24, now 16 days behind Lienhard's group.

The next day, the Donner Party suffered its first official death (the group had yet to form when Sarah Keyes died). While at Fort Bridger, George Donner had agreed to take a young emigrant, Luke Halloran, into his wagon. Halloran had been sick with "consumption"[88] and was coming west to improve his health, but it did not work. On August 25, he died south of Great Salt Lake and was buried next to an emigrant from the Harlan-Young Party who had died 14 days before.

With Halloran buried, it was off to the next challenge. Hastings said it was 40 waterless miles across the Great Salt Lake Desert to Pilot Peak, but Walker's estimate of 75 miles was deadly accurate (Figure 2.5). The route from Skull Valley starts out innocently enough. There is no water, but at least there is vegetation. Soon, though, this is gone, and you are on the edge of Clyman's "most desolate country perhaps on the whole globe"[89] and Bryant's "vast desert-plain . . . which, as far as the eye could penetrate, was of a snowy whiteness, and resembled a scene of wintry frosts and icy desolation."[90] This snowy whiteness represents the salts deposited as the result of the desiccation of an immense lake—Lake Bonneville—some 10,000 years ago. Today, Bryant's scene of desolation is the location of the Bonneville Salt Flats and the famous racetrack that takes advantage of the area's level enormity. Now the area can be fun. In wagons it was hell.[91]

Almost no one took wagons through in a single shot. The only choice was to leave them behind and get the oxen to water, or water to the oxen, and then retrieve the wagons. It was so hot on the salt flats that Lienhard found he could not walk in front of his poor animals: they butted him in

FIGURE 2.5. The view east across the eastern Bonneville Basin and the Donner route, from the base of Pilot Peak.

their attempt to shelter in the shade he threw. His group was the last to cross before the Donner Party took its turn; Lienhard described passing 24 abandoned wagons and dead and dying oxen, some "still moving their ears."[92] Given that Hastings was leading about 70 wagons, these two dozen tell us that about a third of the total had to be abandoned here, the oxen in no shape to continue.

Crossing the salt flats, retrieving the abandoned wagons, and giving the animals time to recover at the base of Pilot Peak cost those preceding the Donner Party about a week. James Mathers, for instance, left Skull Valley on August 16 and left Pilot Peak on the 23rd. Lienhard's group left Skull Valley on August 17 and moved south from Pilot Peak on the 24th.

Next came the Donner Party. They started the drive across on August 30. It is not clear when each family reached Pilot Peak, but we know that some made it to the base of the mountain by September 2. Reed, having left his family and wagons behind to find water, came in that evening. The Donners arrived on the 3rd, but their wagons were still back on the salt flats. Worse, many cattle were simply missing. Reed's men, for instance, had lost control of his animals while driving them toward water; the animals had bolted and disappeared. So even though the people, and some of the animals and wagons, made it across on September 2 and 3, much remained to be done before all of them could continue.

In the end, they could not find all their cattle and so could not retrieve all their wagons. Of the four wagons they abandoned, one belonged to George Donner's family, one to the Kesebergs, and two to the Reeds (it is here that Hawkins and Madsen did the archaeology that, among other things, showed the presence of an outsized wagon).

Worse, though, was the toll on the oxen. Thirty-six were lost, half of which belonged to the Reeds. "The first of my sad misfortune[s]," James Reed later said, discounting the loss of his mother-in-law.[93] Now all Reed had left were an ox and a cow; had it not been for other members of the party who provided him with two yoke, he would have had to abandon his third wagon.

As much as the material loss had cost them, the time lost was even more significant. Between trying to recover their cattle and wagons and waiting until the remaining animals had recovered enough to leave, they spent 12 days in the crossing. The Donner Party left the east side of the lake on August 30 and did not leave Pilot Peak until September 10. They left Fort Bridger five days after the Lienhard group and reached the Oquirrhs 16 days behind, but they started the salt flats only 13 days behind. Now Lienhard's party was 18 days ahead and moving confidently along the Humboldt.

Many who have written on the Donner Party try to fix blame. It is hard not to, even though it does not matter. The usual villain is Hastings, whose cutoff was no cutoff at all. Not only was it longer in terms of the distance it covered,[94] it also took longer to traverse. When Lienhard's group reached the Humboldt, they found that a group that had left Fort Bridger 12 or 14 days after they had left, traveling by way of Fort Hall, was now at the same place on the trail as they were. Hastings Cutoff, Lienhard concluded, "would be better named 'Hastings Long Trip.'"[95] This is a hard conclusion to avoid. For all the good things that Hastings's *Guide* contained,[96] and despite the tremendous effort he made to get people from Fort Bridger to the Humboldt (at which point he simply rode off and left everyone on their own), he had gotten himself in over his head. The Donner Party was to pay the price. Not until 1849, and the gold rush, did anyone try to take wagons across this route again, and they found it no easier than those who tried in 1846.[97]

The other target of blame is Reed. It is clear that even though George Donner was the elected leader of the group, Reed was the effective decision maker into September. It was Reed with whom Clyman mentions talking at Fort Laramie, and it was Reed who rode ahead to find Hastings and then blazed the trail through the Wasatch Range. Those who blame him argue that Reed decided to come this way in the first place; Reed's huge Pioneer Palace and heavily laden wagons slowed them down; Reed's cattle had to be searched for in the desert.

None of these attacks are convincing. There is no evidence that the Reeds' wagon slowed the group down any more than any other of the heavily loaded vehicles, including those of the Donners. Reed did have to look for his cattle, but so did many of the others; after all, his were only half of those lost. To blame Reed for the decisions to which all adhered is inappropriate. Somebody had to make the decisions, and those who did not agree could always go off on their own.

What is clear, though, is what actually led to the disaster: the route they took through the Wasatch, putting them 16 days behind Lienhard's group by the time they left the Oquirrh Mountains. The trip across the salt flats made things worse (18 days behind), but it was the Wasatch Range that meant they would not make it in time.

These delays not only cost them several weeks but left them entirely isolated from anyone in front, from anyone who spoke their own language, from anyone who knew what lay beyond. However, as they set out from Pilot Peak to follow in Hastings's tracks, they knew they were far from their destination and low on supplies. And so it seems to have been on, or soon after, September 10 that two men—Charles Stanton and William McCutchan—were sent ahead to Sutter's Fort to retrieve provisions and return. Stanton, one of several heroes to emerge from this tale, was a single man, a New Yorker, who had been traveling with the Donners. McCutchan, who had joined the group at Fort Bridger after crossing most of the way with what started out as the Russell Party, left behind a young wife and their baby girl, Harriet.

With Stanton and McCutchan gone, the group made its way southwest to Ruby Valley and then south in the valley itself, following the streams that Hastings and Clyman thought must run into the Humboldt River but do not come close to doing so. They continued west over the Ruby Mountains

FIGURE 2.6. Northern Ruby Valley. The Donner Party route hugged the western edge of the valley and then crossed Overland Pass to reach Huntington Valley. Thanks to the National Park Service (2012), signs indicate the location of the Hastings Cutoff in Ruby Valley.

via Overland Pass (which the Pony Express later used) into Huntington Valley, then north, exactly parallel to their southern track one valley over, to reach the Humboldt. This they did on September 26 (19 days behind Lienhard).

The party's second death happened along the Humboldt—the exact place is not known—on October 5. There are several versions of what happened, but all agree on the essentials. In attempting to get over a challenging hill, Reed's wagon tried to pass one driven by the Graves' teamster, John Snyder. Words were exchanged, a fight started; a few minutes later, Snyder was dead, Reed's knife in his chest.[98] It was, in every way, a guy kind of thing of the sort that, minus the death, commonly happened on the trail.

The upshot was that the popular Snyder was dead and the not-so-popular Reed left the group. Some said he was banished. Others said he volunteered to leave and then return with supplies from Sutter's Fort. No matter which is true, leave he did. We have now lost our diarist; another does not appear until November 20. At the time of his departure, the Donner wagons were two days ahead of the rest, and the Donners learned from him what had happened. At the same time, Donner teamster Walter Herron decided to leave with Reed. The group had now also lost six men—Stanton, McCutchan, Reed, and Herron (who had left) and Halloran and Snyder (who had died).

Sharing one horse between them, Reed and Herron soon ran out of provisions. By the time they reached the Sierra Nevada, they were so starved they ate the tar out of a bucket they found attached to an abandoned wagon. Nonetheless, they made it. Edwin Bryant, who had arrived at Sutter's Fort on September 1 and had been busy touring the area ever since, recorded Reed's arrival at the fort on October 28. Reed, Bryant noted, arrived at Johnson's Ranch "so much emaciated and exhausted by fatigue and famine, that he could scarcely walk."[99] Sutter immediately provided Reed and McCutchan with the provisions and pack animals they needed to get back across, but it was too late: snow had closed the pass.

Reed and Herron had made it, but another of the Donner Party was to die soon after they left. Almost nothing is known about Mr. Hardcoop except that he was apparently Belgian, about 60 years old, and traveling with the Kesebergs. Along the Humboldt, Hardcoop was unable to walk, but Keseberg would not let him into his wagon. He was denied access by everyone else as well and was last seen by the side of the trail on October 8.

As they continued down the Humboldt, the Donner Party learned one of the things that made the Humboldt famous among emigrants: Indians and their interest in livestock.[100] Day after day, their animals were stolen or shot. On October 11, they lost some 18 head; two days later, they lost 21. As the oxen disappeared or gave out from their wounds, wagons and goods had to be abandoned. By the time they left the Humboldt Sink on October 13, they had only some 14 wagons with them, and many people were now entirely on foot. They were 19 days behind Lienhard, who was nearing Sutter's Fort.

Jacob Wolfinger, however, did not leave the sink since he was now dead. Wolfinger, whose first name is not known with certainty, was traveling with his young wife, Dorothea. Both were apparently German (or, more accurately, Prussian), and it was commonly believed that they traveled with a significant amount of money. They lost most of their cattle on the 13th and were forced to cache nearly all of their remaining goods. Two other Germans—Augustus Spitzer and Joseph Reinhardt—volunteered to help, but they were the only ones who returned from this supposedly helpful mission. Wolfinger, they claimed, had been killed by Indians, his goods stolen, his wagon burned.

In fact, William Graves and several others soon retrieved the wagon and oxen and returned them to Mrs. Wolfinger. They had seen no sign of Indians near the wagon, and it was widely assumed by Donner Party members that Spitzer and Reinhardt had murdered Wolfinger. Just to report something that is not depressing, I note that Mrs. Wolfinger survived the coming disaster, married George Zins, one of Lienhard's young travelmates, in 1847 and settled in the Sacramento Valley.

One more death would occur before the party made its first approach to the summit of the Sierra Nevada. Around October 20, while camped in Truckee Meadows, where Reno now sits, William Pike and his brother-in-law, William Foster, were getting ready to make a joint run to Sutter's Fort for supplies. When the pistol Foster was loading went off accidentally, Pike was hit in the back. He was dead within the hour. At the time of Pike's burial, Lienhard had already reached Sutter's Fort, having arrived on either the 18th or 19th.

With Pike gone, the group continued to work their way up the Truckee. It took them 49 crossings, but they did it, making the final crossing on about October 22. That evening in camp, a single Indian managed to put arrows into 19 oxen. Eddy caught him, shot him in the back as he ran, and later described the episode to Thornton with vengeful fury: "The ball struck him between the shoulders, and came out at the breast. At the crack of the rifle he sprung up about three feet, and with a terrible yell fell down a bank into a bunch of willows."[101]

Many years later, Sarah Winnemucca Hopkins, born in 1844 and the granddaughter of the Paiute chief Truckee, recounted stories she had been told about the early emigrants who had passed through her homeland. These stories clearly intermingle episodes that involved different people, but one just as clearly relates to the Donner Party:

> This whole band of white people perished in the mountains, for it was too late to cross them. We could have saved them, only my people were afraid of them. We never knew who they were, or where they came from. So, poor things, they must have suffered fearfully, for they all starved there. The snow was too deep.[102]

Given what Eddy's frustration and anger had led him to do, it is no surprise that Truckee's people thought it best to stay away.

In fact, the only potentially good news that the Donner Party would have for many months was the return of Stanton from Sutter's Fort. We do not know exactly when he returned or where he met the Donner Party, but it was somewhere along the Truckee River and sometime after October 20, since he was at Johnson's Ranch on that date. We also know that he brought seven mules and provisions. McCutchan had been ill when Stanton started out, so he was not with him. In his place were two of Sutter's young Indian hands, Luis and Salvador. Although Stanton was related to no member of the Donner Party, it was he who returned.

As the group continued up the Sierra Nevada, the wagons became increasingly separated. By the time the lead wagons had reached what is now Donner Lake, the Donner families were miles behind. They would not have been quite this far behind had one of their wagons not broken an axle. The importance of this was not that it cost the Donners time—it was far too late for that to matter—but that George Donner cut his hand badly trying to repair the damage. The wound was never to heal, an accident that prolonged his life at the same time it shortened that of his wife, Tamzene.

When trying to recall when they had reached Donner Lake, different members of the party gave slightly different dates. The lead wagons were there by October 28 or soon thereafter. For the next several days, those who had made it to the lake tried their hardest to get over the top, but snow stopped them about three miles short of the summit. By November 4, in snow that was soon to become far worse, they had given up and settled down in what they assumed would be temporary camps.

SNOW 8 FEET DEEP ON THE LEVEL

Those camps were established in two very different places (Figures 2.7 and 2.8). Near Donner Lake itself, the Breens occupied the cabin that had protected Moses Schallenberger two years before; the Kesebergs made do with a lean-to affixed to that cabin. Some 500 feet away, the Murphys, Fosters, Pikes, and Eddys occupied a cabin that they built adjacent to a huge boulder, incorporating that boulder into the west cabin wall (Figure 2.9). Archaeologist Donald Hardesty has shown that this cabin was rectangular, about 25 feet by 18 feet, and probably about 8 feet tall.[103]

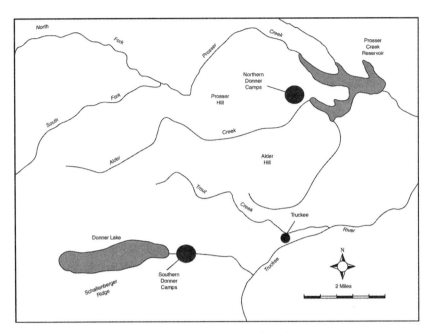

FIGURE 2.7. The general location of the northern and southern Donner Party camps in the Sierra Nevada (after Hardesty 1997).

A third cabin went up about a half-mile down Donner Creek from the Breen structure. This building had two rooms, each about 16 feet by 16 feet, separated by an internal wall.[104] The Graves and McCutchans moved into one end of this cabin, the Reeds and their hired staff into the other.

Hardesty has pointed out that a typical contemporary log cabin meant for a single person would have covered about 320 square feet. At the Donner camps, he notes, as many as 10 to 15 people occupied each of the 256 square-foot rooms of the Graves-Reed cabin (with 15 people, this works out to 17 square feet each). The nine people in the Breen cabin had an estimated 170 square feet (19 each). At these standards, the Murphy cabin, where Hardesty has done important archaeological work, was luxurious. At 450 square feet, it provided its maximum number of occupants (16) with 28 square feet each.[105]

The Donner families encamped some six miles to the northeast, near Alder Creek. Far less is known about the Donner camps than about the situation at Donner Lake. In part, this is because we have Patrick Breen's

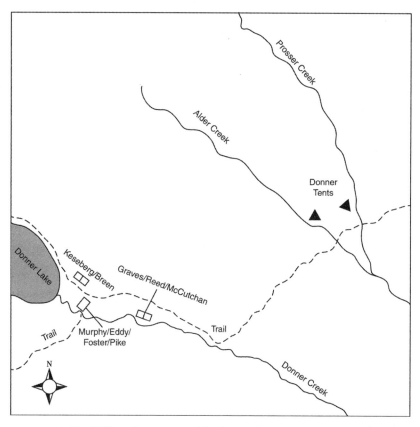

FIGURE 2.8. The William Graves map of the Donner Party encampments in the Sierra Nevada (from Murphy 1980, as modified by Dixon 2011).

diary for November 20 through March 1 for the southern camp, but none from the northern camp (Tamzene Donner and John Denton apparently kept diaries, but, if so, both are lost). In addition, it is because the snows came on the Donners and their traveling companions so quickly that they settled in without building any substantial structures. As Leanna Donner later recalled,

> We had no time to build a cabin. The snow came so suddenly that we had barely time to pitch our tent, and put up a brush shed, as it were, one side of which was open. This brush shed was covered with pine boughs, and then covered with rubber coats, quilts, etc.

FIGURE 2.9. The Murphy cabin location. The flat face on the left side of this massive boulder formed the western wall of the Murphy family cabin (Hardesty 1997).

My uncle, Jacob Donner, and family, also had a tent, and camped near us.[106]

Dorothea Wolfinger apparently lived with George and Tamzene Donner's family, but exactly where each of the Donner family shelters was located is not clear. It is not even known whether a third structure was built to house the Donner teamsters and other single men, though this seems likely.[107]

Even though it was impossible for the members of the Donner Party to get their wagons across, the 81 people in the forced encampments could, and did, take important solace in the fact that three of their party were in the Sacramento Valley: Herron, McCutchan, and Reed. They had, as Eliza Farnham pointed out as early as 1856, "the constant expectation of relief."[108]

Many of them also felt that they could get themselves out, and attempts to do that began soon after the cabins had been built. The first of these attempts occurred about November 12, when 13 men and two women came within about three miles of the summit but returned to camp around midnight. The second attempt began on November 21—we are now within the realm of Patrick Breen's diary—and involved 16 men and six women. This time, they actually made it over the summit, in snow that William Eddy later said was 25 feet deep. They did not, though, get much further than that. They were back in camp late on the 22nd.

A third attempt was planned for November 26, but the evening before saw the start of a massive storm, and the group never got underway. "Still snowing," Breen wrote on the 29th; "killed my last oxen today." "Snowing fast," he wrote on the 30th, "no liveing thing without wings can get about." "Still snowing," he wrote on December 1, "cattle suppose lost in the Snow no hopes of finding them alive."[109] Not until December 4 did it finally end, the snow at the Donner Lake cabins now some seven or eight feet deep.

By now, any livestock that had not been slaughtered and laid up were gone. Attempts to fish were unsuccessful. Hunting provided some small game at first, and Eddy shot a grizzly bear on about November 14 (some of the bones of which were excavated by Hardesty). After that, hunting would be of no help, and people were fully dependent on their rapidly diminishing stores. Not surprisingly, Breen's diary shows that sharing within families was routine, but sharing between families was far less common and, ultimately, often a point of contention. By December 9, Breen was already reporting that some in camp were low on beef and that Stanton was trying to raise something to eat for himself, Luis, and Salvador. "Not likely to get much," Breen concluded.[110] By January 1, Breen began to mention the use of hides for food, and they would soon dominate those aspects of his diary that discuss provisions.

Not coincidentally, soon after Breen mentioned the dwindling supply of beef, he reports the first death in camp. Baylis Williams, one of Reed's employees, succumbed on December 15. Within the week, he also heard that four had died at the Donner encampments. Jacob Donner was now gone, as were three single men: Sam Shoemaker, Joseph Reinhardt, and James Smith. It was to become a familiar entry.

The huge storm that began on November 25 may have delayed the next attempt to walk out, but it did not crush the idea. On December 6, soon after the sun had returned, Breen noted that two men were busy making snowshoes; both Charles Stanton, from upstate New York, and Franklin Graves, from Vermont, knew what they were doing. Another storm hit on

TABLE 2.2. Members of the Forlorn Hope.

Name	Fate
Antonio	Died
Burger, Charles	Returned to camp
Dolan, Patrick	Died
Eddy, William	Survived
Fosdick, Jay	Died
Fosdick, Sarah Graves	Survived
Foster, Sarah Murphy	Survived
Foster, William	Survived
Graves, Franklin, Sr.	Died
Graves, Mary Ann	Survived
McCutchan, Amanda	Survived
Murphy, Lemuel	Died
Murphy, William	Returned to camp
Pike, Harriet Murphy	Survived
Stanton, Charles	Died
Luis	Died
Salvador	Died

the 9th, this one continuing through the 13th ("snow 8 feet deep on the level," Breen recorded[111]), but it cleared on the 14th and froze hard on the 15th. On the morning of the 16th began one of the most remarkable of all Donner Party episodes.

The Snowshoers and the First Cannibalism

Charles F. McGlashan, one of the earliest chroniclers of the Donner Party, called it the Forlorn Hope, and the name is appropriate. On December 16, seventeen people set out for Sutter's Fort on snowshoes, of whom two—Donner teamster Charles Burger and young William Murphy—soon turned back (Table 2.2).

William Eddy provided much of what we know about the sequence of events that occurred during this cruel trip. Reed gave what he termed "A synopsis of the journal of Wm. H. Eddy" to J. H. Merryman, who then incorporated it into an article published in an Illinois newspaper on December 9, 1847. Edwin Bryant published a second version in 1848. This version appeared in a letter from John Sinclair, an important administrator in the Sutter's Fort area, and was built from discussions with survivors and "a few short notes handed me by Wm. H. Eddy."[112] Eddy was also the main source of information for Thornton's version.[113]

The three versions contain many of the same details, but their chronologies differ. George Stewart found the Thornton version the least reliable, largely because it differs from the two remaining versions, which, in turn, seldom differ by more than a day. In addition, a letter by snowshoer Mary Ann Graves, dated May 22, 1847, reports that her father died on December 25.[114] This is the same day recorded in the Eddy journal in Reed's "synopsis" but differs from that provided by Sinclair. Given that it is unlikely that Mary Ann Graves would have forgotten the day her father died, I rely most heavily on Reed's version here for my chronology.

There is no disagreement on the most important details. The snowshoers crossed the summit and began the long descent on December 17, blessed by good weather. "Pleasant sunshine today," Breen noted back at Donner Lake.[115]

This was not to last. Snow began to fall on the 18th and continued. "Feet," Eddy reported the next day, "commenced freezing."[116] Two days later, while the weather had improved, other news was far worse: "Went down the mountain in a southerly direction; provision exhausted."[117]

Stanton was the first to die. He started to suffer from snow blindness soon after they left and had been reaching the evening camps well after the others. On December 21, he never made it; his body was not found until several months later.

Three days later, on the 24th, another major storm hit them. Up at the lake, Breen reported that it started snowing at noon on the 24th. On Christmas Day, he wrote that it had snowed all night and was still coming down: "the prospect is appalling."[118]

The prospect was even worse for the snowshoers. Virtually out of food and without shelter, the storm extinguished their fire on the 24th. On the 25th, Mary Ann Graves's Christmas present was the death of her father. The teamster Antonio died on the same day. Patrick Dolan died two days later; Lemuel Murphy the day after that.

The cannibalism that was to make the Donner Party so famous began during the Forlorn Hope, just a few days after Christmas. The three different Eddy accounts give three different days for the initial decision—the 27th, the 28th, and the 29th—but once it started, it continued until the end. As Mary Ann Graves said in that 1847 letter, they traveled "subsisting on human flesh."[119] With the exception of Stanton, all the adults who died were, to one degree or another, eaten. Had they not been, there is little reason to think that any would have survived.

Jay Fosdick died next. Soon after, Luis and Salvador, apparently fearing for their lives, set out on their own. On January 11, now very close to the snow line, the group encountered them again. In the Bryant version, the two men were dead when they were found. The Reed version is noncommittal: "Saw the dead bodies of the two Indian boys." It is the Thornton version that tells the truth this time: the two were killed, shot by William Foster and then eaten. Mary Ann Graves, whose laconic honesty is remarkable, told it simply: "Two Indians were killed, whose flesh lasted until we got out of the snow and came where Indians lived."[120] These were the fourth and fifth violent deaths of the trip; Mr. Hardcoop might argue it was the fifth and sixth.

It is hard to miss the irony of the fact that after they killed and ate the two Indians, the group emerged at Indian settlements, where they were fed and helped along. By January 18, all the survivors were at Johnson's Ranch. Including the murdered Luis and Salvador, eight of the ten Forlorn men were dead, only Foster and Eddy having survived. All five women made it.

Snowing Death

Up at the lake, Charles Burger died on December 29. On January 4, Margret Reed left her children with the Breens, Graveses, and Kesebergs and tried to walk out with Milt Elliot and Eliza Williams. Eliza was back on the 6th; the others, on the 8th. They were lucky they gave up. Yet another storm moved in on the evening of the 9th, bringing snow that did not stop until the 13th. "It is dredful to look at," Breen wrote.[121] On January 24, Louis Keseberg Jr. died; on the 30th, John Landrum Murphy; on February 2, young Harriet McCutchan; on the 4th, Margaret Eddy; on the 7th, her mother, Eleanor Eddy; on the 8th, Augustus Spitzer; on the 9th, Milt Elliot. And on it went. It was snowing death.

THE FIRST HELP ARRIVES: "DO YOU COME FROM HEAVEN?"

Breen's diary suggests that he lived in the hope, if not the expectation, of help. "In danger if relief dont soon come" was his understatement of January 19.[122] Perhaps this expectation explains his cool response to the arrival of rescuers a month later, though the emotional effects of starvation (Chapter 3) likely played an important role in determining the nature of his reaction:

> Frid. 19th Frozen hard last night 7 men arrived from California yesterday evening with som provisions but left the greatest part on the way to day clear & warm for this region some of the men are gone to day to Doonos Camp will start back on Monday.[123]

This was the First Relief, one of two rescue groups that had been organized in the Sacramento Valley as a result of the efforts of James Reed and William McCutchan and the arrival at Johnson's Ranch of the remnants of the Forlorn Hope.

The 14 members of the First Relief included 12 men who had arrived in California during the 1846 season.[124] One of these, amazingly enough, was William Eddy, sufficiently recovered from the snowshoe ordeal to try to rescue his family. He did not make it all the way up, but it is astonishing that he was even able to try. In fact, of the 14 who started up, only seven arrived at Donner Lake. Three gave up while four others, Eddy among them, were given other tasks to perform, including guarding provisions left along the way.

The men had left Johnson's Ranch on February 5. Traveling on snowshoes, it had taken them two weeks to make the trip. When they arrived, Daniel Rhoads later recalled,

> We looked all around but no living thing except ourselves was in sight and we thought that all must have perished. We raised a loud halloo and then we saw a woman emerge from a hole in the snow. As we approached her several others made their appearance in like manner coming out of the snow. They were gaunt with famine and I never can forget the horrible, ghastly sight they presented. The first woman spoke in a hollow voice very much agitated & said "are you men from California or do you come from heaven."[125]

When the seven men left on February 22, they took 23 people—four men, four women, and 15 children—with them. They did not get far before they realized that Patty and Thomas Reed seemed too weak to make the trip. These two were returned to the Breen cabin, and the First Relief continued downwards with 21 (Table 2.3). Thirty-one were now left at the Alder

TABLE 2.3. Donner Party members who left with the First Relief.

Name	Fate
Breen, Edward	Survived
Breen, Simon	Survived
Denton, John	Died
Donner, Elitha	Survived
Donner, George, Jr.	Survived
Donner, Leanna	Survived
Donner, William Hook	Died
Graves, Eleanor (Ellen)	Survived
Graves, Lovina	Survived
Graves, William	Survived
James, Noah	Survived
Keseberg, Ada	Died
Keseberg, Elisabeth	Survived
Murphy, Mary	Survived
Murphy, William	Survived
Pike, Naomi	Survived
Reed, James, Jr.	Survived
Reed, Margret	Survived
Reed, Martha (Patty)	Returned to camp
Reed, Thomas	Returned to camp
Reed, Virginia	Survived
Williams, Eliza	Survived
Wolfinger, Dorothea	Survived

Creek and Donner Lake camps. With them, though, was the knowledge that another relief was on its way.

It took the First Relief 14 days to get to Johnson's Ranch. Only the rescuers had snowshoes; the others had to follow in the compressed snow left by those in front of them. We have a firsthand account of what the group looked like as they made the trip down. This comes not from Reason P. Tucker, who was in charge of the First Relief and who provided an important account of it, but from James Reed, in charge of the Second Relief.

THE SECOND RELIEF: "TERROR TERROR"

On February 27, Reed was leading the Second Relief upward when he encountered the First Relief on the way down:

I left Camp early on a fine hard snow and proceeded about 4 miles when we met the poor unfortunate Starved people, as I met them Scattered allong the snow trail I distributed Sweetbread that I had backed [baked] the 2 nights previous I give in small quantities here I met Mrs. Reed and two [of my] children two still in the mountains, I cannot describe the death like look they all had Bread Bread Bread Bread was the beging of evry Child and grown person I gave to all what I dared and left for the sene of desolation.[126]

Reed knew that two members of the group had died on the way down: John Denton had to be left behind on the 24th, and little Ada Keseberg died the next day. He did not learn until later that one more was to be lost. Young William Hook Donner broke into the food supplies and literally died of overeating on the 28th. The rest made it out alive.

This was not Reed's first try to reach the camps. In November, he and William McCutchan tried and failed to get through the snow. Now, accompanied by about eleven men (the exact number is not clear, but McCutchan was there, as was former Donner teamster Hiram Miller[127]), he tried again.

The men left Johnson's Ranch on February 23, passed the First Relief on February 27, and arrived at the camps in two separate groups on March 1. What they found was far worse than what they had seen on the way up.

Patrick Breen had mentioned the possibility, on February 26, four days after he reported that the Pikes' child had died on the 20th: "Mrs. Murphy said here yesterday that [she] thought she would commence on Milt. & eat him. I don't [think] that she has done so yet, it is distressing."[128] The Donners, he reported, had told the First Relief that they too would have to eat the dead if they could not find their buried cattle. By the time the Second Relief arrived, all this had come to pass.

There are no trustworthy firsthand accounts of what the Second Relief found. Reed did, though, provide a description of the scene to his father-in-law in Illinois. This account was then rewritten and published in Illinois newspapers in December 1847. While the description has been heavily romanticized from what Reed must have written, it is clear that he had provided the information from which it was built:

Among the cabins lay the fleshless bones and half eaten bodies of the victims of famine. There lay the limbs, the skulls, and the hair

TABLE 2.4. Donner Party members who left with the Second Relief.

Name	Disposition	Fate
Breen, Isabelle	Left at Starved Camp	Survived
Breen, James	Left at Starved Camp	Survived
Breen, John	Left at Starved Camp	Survived
Breen, Margaret	Left at Starved Camp	Survived
Breen, Patrick	Left at Starved Camp	Survived
Breen, Patrick, Jr.	Left at Starved Camp	Survived
Breen, Peter	Left at Starved Camp	Survived
Donner, Isaac	Died before departure from Starved Camp	Died
Donner, Mary	Left at Starved Camp	Survived
Donner, Solomon Hook	Brought in	Survived
Graves, Elizabeth	Left at Starved Camp	Died after rescue
Graves, Elizabeth Cooper	Left at Starved Camp	Died
Graves, Franklin, Jr.	Left at Starved Camp	Died
Graves, Jonathan	Left at Starved Camp	Survived
Graves, Nancy	Left at Starved Camp	Survived
Reed, Martha (Patty)	Brought in	Survived
Reed, Thomas	Brought in	Survived

of the poor beings, who had died from want, and whose flesh had preserved the lives of their surviving comrades, who, shivering beneath their filthy rags, and surrounded by the remains of their unholy feast, looked more like demons than human beings.[129]

The prose came from the editor; the facts from Reed. Indeed, Thornton's account is similar, and Thornton seems to have had Reed as an informant.[130]

Breen reported the arrival of the Second Relief ("10 men arrived this morning from Bear Valley with provisions"[131]) as the last entry in his diary. They were, he said, to leave in two or three days. In the end, the rescuers took 17 people with them (Table 2.4). Left behind were nine people at Alder Creek (Tamzene and George Donner and three of their children, Elizabeth Donner and two of hers, and Jean-Baptiste Trudeau) and five at the lake (Levinah Murphy and her son Simon, Louis Keseberg, and two other children, James Eddy and George Foster).

Reed had taken the three children of Jacob Donner that he thought might be able to make the journey. Tamzene Donner could have made the trip but, in one of the most fabled of Donner Party decisions, told Reed that she would not leave her husband. Three children that Reed described as "Stout harty"[132] stayed with her. Expecting additional relief to arrive soon, Reed left two of his men at Alder Creek (Charles Cady and Nicholas Clark), "one with each tent to cook and as fast as possible resusitate the enfeebled so that they might in a few days Start."[133] At Donner Lake, he left Charles Stone to "take care of the helpless."[134]

We know what happened next at the camps, though we do not know why. Soon after the Second Relief left, Stone made his way to the Alder Creek encampment. Clark was off hunting when he arrived, so it was Stone and Cady who entered into an agreement with Tamzene Donner. She offered to pay them to take her children down, and they agreed. Miller later recalled that Mrs. Donner had offered any one in the Second Relief $500 to rescue her children.[135] Eliza Donner reported that Stone and Cady were offered $500 in coin.[136] The two accounts are at least consistent, and the two men did take the three children as far as the Donner Lake camp. There, however, they left them with Levinah Murphy and then left by themselves, their packs apparently full of items they had gotten from Tamzene Donner. The kind interpretation—and it is the one McGlashan gives—is that the men saw the storm coming and realized that they could not bring the children down.[137] It may be true.

Reed certainly saw it coming as he struggled to get back. Three men had been sent ahead to the food caches that had been left lower down, and the group had arrived at the head of the Yuba River on the evening of March 4. Reed's journal entry for the day is of biblical intensity, one of the most moving passages to emerge from all that happened:

> Here the men began to fail being for several days on half allowance, or 1 1/2 pints of gruel or sizing per day. the Sky look like snow and everything indicates a storm god for bid wood being got for the night & *Bows* for the beds of all, and night closing fast, the Clouds still thicking terror terror I feel a terrible foreboding but dare not Communicate my mind to any, death to all if our provisions do not Come, in a day or two and a storm should fall on us. Very cold, a great lamentation about the Cold.[138]

The storm came that night, and in his journal entry for the 5th (not surprisingly, the days may be one off), Reed continued:

The last of our provisions gone looking anxiously for our supplies none. My dreaded Storm is now on us comme[nce]d snowing in the first part of the night and with the Snow Commed a perfect Hurricane in the night. A great crying with the Children and with the parents praying Crying and lamentations on acct of the Cold and the dread of death from the Howling Storm . . . still the storm Continues the light of Heaven, is as it ware shut in from us the snow blows so thick that we cannot see 20 feet looking against the wind I dread the Coming night.[139]

At what Reed himself called Starved Camp, the fire burned 15 feet into the snow; young John Breen actually fell into the pit. By the time the storm ended, Isaac Donner had died and many were no longer in any condition to travel. Relief was still expected from below, so 13 members of the group were left behind (Table 2.4). Only the two Reed children and Solomon Hook Donner, who could walk, went with the four rescuers. They were down safely by March 10.

It was otherwise at Starved Camp. There, Elizabeth Cooper Graves and her son Franklin died the night that Reed left. Soon the eleven who were still alive ate them and little Isaac Donner. Fortunately, the Third Relief was soon to find them.

THE THIRD RELIEF: "GOD AND STARK AND THE VERGIN MARY"

The third rescue was organized around William Eddy and William Foster, both of whom had children at the lake. Unlike the First and Second Reliefs, the Third left us with no journal, and so the timing of the events that occurred is not well known, though the major events are clear enough.

Seven men formed this group. In addition to Eddy and Foster, they included two men who had just returned from the Second Relief, Hiram Miller and Charles Stone. Then there was John Stark, who emerged as a hero. Stark had come to California in 1846 and was reported by all to be both huge (224 pounds, Thornton reported[140]) and powerful.

The seven set out around March 11. They came across John Denton's body the next day and arrived at Starved Camp around the 13th. They found 11 people alive, more than they had expected. For obvious reasons, Eddy

TABLE 2.5. Donner Party members who left with the Third Relief (those left at Starved Camp were also brought in by this relief; see Table 2.4).

Name	Fate
Donner, Eliza	Survived
Donner, Frances	Survived
Donner, Georgia	Survived
Murphy, Simon	Survived
Trudeau, Jean-Baptiste	Survived

and Foster were anxious to get to the lake. The next morning, they and two others went ahead, leaving Stark, Stone, and Howard Oakley to deal with the weak survivors. Stone took the baby, Elizabeth Graves. Oakley took Mary Donner. Stark took the rest.

John Breen later recalled that, in the end, Stark was simply left alone: "To his great bodily strength, and unexcelled courage, myself and others owe our lives. . . . He was as strong as two ordinary men. On his broad shoulders, he carried the provisions, most of the blankets, and most of the time some of the weaker children."[141] Often bringing them down in relays, he got them all in safely. William Graves recalled that Margaret Breen had vowed that she would "thank no boddy but God and Stark and the Vergin Mary" for her rescue.[142]

Eddy later said that it took the Third Relief only six hours to get from Starved Camp to Donner Lake.[143] The day they arrived is not known, but it would have been around March 14. It did not take them long to learn of new tragedies. James Eddy and George Foster were dead and cannibalized. Also gone were Elizabeth Donner and her son Lewis; Samuel Donner was either gone or close to it.

The four men left as quickly as they could. With them they took Jean-Baptiste Trudeau and four children (Table 2.5); Nicholas Clark, a member of the Second Relief who had stayed behind, joined them.

Of the four members of the Donner Party known to have been alive when the Third Relief left, three simply could not travel: George Donner, Levinah Murphy (to whom the Donner children now owed their lives), and Louis Keseberg. Tamzene Donner could travel but, as before, would not leave her husband. This was to be her last chance.

The Third Relief reached safety on March 17.[144] Yet another relief was organized for late March but had to turn back because the men could not get through the soft snow.

A SALVAGE OPERATION

A month passed between the return of the Third Relief and the next successful attempt to reach the encampments. This party is always referred to as the Fourth Relief. In fact, the prime goal of most of the members of this group, led by the distasteful—and soon murdered—William Fallon, was not to bring back people but to bring back property, especially that of the wealthy Donner families. Fallon and two others entered into a formal agreement with John Sinclair that provided the estates of George and Jacob Donner with half of the salvaged value of any retrieved goods and the cosigners with the other half. The agreement was to be modified if either George or Tamzene Donner were found alive. William Foster was part of this relief effort; when he had left with the Third Relief, his mother-in-law, Levinah Murphy, was still alive.

The group left Johnson's Ranch on April 13, went as far as they could on horseback, and then walked over the snow to reach the encampments on April 17. When they arrived, the only person alive was Louis Keseberg, and he had survived by eating the dead. Later, Keseberg recalled that Levinah Murphy had died about a week after the Third Relief left (Stewart estimated the date as March 20[145]) and that Tamzene Donner had appeared at his cabin about a week after that. Reporting that her husband had just died, she herself died the next day.[146] Keseberg then cannibalized her.

After the Fourth Relief returned safely with Keseberg, Fallon accused him of theft, asserted that he had expressed a preference for human flesh over any other kind of meat, said that he had been found with two buckets of fresh human blood, and strongly implied that he had killed Tamzene Donner. Indeed, one of the members of the Fourth Relief, Edward Coffeemire, explicitly accused him of murder. Keseberg successfully sued him for defamation of character but was granted only $1 in damages and had to pay court costs. It did not help that Keseberg was found with significant amounts of the Donner family possessions—including cash—nor did it help that he had a violent temper and was thought to have beaten his wife. Kristin Johnson has pointed out that he was tried for assault in 1856 and 1863 and that he once hit a little girl so hard that she was scarred for life.[147] Keseberg gained a reputation that followed him beyond death and well into this century.[148] Eliza Donner had come to his defense by 1880,[149] as have others since,[150] but, as Johnson has concluded, he was hardly an admirable person.

THE FINAL RELIEF

Edward Bryant left California in the summer of 1847, traveling east with Gen. Stephen Watts Kearny's party, John Charles Frémont in tow and on his way to a court-martial for what Kearny claimed was mutiny.[151] On June 22, they reached the place where it had all happened. Kearny ordered a halt so that the remains then so visible could be gathered and buried.

Near the cabins, Bryant reported, were seen

> two bodies, entire with the exception that the abdomens had been cut open and the entrails extracted. Their flesh had been either wasted by famine or evaporated by exposure to the dry atmosphere, and they presented the appearance of mummies. Strewn around the cabin were dislocated and broken bones—skulls, (in some instances sawn asunder with care for the purpose of extracting the brains),—human skeletons, in short, in every variety of mutilation. . . . The remains were, by an order of Gen. Kearny, collected and buried under the superintendence of Major Swords. They were interred in a pit which had been dug in the centre of one of the cabins for a *cache*. These melancholy duties to the dead being performed, the cabins, by order of Major Swords, were fired, and with every thing surrounding them connected with this horrid and melancholy tragedy, were consumed.[152]

Important archaeological work by Hardesty and Kelly Dixon and her colleagues has shown that the cleansing was not nearly as complete as this description suggests.[153] Nonetheless, when the flames died down, the fifth and final relief had ended. Of the 87 members of the Donner Party, 40 had died.

CHAPTER 2 NOTES

1. Hastings 1845:137–138.
2. Carey 1932; Andrews 1968:33.
3. See Nunis 1991 and Bagley 2010 on the Bidwell-Bartleson Party and Hafen 1973 on Fitzpatrick.
4. Bagley 2010:88.
5. Nunis 1991:110.
6. Ibid., 111.
7. The detailed route is shown in DeLafosse 1994.
8. Stewart 1962; Bagley 2010.
9. For the details of Walker's route to and from California in 1833–1834, see Stine 2015.
10. Frémont 1845:271; Jackson and Spence 1970.
11. Egan 1985:250. For a review of Walker's accomplishments, see Bagley 2010.
12. Gilbert 1983.
13. Ibid.; Stewart 1962; Bagley 2010.
14. Unruh 1979. The numbers are provided by Stewart 1962 and Bagley 2010.
15. Stewart 1962; Bagley 2010.
16. Camp 1960:318.
17. Stewart 1953:70.
18. Stewart 1962. See also Bagley 2010.
19. Stewart 1953:64; Stewart 1962:78.
20. Bancroft 1886:574–578.
21. Cooke 1859:284.
22. Unruh 1979.
23. Stewart 1962 suggests that this was the case; Bagley 2010 argues otherwise.
24. Palmer 1906:87–88.
25. Ibid., 88.
26. Lockley n.d.:4.
27. Ide 1944:22.
28. Palmer 1906:88.
29. Bagley 2010.
30. Ibid., 251.
31. Andrews 1970:23–25.
32. Johnson 1996:20.
33. Hastings 1845:40.
34. Ibid., 133.
35. Ibid., 137.
36. Ibid.
37. Morgan 1963:33.
38. Spence and Jackson 1973.
39. Ibid., 20.
40. Ibid., 21.
41. Andrews 1973; Spence and Jackson 1973:44n11; Bagley 2010.
42. Spence and Jackson 1973:21 (emphasis in original).
43. Hasselstrom 1984; Korns and Morgan 1994; Bagley 2010.
44. Korns and Morgan 1994.
45. Camp 1960:18.
46. Ibid., 138.
47. Hasselstrom 1984:241.
48. Camp 1960:213.
49. Ibid., 214.
50. Ibid., 215.
51. Ibid., 216.
52. Bagley 2010:246.
53. Camp 1960:216; the bird was probably a Western Meadowlark (*Sturnella neglecta*).
54. Morgan 1963:533.
55. Gilbert 1983:222.
56. Bryant 1985:143.
57. Ibid., 143.
58. Ibid., 144.
59. See, for instance, Andrews 1973.
60. Camp 1960:179.
61. Morgan 1963:174.
62. Ibid., 215.
63. Camp 1960:335.
64. Gudde and Gudde 1961:70.
65. Bryant 1985:114.
66. Camp 1960:225.
67. Ibid., 266. See also the discussion in Andrews 1973:137.
68. Camp 1960:202.
69. The spelling of all Donner Party names, including "Tamzene" rather than "Tamsen," "McCutchan" rather than "McCutchen," and "Dorothea"

rather than "Doris" Wolfinger, follows Johnson 2011. See also Novak and Dixon 2011:24n1.
70. Murphy 1980.
71. Stewart 1960:12 observes that both the reputation of California's climate and business difficulties led Reed to bring his family west. Dirck 2007 outlines these business difficulties and Abraham Lincoln's role in assisting him as his attorney. For an early account of Reed's life, see *History of Sangamon County, Illinois* (1881:853–854). I thank Will Bagley for emphasizing to me the importance of Reed's financial setbacks in leading him west.
72. Johnson 1994, 1996.
73. Hawkins and Madsen 1990.
74. Camp 1960:210.
75. Morgan 1963:256.
76. Unruh 1979.
77. Bryant 1985:46.
78. Morgan 1963:278.
79. Camp 1960:228.
80. McGlashan 1947:25.
81. Morgan 1963:258.
82. Ibid., 278.
83. Ibid., 279–280.
84. Korns and Morgan 1994. The maps accompanying this volume make the Bryant-Russell (and Donner) routes clear.
85. Morgan 1963:261.
86. Gudde and Gudde 1961:103.
87. Morgan 1963:263.
88. Johnson 1996:188.
89. Camp 1960:216.
90. Bryant 1985:173.
91. For a history of Pleistocene Lake Bonneville, see Grayson 2011.
92. Gudde and Gudde 1961:116.
93. Johnson 1996:189.
94. Mullen 1997:160 estimates Hastings's route to have been about 125 miles longer than the "standard" route via Fort Hall. He probably took this figure from Stewart (1962:183), who does not tell us how he arrived at this number. Bagley (2010:312), using historical estimates, puts the difference at only 10 miles. James Reed estimated the distance from Fort Bridger to the Humboldt via Hastings cutoff to be 461 miles (Korns and Morgan 1994:232–233).
95. Gudde and Gudde 1961:137. See also Korns and Morgan 1994:184.
96. Andrews 1968.
97. Bagley 2012:202–204. Emigrants used the route again in 1850, with similar results; no emigrants are known to have tried after that date (Bagley 2012:278–285).
98. On the possible location of John Snyder's grave, see Grebenkemper, Johnson, and Morris 2012.
99. Bryant 1985:346.
100. Unruh 1979:141–142 and Bagley 2012:150–151 describe Indian attacks on emigrant animals.
101. Johnson 1996:43.
102. Hopkins 1969:13.
103. Hardesty 1997.
104. Ibid.
105. Ibid.
106. McGlashan 1947:63.
107. Hardesty 1997; Johnson 2011a.
108. Johnson 1996:154.
109. King 1998:54.
110. Ibid., 55.
111. Ibid.
112. Bryant 1985:251.
113. Johnson 1996.
114. Johnson 1996:130.
115. King 1998:62.
116. Morgan 1963:294.
117. Ibid., 294.
118. King 1998:65.
119. Johnson 1996:130.
120. Ibid., 130.
121. King 1998:71.
122. Ibid., 72.

123. Ibid., 79.
124. Ibid.
125. Morgan 1963:328.
126. Ibid., 345.
127. King 1998.
128. Ibid., 91.
129. Morgan 1963:298.
130. Johnson 1996.
131. King 1998:92.
132. Morgan 1963:346.
133. Ibid., 346.
134. Ibid.
135. McGlashan 1947.
136. Houghton 1997.
137. McGlashan 1947.
138. Morgan 1963:347.
139. Ibid., 347–348.
140. Thornton 1986:80, Johnson 1996:103.
141. Morgan 1963:356.
142. Johnson 1996:226.
143. Stewart 1960.
144. Morgan 1963:358.
145. Stewart 1960.
146. McGlashan 1947.
147. Johnson 1996:256.
148. See, for instance, the portrait of him by Stewart 1960.
149. McGlashan 1947. See also Houghton 1997.
150. Rarick 2008.
151. For discussions of this episode in Frémont's life, see Spence and Jackson 1973, Egan 1985, Rolle 1991, and Chaffin 2002.
152. Bryant 1985:263.
153. Hardesty 1997; Dixon, Schablitsky, and Novak 2011.

3

PREDICTIONS OF DEATH

The Donner Party was fully formed in early August when the Graves family joined the others in the Wasatch Range. Their ordeal did not end until nearly nine months later. Forty-three deaths were associated with the group during these months, but three of these did not involve any of its members. All three were murders, and all three involved Indians: the man Eddy killed in Truckee Meadows and Sutter's two employees, Luis and Salvador (see Chapter 2).

Of the 40 deaths that occurred within the Donner Party, five occurred before the forced encampment. Luke Halloran died of consumption—presumably tuberculosis—but the remaining early deaths involved passive or active violence. Snyder was knifed by Reed, Hardcoop was forced to walk, Wolfinger was murdered, and Pike was accidentally shot.

The remaining 35 deaths happened after the establishment of the winter encampment. Of these, 22 occurred in the encampment itself, as members of the group awaited rescue or a chance to escape on their own. The remaining 13 deaths took place during the Forlorn Hope (six, not including Luis and Salvador; see Table 2.2) and the rescues (six; see Tables 2.3 and 2.4) or, in the case of infant Elizabeth Graves, at Sutter's Fort soon after rescue.

The exact causes of these 35 deaths are unknown. The general cause, however, is quite clear. Even though young William Hook Donner died after gorging himself when rescuers made food available, all, or nearly all, died of the results of some combination of starvation and exposure to cold. I explore the pattern of death within the Donner Party in the next chapter. Here I ask a more basic question: What does our understanding of human biology tell us about what the pattern of death should have been like?

PREDICTING DONNER PARTY DEATHS

THE WEAKER SEX

"Frailty," said Hamlet, "thy name is woman." Hamlet, of course, made many mistakes, and this was one of them. Measured in terms of mortality, frailty is a decidedly male characteristic. Take, for instance, life expectancy at birth. The most recent United Nations survey shows that of 196 countries and dependencies, males can expect to outlive females in only five (Botswana, Lesotho, Qatar, Swaziland, and Zimbabwe). In Europe as a whole, female life expectancy exceeds that of males by 7.9 years, in South America by 7.2 years, in the United States by 5.1 years, in Oceania by 4.7 years, in Asia by 3.7 years, and in Sub-Saharan Africa by 2.1 years. In the world as a whole, females can now expect to live 4.4 years longer than males.[1]

This is not some temporary state of affairs that just happens to characterize the world today. The life expectancy differential changes through time, just as it changes across space. But as far back as records allow the numbers to be assessed, females come out ahead. For instance, in the United States since 1900, the differential has fluctuated from a low of 1 year in 1920 to a maximum of 7.8 years in 1975, but in every year, females have the advantage. Changes in the magnitude of the difference have been driven largely by improvements in women's health care, especially during childbirth earlier in the century and, more recently, by declines in the adult male mortality rate.[2] Today, according to the United Nations, the difference stands at 5.1 years.[3]

Trustworthy records from other centuries show the same female advantage. In 1850, females born in Massachusetts could expect to live 2.2 years longer than males. In Sweden, female life expectancy from 1751 to 1790, when the first records became available, exceeded male life expectancy by 2.9 years. The advantage is less for the first data available for the British peerage—1700–1724—but here as well it is for females, by 0.4 years.[4] It is not true, as some have said, that women outlive men in all societies,[5] but the truth is not far from that.

Not only can males expect to have shorter lives than females, but they can expect to have higher mortality rates at every age, including infancy,[6] though female mortality is greater than that suffered by males before birth.[7] That is, males almost always have lower life expectancies than females and, far more often than not, die at higher rates across all ages. As Steven N. Austad has noted,

> Possibly no feature of human biology is more robust than women's survival advantage over men. Women live longer than men in cultures with short life expectancies and those with long life expectancies. Women live longer through periods of war, famine, and pestilence. They are the superior survivors when they are old, when they are young. . . . Women in modern societies die at lower rates from virtually all of the major causes of death.[8]

Women, Austad concludes, are better designed for survival than men.[9]

But what causes these differences? The answer to that depends on what we consider a cause.

On the easiest level—the actual proximate causes of the deaths themselves—it is well known that males die at a greater rate from most causes that can affect both sexes (that is, excluding such things as mortality associated with childbirth or with cancers that affect the reproductive organs). Females are more susceptible to such autoimmune diseases as lupus and rheumatoid arthritis,[10] but males die at higher rates from ischemic heart disease (produced by obstruction of blood flow), cancer, epilepsy, homicide, suicide, accidents, and a wide variety of infectious and parasitic diseases. Indeed, even though women are more susceptible to multiple sclerosis, men may die at higher rates from it.[11]

Figure 3.1 shows the average male/female sex ratios for the 15 leading causes of death in the United States in 2010[12] ("age-adjusted" here simply means that these values take into account the fact that different populations have different age structures). Figure 3.2 shows comparable data on the leading causes of death on a global basis for the year 2012, incorporating the member states of the World Health Organization.[13] Clearly, in all these countries at this time, male mortality rates were higher across the vast majority of the leading causes of death, reaching their peaks in deaths due to violence, cirrhosis, tuberculosis, suicide, and accidents.

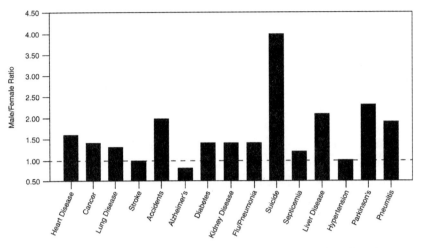

FIGURE 3.1. Male/female mortality ratios for the 15 leading causes of death in the United States in 2010 (Murphy et al. 2013).

This is not to say that sex ratios associated with particular causes of death are immutable. As I have said, they can and do change, both across space and through time. In the United States, for instance, the increase in the sex differential in life expectancy—from 2 years at the beginning of the century to 7.8 years in the mid-1970s—is associated with a decrease in deaths due to childbirth, driving down female mortality rates, and a proportionally greater increase in cigarette smoking by men, driving up male deaths due to lung cancer and heart disease.[14] But even though cause-specific ratios change through space and time, they nonetheless illustrate the strong tendency for males to die at higher rates across a diverse set of mortality-producing factors.

So, at one level, we can say that males tend to die at higher rates and at younger ages because they are vulnerable to such a wide range of life-threatening factors, from epilepsy to violence. The more difficult question, of course, is why this is the case—why it is males, not females, whose name is frailty.

No answer to this question has found widespread agreement. There are those who claim that the differences are entirely behavioral in origin. For instance, H. O. Lancaster has suggested that "in a human society without sex differences in automobile behavior and occupational risks, and with no tobacco smoking, a plausible case can be made that there would be little

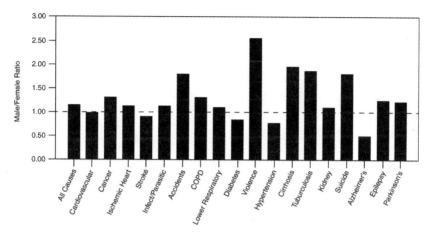

FIGURE 3.2. Male/female global mortality ratios for the leading causes of death (World Health Organization 2014).

difference in longevity or, rather, in the age-specific mortality rates between the sexes."[15] In this view, if men would just change how they behave, the sex differential in longevity would disappear.

This, the "gender argument," has virtually no support. Even though debate continues over the ultimate reasons for greater female than male longevity, all explanations focus heavily on the biological differences between the sexes.

At one time, it seemed that male hormones might lie behind these differences. Take, for instance, the analysis that J. B. Hamilton and G. E. Mestler did of the lifespans of "mentally retarded" people who had the misfortune of being institutionalized at a time when castration was considered to be an acceptable way of making males easier to control. Of the 1,032 males born between 1871 and 1920 that they studied, 297 had been castrated between the ages of 8 and 59.

The impact of castration on the longevity of these males was remarkable. Those who had been castrated lived an average of 13.6 years longer than those who had not. In addition, Hamilton and Mestler found that life expectancy was higher at every age for those who had been castrated than for those who had been left intact. Given all this, perhaps it is not surprising that they also found that among the castrated males who survived beyond 40, the later they had been castrated, the less the increase in life expectancy they received. In particular, each additional year of delay in castration cost 0.28 years of longevity.[16]

An analysis of Korean eunuchs born between 1556 and 1861 provided very similar results. The lifespan of the 81 eunuchs analyzed by K.-J. Min and his colleagues was between 14.4 and 19.1 years longer than the lifespans of intact men of similar socioeconomic status, depending on the exact group chosen for comparison.[17]

Not all such studies agree, however. A study of 50 Italian castrati born between 1581 and 1858 found no difference in average lifespans between these individuals and members of their intact cohorts.[18] In addition, a study of nearly 1,000 Danish men castrated between 1929 and 1968 found that, while castrated men had a lower death rate from heart attacks (myocardial infarction), they had higher death rates from all other causes combined.[19] And if castration increases male life expectancy by lowering the level of male sex hormones, then how might this be reconciled with studies showing that low levels of testosterone in males are associated with increased mortality?[20]

Rather than focusing on the curative aspects of low levels of sex hormones in males, recent approaches to understanding differential mortality in men and women focus on a wide variety of other possible underlying biological causes. These include the differential accumulation of mutations in the mitochondrial DNA that males inherit from their mothers; the biological burden borne by males as a genetic consequence of having a Y chromosome; the possibility that males suffer greater oxidative stress than females; the fact that the DNA caps that help protect the ends of chromosomes (telomeres) shorten more rapidly in males than they do in females as people age; and the potentially protective powers that females gain from estrogen.[21]

No one doubts that biology mediates longevity in general and differential male and female mortality specifically.[22] But is it fair to suggest that biology mediates virtually all the differences in mortality between human males and females?

It is certainly true that males engage in an extraordinarily wide variety of risky behaviors, behaviors that frequently cause them to die prematurely. As I have noted, men die at higher rates from homicide, suicide, and accidents (Figures 3.1 and 3.2); they also die at higher rates from such things as alcohol and tobacco use. They even die at higher rates from dog attacks.[23] The sex differentials in these categories can be substantial.[24]

Automobile accidents in the United States provide a good example. Between 1975 and 2012, men were involved in approximately 3 times as many fatal accidents as were women (the actual numbers vary from 2.7 times as many in 1998 to 4.1 times as many in 1975; in 2012, the ratio was 2.9). These differences exist whether they are measured in terms of fatal accidents per 100,000 licensed drivers[25] or in terms of numbers of miles driven,[26] and they exist even though women are involved in more accidents per million miles driven than are men.[27]

Greater male mortality in traffic accidents in the United States is not some oddity of our society today. In Norway in 1946, the male death rate from this cause was 2.5 times that of the female death rate; in Japan in 1951, 3.3 times; in Venezuela in 1960, 4.4 times; in Canada in 1964, 2.9 times.[28] The reason for this difference is fairly clear. Men drive faster and less cautiously than women; they also drive under the influence of alcohol more often.[29]

In other words, men die at higher rates in automobile accidents because they drive more aggressively and take more risks on the road than women do. They also drown more often (globally, 2.1 times more often in 2012 and 3.4 times more often in the United States during the same year[30]). In the United States in 2003–2004, men died from falls at far higher rates than women at every age and died from poisoning at higher rates at almost every age.[31] The ultimate risky behavior is suicide, and males kill themselves at far higher rates than females do (Figures 3.1 and 3.2). In the United States in 2010, males committed suicide at four times the female rate.[32] In the year 2000, the ratio was 4.4 male to female suicides; in 1990, it was 4.5; in 1980, 3.5; in 1950, 3.8.[33]

Men are also murdered more often. In the United States in 1950, men were murdered 3.3 times more often than women; they were murdered 3.9 times more often in 1970 and 3.8 times more often in 1980 and 2005.[34] They also murder more often. FBI data shows that from 1976 to 1987, men committed 85.3 percent of all homicides committed by people aged 16 or older, and 77 percent of all victims were men. For that data set, the male/female mortality ratio from homicide was 3.7.[35] These differences in male/female violence, psychologists Martin Daly and Margo Wilson observe, characterize every known human society.[36]

The risky behaviors in which men engage go far beyond such things as driving recklessly, killing one another, and purposefully killing themselves. Male Dutch bicyclists ride at night without lights far more often than their female counterparts and are far more likely than women bicyclists to cross railroad tracks when trains are coming.[37] Likewise, men cut waiting times for buses much shorter than females (and miss them more often as a result) and cross roads regardless of traffic more often than women.[38] Such risky behaviors likely account for why males are more frequently struck by bicycles than females.[39] The famous Darwin Awards honor those who "improve our gene pool by removing themselves from it in a particularly stupid manner"[40]—for instance, by lying down in the middle of a busy highway to stop traffic and dying as a result.[41] Of all such awards that were made between 1995 and 2014, 88.7 percent were earned by men, supporting, according to some, the belief that male risk-taking behavior stems from the fact that men are idiots.[42]

No one suggests that idiotic behavior is confined to males—for instance, females end up in hospital emergency rooms more often than males as a result of using cell phones while walking[43]—but males most certainly display such behavior in far greater frequencies than females do. And, of course, it is not just idiotic behavior that men display more frequently than women. The Carnegie Hero Fund recognizes "civilians who risk their lives to an extraordinary degree saving or attempting to save the lives of others."[44] By April 2003, 8,706 Carnegie Medals had been awarded. Of these, 91.1 percent went to men,[45] a proportion that is statistically identical to the proportion of Darwin Awards honoring men.[46]

Risk-taking and aggressive behavior are almost universal male attributes. Compared to one another, men are routinely risk-takers and women are risk-avoiders. Cross-cultural studies show that even though levels of male and female aggression vary substantially from society to society, young boys are routinely more aggressive than young girls within particular societies,[47] a difference that continues into adult life.[48] In addition, females routinely participate in activities that are low in risk compared to those in which males participate. Virginia Burbank's cross-cultural studies of female aggression show that, in contrast with male aggressive behavior, female aggression that becomes physical routinely involves weapons that are far more likely to injure than kill—sticks and stones, for instance.[49] Male aggression leads to high male involvement in homicide; more generally, male risk-taking leads to greater male involvement in deaths resulting from everything from homicide to hunting, automobile accidents to true heroism, and, yes, lying down in the middle of a busy highway to stop traffic.

Again, these patterns are not just Western ones. The male death rate from accidents in the United States in 2010 was 2.0 times that of the female death rate.[50] Among the forest-dwelling Ache of Paraguay, males suffered 2.4 times the number of accidental deaths than females did between 1890 and 1971.[51] At the time, the Ache earned their living entirely by hunting and gathering. In Uganda between 1923 and 1994, large carnivores (lions, leopards, and hyenas) attacked men 13.8 times more often than they attacked women, apparently because men put themselves at risk for such attacks far more often than women did.[52]

If only men would learn to be less aggressive and take fewer risks, the behavioral argument goes, their death rates would be reduced to a level that could be accounted for by biology alone. But why are men so aggressive; why do they so frequently engage in risky behavior that ends their lives far more often than it ends the lives of their female counterparts?

EXPLAINING MALE AGGRESSION

There are two very different, but overlapping, approaches to explaining why males so often engage in risky and aggressive behavior. The biosocial theory, championed by Alice H. Eagly and Wendy Wood, contends that the roles adopted by males and females in human societies result from the biological differences between the two sexes. Women have and then nurse and nurture children; men are physically larger, faster, and stronger. These very different biological attributes lead to a particular division of labor within societies (men hunt, women gather) as well as to very different general beliefs about the inherent nature of men and women. Men, for instance, are taken to be dominant, aggressive, forceful, and, as part of this behavioral package, risk-takers. Women are taken to be warm, caring, and far more skilled at building and maintaining social relationships. Children are raised to conform to these beliefs about the innate nature of human beings.[53] In this view, biological differences between the sexes lead to stereotyped gender differences to which people then conform.

The sexual selection theory sees male aggression and risk-taking in a very different light. This approach sees these quintessential male attributes as evolving as a result of competition between males for mates and as a means of restricting access of other males to those mates and potential mates. In this view, risky and aggressive behavior helps advertise underlying characteristics indicative of greater biological fitness and deters other men from messing around with one's own mates or possible mates: "I am a powerful guy who has a Rolex and a Maserati; I can provide for however many children you wish to have."[54] This explanation of risk-taking behavior gains support from evidence that men who engage in it have more mates[55] and evidence that males engage in riskier behavior in the presence of potential female mates than they do in their absence.[56]

There is nothing that prevents both biosocial and sexual selection explanations from being true. In the opening pages of this book, I pointed out that when I have gotten stuck in remote areas during my field projects, the men and women on those projects tended to respond in very different ways. The men acted aggressively to fix the problem—dig the vehicle out or change the tire—while the women stood back and watched. If the men could not fix the problem, their behavior became less productive while, at the same time, the women tended to take everything in stride and provide what I referred to as psychic glue, creating group cohesiveness where far less would have otherwise existed.

Perhaps the men in these settings were signaling their physical fitness to the women, just as the sexual selection theory suggests. On the other hand, perhaps the women were hanging back at first because men in general are better suited to tasks that require significant amounts of upper body strength, just as the biosocial theory suggests. Most likely, both things were happening.

It is also possible that male aggressiveness in this setting reflects the famous fight-or-flight response, in which a significant threat causes your body to become awash in chemicals, including adrenaline, that allow you to confront that threat head-on or retreat from it as fast as possible.

Psychologist Shelley E. Taylor and her colleagues have pointed out that a fighting response by females might put them and their offspring in serious jeopardy, while effective flight might be hindered by pregnancy or the need to attend to dependent offspring. Aggressive hyperarousal might make good sense for men but makes little sense for women.

Instead, Taylor and her team suggest that women respond to threatening situations by what they refer to as tend-and-befriend.[57] In this view, women in these contexts will do all they can to safeguard themselves and their offspring. That is the "tend" part. In addition, they will depend heavily on the creation and maintenance of social groups—especially groups of females—that can help them manage stressful situations. That is the "befriend" part, the psychic glue. Just as with the fight-or-flight reaction, Taylor and her colleagues argue, the tend-and-befriend response is mediated by a suite of stress-induced chemicals, including the hormone oxytocin.

The behavioral impacts of this hormone on women are complex and context dependent,[58] but they include increasing maternal care, enhancing the need for affiliation with others (it has been called both the affiliation and the social hormone[59]), and reducing anxiety in stressful situations. Women, Taylor and her team suggest, produce greater amounts of oxytocin in stressful situations than men do, and it is this chemical, among others,[60] that supports the tend-and-befriend response. In this view, some aspects of the biosocial explanation of gender roles—in particular, the expertise women seem to have in fostering positive social relationships—are to be explained biochemically, as a result of our deeper evolutionary history.

There is, in short, no reason to think that arguments based on sexual selection and those based on other aspects of human biology cannot combine to provide powerful explanations of some very basic behavioral differences between men and women, including the degree to which they display risky and aggressive behavior.

Where does this leave us as regards the argument that without gender differences in behavior, the sex differential in mortality would not exist? This argument, it turns out, is simply another way of saying that if the sexes were the same, the mortality rates would be the same.

This is not to say that human behavior cannot be modified. One of the most remarkable things about people is the degree to which their behavior can change. During the past few decades, the increase in female participation in one of the riskiest behaviors people routinely undertake—smoking—has had a significant impact on reducing the difference in male and female life expectancies in the United States.[61] But even though human behavior is remarkably plastic, the strong tendency of males to behave in ways detrimental to their longevity is very much biological in origin.

"A male's career," Martin Daly and Margo Wilson observe, is "short and sweet."[62] Under usual conditions, males live shorter lives than females and suffer greater mortality across all age classes. As a result, we would expect more males than females to have died within the Donner Party. But what might be expected to happen to this pattern under conditions of extreme cold and famine?

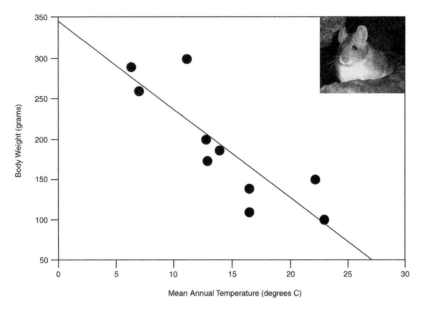

FIGURE 3.3. The relationship between body weight and mean annual temperature in western woodrats (after Brown and Lee 1969); the bushy-tailed woodrat (*Neotoma cinerea*) lurks in the corner (photograph by Ken Hickman).

DIFFERENTIAL MORTALITY AND EXPOSURE TO COLD

Men and women are built in such different ways that there are many reasons to think that their physiological reactions will also differ, perhaps substantially, when exposed to extreme cold for significant amounts of time. Some of these are obvious, some not, but all are likely to be important in such settings.

Surface area
Toward the end of the Pleistocene epoch or Ice Age in North America, many species of large mammals—including camels, mammoths, and mastodons—became extinct.[63] Among those that survived, a number decreased in size, including bison, bobcats, and jaguars.[64] These decreases in size, some have argued, reflect Bergmann's Rule in action.

Bergmann's Rule is straightforward. It states that within given species or closely related species of warm-blooded animals, those populations that live in cooler climates have larger average body sizes than those that live in

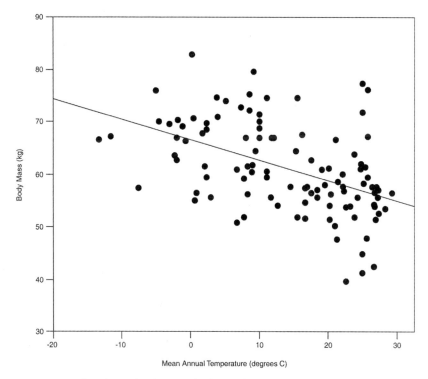

FIGURE 3.4. The relationship between body weight and mean annual temperature in a sample of human groups (after Foster and Collard 2013).

warmer climates.[65] Figure 3.3, for instance, shows the relationship between mean annual temperature and body size in four species of the squirrel-sized rodents called woodrats (genus *Neotoma*) in western North America. Larger woodrats live in areas marked by lower annual mean temperatures and vice versa.[66] Figure 3.4 shows a similar relationship for a variety of human populations, suggesting that the same kind of response is at work here as well.[67]

Bergmann's Rule does not always work in situations where it seems like it should,[68] but biologists Shai Meiri and Tamar Dayan have shown that it does apply to about two-thirds of the 149 mammal species they investigated.[69] One of the reasons that it works so often is likely to be the relationship between an animal's mass and surface area, on the one hand, and its ability to generate and retain heat, on the other.

Mammals tend to produce roughly the same amount of heat per unit of weight.[70] However, as mammals become larger, their volume increases as a cube, but their surface area increases only as a square. As a result, if we calculate the ratio between surface area and weight, smaller individuals have a higher ratio than larger ones. This higher ratio means that smaller mammals have a relatively greater area from which to lose heat than do larger animals per unit of heat production. Many argue that this relationship accounts for those instances in which Bergmann's Rule seems to apply.

There are several formulas for calculating human surface area. One of the standards is

$$BSA = W^{.425} \times H^{.725} \times .007184, \text{ where}$$
$$BSA = \text{body surface area;}$$
$$W = \text{weight in kilograms (kg); and}$$
$$H = \text{height in centimeters (cm).}[71]$$

Table 3.1 shows the result of the application of this formula to six hypothetical individuals ranging from 50 kg (110 pounds) to 100 kg (220 pounds) in weight and from 160 cm (5 feet 3 inches) to 185 cm (6 feet 1 inch) in height. Here, as weight and height have increased, so has surface area, but the surface area/body mass ratio has decreased by as much as 25.3 percent. Clearly, smaller people have more surface area per unit of heat production than larger people do. As a result, they also have a relatively greater surface area from which heat can be lost.

On average, women are, of course, smaller than men: roughly 8 percent shorter and 25 percent lighter.[72] It follows that they also have higher surface area/body mass ratios. Since the amount of heat that a person can produce is largely a function of body mass, and the amount of heat a person can lose is a function of the surface area/body mass ratio, it would seem that, on average, women would be at a greater disadvantage in cold environments. Many people have, in fact, reached just this logical conclusion.[73]

Body Fat: White Adipose Tissue
Not only are women smaller than men, but they also have a higher proportion of white adipose tissue, or white fat and the stuff we all think of as body fat. The actual figures vary from population to population (and across ages), but in general, women's bodies average around 25 percent fat by weight, while men's bodies average around 15 percent.[74] In addition, the distribution of fat within the body differs between men and women. In women, fat tends

TABLE 3.1. An example of the relationship between human body size and body surface area (BSA).

Weight (kg)	Height (cm)	BSA	(BSA/kg)(100)
50	160	1.50	3.00
60	165	1.66	2.76
70	170	1.81	2.59
80	175	1.96	2.45
90	180	2.10	2.33
100	185	2.24	2.24

to be distributed subcutaneously, just beneath the skin. In men, fat tends to be located more deeply within the body, especially within the abdomen (think beer belly).

For instance, an analysis of the distribution of fat in 121 Japanese men and 93 Japanese women, all between 18 and 23 years old, found that the women had a greater absolute amount of body fat (11.4 kg [25 pounds] compared to 7.7 kg [17 pounds] for the men) as well as a greater relative amount of body fat (20.9 percent compared to 12.4 percent). Of that fat, a relatively higher proportion was distributed subcutaneously in the women: 63 percent, compared to 54 percent in the men.[75] While studies done on different human populations, and different age classes within those populations, provide different numbers,[76] the general results are the same. Women have more fat than men in an absolute sense, and more of that fat is distributed just beneath the skin than it is in men. In particular, more of that fat is found just beneath the skin in the abdominal, gluteal (buttocks), and femoral (thigh) regions of the body.[77]

The potential significance of this fact for adaptation to extreme cold is simple. Because subcutaneous fat is not well supplied with blood vessels, it provides a significant layer of insulation between skin and the interior of the body. In general, people with greater amounts of subcutaneous fat maintain lower skin temperatures under cold conditions and thus shed less heat to the environment. That, in turn, means they need to produce less heat to maintain appropriate core temperatures. Because women have greater amounts of subcutaneous fat than men do, they should be able to withstand cold environments better than men.[78] Indeed, physiologist W. R. Keatinge has argued that "surface fat thickness is usually the only important individual factor determining heat loss when normal people are exposed to a cold environment."[79] It is for this reason, some have argued, that the cold water divers of Japan and Korea are women, not men.[80]

Reading all this might make you think of polar bears swimming happily in icy waters and of the protection they must get from extra-thick layers of fat. Mammalogists have at times thought the same way,[81] and it is true that these animals are extremely well insulated.[82] However, biologist Caroline Pond and her colleagues have shown that polar bears have no more superficial fat than would be expected given their huge size.[83] In fact, Pond sees no reason to believe that "superficial adipose tissue has evolved as an adaptation to thermal insulation" in any terrestrial mammal (thus excluding whales and seals, about which there is little doubt).[84]

Terrestrial mammals, of course, include people, and Pond means for her argument to include us as well.[85] Indeed, there is no evidence that the peoples of the Far North can be distinguished from those to the south in terms of the distribution and abundance of their fat deposits. For example, the Inuit, native to the American Arctic, have no greater amount of subcutaneous fat than do people whose ancestry lies in more temperate realms.[86] Instead, the greater amount of fat, including subcutaneous fat, that women have seems to be largely an adaptation to the demands of pregnancy and lactation.[87] In addition, some aspects of fat distribution in women seem to serve as signals to potential mates.[88] The particular distribution of body fat in women, independent of the total amount of that fat, may also provide protection against certain kinds of diseases.[89]

For both males and females, white adipose tissue represents one of our physical risk management systems, providing a source of energy in times of need.[90] As Pond and C. A. Mattacks noted long ago, however, it appears as if "women may be designed to be fatter than men."[91] If so, there are good reasons for that design, and any thermal protection that women might gain when exposed to severe cold would simply represent a secondary benefit from a feature that exists for very different reasons.

Body Fat: Brown Adipose Tissue
Whether distributed subcutaneously or more deeply within the body, white adipose tissue serves as a fuel storage site, releasing calories if and when they are needed. Although not the reason for its existence, white adipose tissue also serves as an insulator.

Brown adipose tissue, or brown fat, is distinctly different. It has a much better blood supply (accounting, in part, for its brown color) and is far more restricted in distribution, with much of it found in the neck and upper chest. Given this more restricted distribution, it is not surprising to learn that while human bodies might be about 20 percent fat by weight, brown adipose tissue provides no more than about 0.5 percent of that weight.

Brown fat also has a very different function from its white cousin. It exists to protect the body's core temperature by generating heat in response to even mildly cold environmental conditions. This it can do rapidly through non-shivering thermogenesis, a process that might have evolved to warm blood flowing to vital organs (there are functionally similar adipocytes that develop within white adipose tissue, called brite, or beige, cells).

We know less about brown adipose tissue than we do about its white counterpart, in large part because it was not until 2009 that it was shown that such fat exists in adults.[92] What we do know suggests that women have more of it[93]—though there is some disagreement in this realm[94]—and that both men and women retain less of it as they age, with men seeming to lose it more rapidly than women.[95] From the perspective of cold adaptation, women again appear to be on the winning side of the fat war between the sexes.

Some Other Factors

Bergmann's Rule tells us that within a single species, or closely related species, of warm-blooded animals, populations that live in cooler climates have larger average body sizes than those that live in warmer ones. The rule seems to work as well as it does because of the relationship between body surface area and body mass discussed previously. Much the same can be said about Allen's Rule, which applies not to whole bodies but to parts of them. This rule tells us that within a single species, or closely related species, of warm-blooded animals, those populations that live in cooler climates have shorter protruding body parts—ears, arms, and legs, for instance—than those who live in warmer climates.[96]

For instance, Michael Tilkens and his colleagues have shown that, among people, longer legs are associated with higher resting metabolic rates in both men and women. In line with Allen's Rule, this suggests that shorter legs are metabolically less expensive than longer ones.[97] Since women tend to have legs that are both absolutely and relatively shorter than those of men, and since the upper parts of women's limbs tend to be better insulated with fat than those of men,[98] this implies that women should gain yet another advantage over men in conditions of extreme cold.

The Empirical Evidence: Experiments

How do males and females who are not acclimated to cold environments respond to them? The experimental studies of unacclimated subjects have been of two sorts: those that immerse people of both sexes in cold water and those that expose them to cold air. The results of these two kinds of studies differ somewhat, and, since the cold air studies are far more relevant to the Donner Party experience, I focus on those results here.[99]

The cold air studies have shown that under cold conditions, the average skin temperatures of women fall more than those of men do, both at rest and during exercise.[100] The difference is often on the order of 1°C–2°C, but there is more to it than just this average difference. If women's skin temperature decreased to a greater extent than men's across all parts of the body, then it would seem that women would be at greater risk from such cold injuries as frostbite than men. Richard Burse hypothesized just this risk in 1979, before much work had been done in this area. However, it turns out that this is not the case. Peripheral sites—nose, chin, fingers, and toes—cool to an equal degree in both men and women. It is average, not peripheral, skin temperature that shows the difference.[101]

Thus, under cold conditions, the average skin temperatures of unacclimated women drop more than those of unacclimated men, except for those parts of the body that would be most prone to cold-related injuries. Much evidence suggests that this difference is a direct result of the greater thermal insulation provided to women by subcutaneous fat.[102] Although some studies do not support this conclusion,[103] it has been shown that the greater the amount of subcutaneous fat possessed by a long-distance cold water swimmer, the longer that person can remain in the water.[104] In addition, analyses of skin temperatures in men and women in response to whole body cryotherapy—in which individuals can be exposed to temperatures as low as −110°C for brief periods of time—have shown that the greater the amount of subcutaneous fat an individual possesses, the greater the decrease in that individual's skin temperature. Because women have greater amounts of that fat, their skin temperatures decrease more than those of men do.[105]

The full run of cold air studies suggests that subcutaneous fat mediates skin temperatures in cold conditions. No matter what mechanism accounts for the difference, the difference is real, and its potential impact on survival in cold air is quite significant. Because women maintain colder skin temperatures than men do in these settings, the thermal gradient between skin and air temperature is greater in men than in women, and the rate at which heat is lost from the body is thus greater in men than in women.[106]

Looking from the skin inward toward core temperatures rather than from the skin outward toward ambient temperatures, C. H. Wyndham and his colleagues calculated that the heat loss per unit surface area in women at 5°C is 15.3 percent less than that for men.[107] Perhaps this is why the great majority of studies have found that at rest under cold conditions, women maintain core temperatures that are either similar to or higher than those maintained by men.[108] Under exercise conditions, however, this relationship seems to break down, since no consistent relationship has been found between sex and relative core temperatures in this context. When at work, the increased blood flow from the body core to the skin would tend to remove any advantage provided by greater subcutaneous insulation, and this fact may explain the conflicting results of the cold air exercise experiments.

Since the Donner Party was exposed to cold air and not cold water, it is the cold air studies that are most relevant to understanding how members of that party might have reacted to the situation in which they found themselves. In cold water, the skin temperatures of men and women take on the temperature of the water itself, thus depriving women of a major relative advantage that they have in cold air. It is, however, relevant to observe that the body temperatures of women drop further than those of men in cold water, perhaps in part because of their smaller mass and larger surface area/ mass ratio. In addition, men show a greater metabolic response to a given degree of cooling in water, whether at rest or during exercise. This response also occurs in cold air studies involving exercise. That is, men burn more calories in cold contexts to maintain core temperatures than women do.[109]

Even though it has been argued that women are at a great disadvantage in the cold,[110] these experimental results suggest otherwise. In particular, they show that in cold air, women maintain lower skin temperatures, lose less heat per unit of surface area, maintain core temperatures as high as or higher than those maintained by men, and burn fewer calories in accomplishing all this. No wonder, then, that physiologist Lewis Pugh, in his subjective analysis of cases of accidental hypothermia in Great Britain, was struck by the apparent high survivorship of women. Subcutaneous fat, he speculated, was the critical variable here, and while it seems very likely that other variables are also at play, the role that subcutaneous fat plays in providing insulation seems key.[111]

In short, a wide range of experimental studies of the differential reactions of unacclimated males and females to cold suggest that females should do better than males in these settings.

The Empirical Evidence: The Real World

The biology of human responses to exposure to extreme cold has been well studied—especially in experimental settings—and suggests that women should survive such settings at higher rates than men. However, what really happens during times of extreme cold does not necessarily conform to these expectations.

The results of some studies of differential human mortality under conditions of extreme cold in urban settings can be used to argue that females do survive such cold at higher rates than males do.[112] However, other studies can be used to argue that females are the weaker sex in these contexts[113] or that there is no difference in male/female mortality ratios in prolonged cold.[114]

It is not at all clear why the results of such studies vary so widely. If, as the underlying biology suggests, women should die at lower rates than men under cold conditions, then perhaps women are lost at unexpectedly high rates simply because cold-related mortalities fall so very heavily on the elderly, and so many of the elderly are women.[115] It might also be because such important factors as access to medical care and social support systems have gone unmeasured and work to the disadvantage of women in certain urban settings.[116] It might even be because, in some cultural contexts, men clothe themselves in more weather-appropriate ways.[117]

No matter what the reasons, patterns of cold-induced mortality in modern urban settings seem to show little global advantage to either females or males and so give us little guidance as to what to expect in the horrendous conditions encountered by the Donner Party.

Famine

A wide variety of biological factors suggest that females should do better than males in the face of starvation and that this should be especially true for adults—that is, for women and men. Most obviously, women are smaller than men (again, by about 25 percent by body weight), and this fact alone means that their nutrient and energy needs are less than those of men. In addition, a greater amount of body fat provides women with relatively greater energy stores. At the same time, that high proportion of fat decreases women's energy requirements since, everything else being equal, the greater the amount of fat, the less the proportion of metabolically active lean tissue. Females above the age of five or so also have lower basal metabolic rates than males do.[118]

For all these reasons, males have higher nutrient and energy requirements than females do. Thus, anthropologist William Stini notes that a 70 kg man will expend about 540 kcal during eight hours of sleep, while a 58 kg female will expend only about 440 kcal during the same period.[119] Likewise, the same man will expend about 300 kcal per hour in moderate labor, while the same woman will expand 60 kcal less per hour while engaged in that labor. These are significant differences. Indeed, evidence even shows that males will use a greater proportion of body protein than females (who will use fat) to meet their energy requirements.[120]

All other things being equal, it follows that females, especially adult women, should be more robust in the face of starvation than males, especially adult men. It is presumably for this reason that males routinely suffer greater increases in mortality in times of severe famine than females and that they have done so both through time—extending back at least into the nineteenth century—and on a virtually global basis. While mortality during famines tends to fall most harshly on the oldest and youngest members of the affected groups, the greatest increases in mortality over background rates tends to be for males in the prime of life—those between about 15 and 40 years of age.[121]

There certainly have been episodes of famine with higher female than male mortality.[122] As J. P. W. Rivers observed long ago, and as others have since stressed, the reason for this appears to involve differential male access to food and other resources.[123] In situations in which both sexes share resources, starvation-induced mortality should differentially remove males from any given human population.

Age
In normal situations, relatively high death rates characterize both the youngest and oldest members of human societies (Figure 3.5). Mortality tends to

be high between birth and about five years of age, decreases through the early teen years, then begins to rise and become increasingly higher among older adults.[124]

Conditions of cold and/or famine exacerbate this pattern. Young children, for example, have smaller nutrient and energy stores than adults, and this alone makes them more prone to starvation-caused mortality. And, as noted above, it is the oldest and youngest members of society who tend to suffer the most during episodes of famine.

Children are also among the most susceptible to cooling. While they do have relatively substantial stores of heat-producing brown adipose tissue, they also have a high surface area/body mass ratio, relatively small amounts of subcutaneous fat, and, because of their small muscle mass, a low rate of metabolic heat production.[125] As a result, they can lose heat quickly and have a relatively low ability to replace it.

The studies that have been done on the reaction of older men and women to cold show that older people are less able than younger ones to respond to heat loss by vasoconstriction,[126] perhaps as a result of structural changes to blood vessels, and that this decreasing ability may impact men more than women. It does not help that basal metabolic rate decreases as we age, though this is a function of decreasing muscle mass in the elderly and is of less importance for physically fit individuals in cold contexts.[127] Older men may also gain little from the body fat insulation they do have. In an analysis conducted by J. A. Wagner and S. M. Horvath, for instance, the core temperatures of men older than 50 fell much further than did those of men between the ages of 20 and 30, even though the older men had twice as much insulating body fat.[128] Older people—and especially older men—seem to be at greater risk than younger ones in cold contexts.

Thus, all that we know about the interrelationships between sex, on the one hand, and cold and famine, on the other, leads us to expect that deaths within the Donner Party should have taken the heaviest toll on the old and young. We should also expect that, unless males gained differential access to resources, they should have died at much higher rates than females. It is also reasonable to expect that males would have died sooner than females, given the greater rates of energy expenditure they would have undergone. This might be expected to have happened even if the activity levels of males and females had been equal.

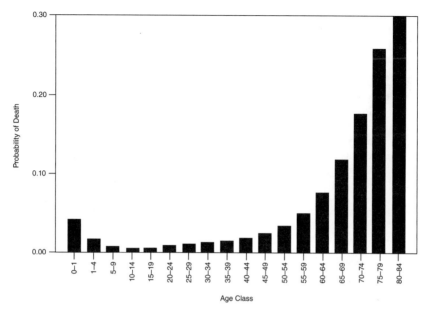

FIGURE 3.5. Global probabilities of death by age class, 2005–2010 (United Nations 2013).

The Potential Role of Social Ties

For nearly 150 years, it has been known that married men and women have lower mortality rates than those who remain single. Historically, while both married men and women tended to live longer than their unmarried counterparts, men have gained greater longevity benefits from marriage than women have, though this differential seems to be disappearing in economically developed societies.[129] Not only does marriage increase longevity, but the longer individuals remain married, the greater the increase seems to be (see Table 3.2 and Figure 3.6).[130]

In general, there are two possible reasons for this. First, people with poor health or with unhealthy or dangerous lifestyles may simply find it difficult to attract spouses. This is not surprising given that people use a wide variety of cues to choose their mates and that choosing a healthier mate can increase one's own genetic fitness by increasing the likelihood that offspring will themselves survive to reproduce.[131]

Marriage also clearly provides direct protection against death. Marriage leads to a reduction in risk-taking and the pursuit of healthier behaviors,

TABLE 3.2. Deaths per 100,000 U.S. citizens, 1966–1968, ages 35 to 74, and associated mortality rates of married and unmarried people (from Kobrin and Hendershot 1977).

Age	35–44	45–54	55–64	65–74
Male deaths per 100,000				
Married	323	814	2,042	4,456
Unmarried	1,008	2,125	4,276	5,944
Unmarried/married ratio	3.12	2.61	2.09	1.33
Female deaths per 100,000				
Married	212	464	910	2,379
Unmarried	408	757	1,278	2,595
Unmarried/married ratio	1.92	1.63	1.40	1.09

particularly among married men. Marriage, for instance, can lead people to decrease their use of alcohol and tobacco, drive more carefully, and exercise more. Marriage can also lead to an increase in socioeconomic well-being and that, in turn, can lead to improved nutrition, better access to health care, increased possibilities for nurturing during times of ill health, and reduced stress related to economic needs.[132]

The longevity benefits of marriage have been well studied and are quite clear. However, marriage can be seen as just one subset of a broad group of quintessentially human social behaviors that have a longevity payoff. A diverse set of studies has shown that under normal living conditions, the greater the number of social ties a person has, the greater the increase in his or her longevity. Marriage provides just one kind of life-enhancing social tie; others include religious involvement, contacts with friends, and participation in informal social groups.

Religious involvement has been particularly well studied. For instance, Robert A. Hummer and his colleagues have shown that those who attend religious services once a week can expect to live about 6.6 years longer than those who never attend such services.[133] Similarly, Marc Musick and his team reported that people who attended religious services at least once a month had their risk of death during the following 7.5 years (the follow-up period of the study) cut by about a third compared to those who never attended.[134] Study after study has shown that the more a person is embedded in a web of richer and more complex social relationships, the longer that person is likely to live.[135]

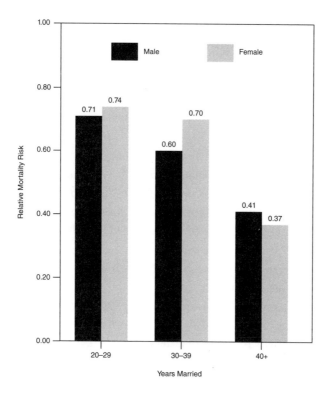

FIGURE 3.6. The marriage benefit by length of marriage; a mortality risk of 1.0 would indicate no benefit (after Dupre et al. 2009).

Although it is not always clear why this effect exists, some pathways are obvious. Enhanced social ties increase access to information, some of which may be health enhancing and increase the likelihood of receiving assistance in a timely manner. Positive social relationships, deep religious beliefs, and a sense of well-being can decrease stress and the negative cardiovascular consequences of stress (having a dog as a pet can help here as well).[136] Adherence to religious norms may decrease participation in certain kinds of risky behaviors. To give but one example, members of the Church of Jesus Christ of Latter-day Saints neither drink alcohol nor use tobacco. Some studies also suggest that such relationships may enhance immune systems.[137]

It should come as no surprise that in disaster settings, families and friends play a known role in providing information and assistance.[138] It is not pleasant reading, but firsthand accounts of starvation episodes during World War II show the hierarchical relationships of friends, family, and self in times of overwhelming need. They also provide remarkably strong parallels to the Donner Party experience.

Take, for instance, this firsthand account of the results of starvation at Bergen-Belsen, the Nazi concentration camp, in 1945:

> The most conspicuous psychological abnormality was a degradation of moral standards characterized by increasing selfishness, and it was more or less proportional to the degree of undernutrition. In the first stage consideration for others was limited to personal friends, then the circle contracted to child or parent, and finally only the instinct to survive remained. Emotional response became progressively lowered and consciousness of sex was lost. Eventually all self-respect disappeared and the only interest left was to obtain something which could be eaten, even human flesh. Even among those not grossly under-nourished, there was a blunting of sensitivity to scenes of cruelty and death.[139]

The lessons from all this seem clear. Increased social ties, including those provided by one's family, are associated with decreased mortality. The predictions for Donner Party deaths follow directly. All other factors being equal, we should expect that the larger the family to which a person belonged and with which he or she traveled, the greater the chances of surviving. Other factors may intervene, but this is the general expectation. If this is not what we find, then we will be alerted to search for those other factors that may not be equal.

EXPECTATIONS OF DEATH

Given all this, we now have a strong set of expectations about what the pattern of deaths within the Donner Party, and other groups like it, should have been. We expect high mortality among the youngest and oldest members of the group. We expect higher mortality among the males than the females. Finally, we expect higher survivorship among those who traveled with larger kin groups than those who traveled with smaller ones. We might even expect that those who traveled with the smallest support groups died before those who traveled with larger ones, since these people would have diminished access to family-based assistance.

CHAPTER 3 NOTES

1. United Nations 2011.
2. Verbrugge and Wingard 1987; Trovato and Lalu 1996; Luy 2003; Kruger and Nesse 2004; Austad 2011; Thorslund et al. 2013.
3. United Nations 2011.
4. Trussell 1995.
5. E.g., Hazzard 1986.
6. McMillen 1979; Waldron 1983, 1986; Wingard 1984; Stinson 1985; Verbrugge and Wingard 1987; Austad 2006, 2011.
7. Orzack et al. 2015; Austad 2015.
8. Austad 2011:479.
9. Ibid., 484.
10. Whitacre et al. 1999; Austad 2011.
11. Whitacre et al. 1999; Scalfari et al. 2013; Kingwell et al. 2012.
12. Murphy et al. 2013.
13. World Health Organization 2014.
14. Waldron 1983, 1986, 1993.
15. Lancaster 1990:372.
16. Hamilton and Mestler 1969.
17. Min, Lee, and Park 2012.
18. Nieschlag, Nieschlag, and Behre 1993. See also Paternostro 1994.
19. Edler von Eyben, Graugaard, and Vaeth 2005.
20. Shores et al. 2006; Laughlin, Barret-Connor, and Bergstrom 2008; Yeap et al. 2014.
21. E.g., Kruger and Nesse 2004; Stindl 2004; Eskes and Haanen 2007; Vaupel 2010; Austad 2006, 2011; Barrett and Richardson 2011; Seifarth, McGowan, and Milne 2012; Maklakov and Lummaa 2013; Regan and Partridge 2013.
22. E.g., Kirkwood 2005; Chen et al. 2010; Chung et al. 2010; Montesanto et al. 2011; Slagboom et al. 2011; Sebastiani and Perls 2012; Sebastiani et al. 2012; Beekman et al. 2013.
23. Langley 2009.
24. Wisser and Vaupel 2014.
25. National Center for Health Statistics 2012; National Highway Traffic Safety Administration 2014, 2015.
26. Li et al. 1998.
27. Ibid.
28. Preston, Keyfitz, and Schoen 1972.
29. Waldron 1986.
30. World Health Organization 2014.
31. Bergen et al. 2008.
32. Murphy et al. 2013.
33. National Center for Health Statistics 2012.
34. National Center for Health Statistics 2011. See also Cooper and Smith 2011.
35. Kellerman and Mercy 1992.
36. Daly and Wilson 1988.
37. Cobey et al. 2013.
38. Pawlowski, Atwal, and Dunbar 2008.
39. Tuckel, Milszarski, and Maisel 2014.
40. Northcutt 2003:2.
41. Ibid., 65; http://darwinawards.com/darwin/darwin2001-34.html.
42. Lendrem et al. 2014.
43. Smith et al. 2013.
44. http://www.carnegiehero.org/about-the-fund/carnegie-medal/.
45. Becker and Eagly 2004; Wood and Eagly 2012.
46. Chi-square = 2.18, p = 0.14.
47. Rohner 1976; Maccoby 1998.
48. E.g., Burbank 1987; Campbell 1993.
49. Burbank 1987. See also Burbank 1994.
50. Murphy et al. 2013.

51. Hill and Hurtado 1996.
52. Treves and Naughton-Treves 1999.
53. Wood and Eagly 2002, 2012; Eagly and Wood 2009.
54. E.g., Daly and Wilson 1983, 1988; Hawkes and Bliege Bird 2002; Smith, Bliege Bird, and Bird 2003; Bliege Bird and Smith 2005; Archer 2009; Jones, Bliege Bird, and Bird 2013.
55. E.g., Smith, Bliege Bird, and Bird 2003.
56. Baker and Maner 2008, 2009; Pawlowski, Atwal, and Dunbar 2008; Ronay and von Hippel 2010; Cobey et al. 2013. For a female behavioral counterpart, see Hudders et al. 2014.
57. Taylor et al. 2000.
58. Olff et al. 2013.
59. Miller et al. 2015; Li et al. 2016.
60. The others include the opioids that the body is able to produce—the endorphins are probably the most famous example (Taylor et al. 2000).
61. Waldron 1993, 2009.
62. Daly and Wilson 1983:92.
63. For a review, see Grayson 2016.
64. E.g., Kurtén 1965.
65. Meiri and Dayan 2003; Meiri, Yom-Tov, and Geffen 2007; Meiri 2011.
66. Brown and Lee 1969.
67. D. F. Roberts 1953, 1978; Leonard and Katzmarzyk 2010; Foster and Collard 2013.
68. E.g., Dayan et al. 1989; Paterson 1990; Meiri, Yom-Tov, and Geffen 2007.
69. Meiri and Dayan 2003.
70. The amount of energy produced per unit weight of tissue varies with body size across mammals, but that variation is far less than the variation in body mass across those mammals (see Speakman 2005).

71. Harrison et al. 1988.
72. Archer 2009.
73. E.g., Burse 1979; Greene and Bell 1987; Stocks et al. 2004; Kaciuba-Uscilko and Grucza 2001; Taylor, Mekjavic, and Tipton 2008; Kingma, Frijns, and van Marken Lichtenbelt 2012.
74. Wardle, Gloss, and Gloss 1987; Lassek and Gaulin 2006; McArdle, Katch, and Katch 2007; Karastergiou et al. 2012; Zihlman and Bolter 2015.
75. The actual figures are 62.6 percent and 53.7 percent, respectively (Hattori et al. 1991).
76. E.g., Sjöström 1988; Schreiner et al. 1996; Rattarasarn et al. 2004; Malina 2005; Demerath et al. 2007.
77. Karastergiou et al. 2012; Bloor and Symonds 2014.
78. Keatinge 1960, 1978; Kaciuba-Uscilko and Grucza 2001; Stocks et al. 2004; Taylor, Mekjavic, and Tipton 2008; Kingma, Frijns, and van Marken Lichtenbelt 2012; Castellani and Young 2016.
79. Keatinge 1978:299.
80. Rennie et al. 1962. See also Bae et al. 2003.
81. E.g., DeMaster and Stirling 1981.
82. Stirling 1988.
83. Pond 1992, 1997, 1998; Pond and Ramsay 1992; Pond et al. 1992, 1993.
84. Pond 1992:372.
85. Pond 1997, 1999; Pond and Mattacks 1987.
86. Shephard and Rode 1976; Schaeffer 1977; Leonard and Katzmarzyk 2010.
87. E.g., Hrdy 1981; Caro and Sellen 1990; Dewey 1997; McFarland 1997; Zihlman 1997; Sidebottom, Brown, and Jacobs 2001; Lassek and Gaulin 2006; Pike and Milligan 2010; Florido, Tchkonia, and Kirkland 2011; McClure et al. 2012.

88. Pond 1997; Low 2000.
89. Karastergiou et al. 2012.
90. Wells 2012.
91. Pond and Mattacks 1987:182.
92. Cypess et al. 2009; van Marken Lichtenbelt et al. 2009; Virtanen et al. 2009.
93. Cypess et al. 2009; Celi, Le, and Ni 2015.
94. van der Lans et al. 2013.
95. Florido, Tchkonia, and Kirkland 2011; Van Someren 2011; Saely, Geiger, and Drexel 2012; van Marken Lichtenbelt and Schrauwen 2011; Chen et al. 2013; Harms and Seale 2013; Bloor and Symonds 2014; Betz and Enerbäck 2015; Celi, Le, and Ni 2015. For a brief general review, see Castellani and Young 2016.
96. Mayr 1966.
97. Tilkens et al. 2007. See also Roberts 1978; Burse 1979; Stephenson and Kolka 1993; Leonard and Katzmarzyk 2010.
98. Eveleth and Tanner 1990:35; Arendt 1994; Stocks et al. 2004.
99. See Castellani and Young 2016:64 on differences between cold air exposure and cold water immersion studies.
100. Graham 1988.
101. E.g., Wyndham et al. 1964; Graham 1988; Graham et al. 1989. Bartelink et al. (1993) found a greater reduction in finger surface temperature in premenopausal women than in men when only hands were cooled (as opposed to total body cooling in other studies).
102. E.g., Wyndham et al. 1964; Haymes and Wells 1986; Stephenson and Kolka 1993.
103. Graham 1988.
104. Keatinge et al. 2001; Brannigan et al. 2009.
105. Hammond et al. 2014.
106. Women more frequently complain of being cold or hot than men do under the same thermal conditions. The generally lower skin temperatures maintained by women might account for complaints about being cold. Complaints about being too warm may follow from the fact that women maintain higher core temperatures and sweat less than males of the same body surface area. There is a substantial amount of literature on this topic. See, for instance, Hashiguchi, Feng, and Tochihara 2010 and Karjalainen 2012.
107. Wyndham et al. 1964.
108. Graham 1988; Stephenson and Kolka 1993.
109. Graham 1988; Stephenson and Kolka 1993.
110. E.g., Burse 1979; Frisancho 1993.
111. Pugh 1966.
112. E.g., Centers for Disease Control and Prevention 1985; Kilbourne 1997; Deschênes and Greenstone 2011; Berko et al. 2014.
113. E.g., Schwartz 2005; Davie et al. 2007; Deschênes and Moretti 2009; Ou et al. 2013; Xuan et al. 2014; Zhou et al. 2014.
114. O'Neill et al. 2003; Ma et al. 2013; Huang et al. 2014 (from cardiovascular disease only).
115. E.g., Deschênes and Moretti 2009:675; Zhou et al. 2014:10.
116. E.g., Xuan et al. 2014:6.
117. E.g., Schwartz 2005:71.
118. Rivers 1982, 1988; Dyson and Ó Gráda 2002; Macintyre 2002; Ó Gráda 2009.
119. Stini 1981.
120. Widdowson 1976; Rivers 1982, 1988.
121. Dyson and Ó Gráda 2002; Hionidou 2002; Macintyre 2002; Ó Gráda 2009.

122. Macintyre 2002; Neumayer and Plümper 2007.
123. Rivers 1982; Neumayer and Plümper 2007.
124. Bogue 1969.
125. Stocks et al. 2004; Cypess et al. 2009; Cowgill et al. 2012; Taylor, Mekjavic, and Tipton 2008; Betz and Enerbäck 2015.
126. Vasoconstriction refers to the narrowing of blood vessels by muscle contraction. By reducing blood flow, vasoconstriction can also reduce heat loss to the external environment.
127. Collins et al. 1977; Wagner and Horvath 1985; Florez-Duquet and McDonald 1998; Kenney and Munce 2003; Taylor, Mekjavic, and Tipton 2008; Van Someren 2011.
128. Wagner and Horvath 1985.
129. Waite and Lehrer 2003; Murphy, Grundy, and Kalogirou 2007; Rogers et al. 2010. On the decreasing male/female longevity gain, see Liu and Umberson 2008 and Dupre, Beck, and Meadows 2009.
130. Dupre, Beck, and Meadows 2009.
131. Kisker and Goldman 1987; Hu and Goldman 1990; Goldman 1993; Lillard and Panis 1996; Waite and Lehrer 2003; Liu and Umberson 2008.
132. Gove 1973; Kobrin and Hendershot 1977; Zick and Smith 1991; Lillard and Panis 1996; Dupre, Beck, and Meadows 2009.
133. Hummer et al. 1999.
134. Musick, House, and Williams 2004.
135. Berkman and Syme 1979; House, Robbins, and Metzner 1982; Berkman 1984; Schoenbach et al. 1986; House, Landis, and Umberson 1988; Hummer et al. 1999; Waite and Lehrer 2003; Hummer et al. 2004; Holt-Lunstad, Smith, and Layton 2010.
136. Levine et al. 2013. Cats might also have beneficial effects (Qureshi et al. 2009). However, dogs appear to bring a wider array of health benefits, in part because it is hard to walk a cat (Levine et al. 2013; see also Nagasawa et al. 2015 and the review in Hodgson et al. 2015). That dogs are superior to cats in nearly all ways does not appear relevant to health-related issues.
137. House, Landis, and Umberson 1988; Kaplan and Toshima 1990; Kennedy, Kiecolt-Glaser, and Glaser 1990; Berkman 1984; Hummer et al. 2004; Musick, House, and Williams 2004.
138. Neal et al. 1988.
139. Keys et al. 1950:798.

4

"A CURIOUS FEATURE OF THE DISASTER"

The Donner Party has been famous ever since its members became stuck in the Sierra Nevada. California newspapers had begun reporting on their situation by January 16, 1847, and continued to do so until well after the last survivor—Louis Keseberg—had been rescued. A book-length account of the tragedy appeared as early as 1849 and remains an important source of information on the Donner Party experience.[1] Because of all the attention the group has received for the last 150 years, we not only know the names of all the members of the group, but we also have detailed information on who was related to whom, where most of them came from, and, with a reasonable degree of accuracy, the ages of all but one of the people involved.

This is not to say that we know all there is to know. Jacob Wolfinger is a good example. Not only do we lack even an estimate of his age, but we are also not sure of his first name. Mr. Hardcoop's age is estimated at 60, and we also don't know his first name; it is not even certain that he was Belgian, as J. Quinn Thornton asserted. We do, in short, have a number of holes to fill.

When I first studied mortality patterns in the Donner Party, I used the age estimates provided by George Stewart in 1960.[2] In the years that have passed since that time, new research by Joseph King, Kristin Johnson, and others has provided more accurate ages for a number of the people involved. The list I present in Table 2.1 relies most heavily on information provided by Johnson.[3]

Of the 87 people in the group, the majority (47) were from Illinois; an additional 26 were from adjacent Missouri (16) and Iowa (10). Because of these origins, I assume that the population of Illinois in 1850, the year of the closest U.S. Census, provides an adequate picture of the population from which the Donner Party was drawn. How does the age and sex composition of the Donner Party compare with that source population?

The distribution of the Euro-American ("white") population of Illinois by the age classes used in the 1850 (Seventh) U.S. Census is shown in Table 4.1. This table also shows the distribution of Donner Party members across those age classes. To emphasize how similar these two distributions are, the last columns in Table 4.1 ("Donner scaled") show the number of people in each age class that the Donner Party would have had if the 86 people of known age in that group were distributed across these classes in exactly the same proportions that characterized Illinois at the time.[4] The general similarity between the age structure of the actual Donner Party and the Euro-American population of 1850 Illinois is clear. In fact, the two distributions are statistically identical.[5]

On the other hand, males as a whole were far better represented in the Donner Party than they were in the contemporary Illinois population.[6] In fact, 69 percent of Donner Party members between 20 and 39 years of age were men, compared to about 46 percent of the general Illinois population of this age (Tables 4.2 and 4.3).

It is no great surprise that the Donner Party was loaded with men, particularly men between 20 and 39 years old. Men contributed a disproportionate share of the western immigration in general.[7] Oregon and California were the two prime targets for western emigrants at this time, and the greatest sex ratio imbalances are for these two areas.

In 1850, the greatest imbalance was for California, as Table 4.4 shows. Here, men between the ages of 20 and 39 outnumbered women of that age by 25 to 1. These figures, though, reflect the "flood of male fortune hunters and freebooters" that marked California gold fever,[8] and there are no pre-gold rush figures for this region. But even in more agrarian Oregon, men between 20 and 39 outnumbered women by about 3 to 1.

Preponderantly male emigration characterized the early American movement west, and the Donner Party was no different. In fact, the proportion of males between 20 and 39 years old in the Donner Party (69 percent)

TABLE 4.1. Ages of Donner Party members and of people identified as Euro-American ("white") in the Seventh U.S. Census by Seventh Census age class (see text for explanation of "Donner scaled").

Age class	Illinois		Donner Party		Donner scaled	
	Total	%	Total	%	Total	%
1–4	141,360	16.72	16	18.60	14.4	16.72
5–9	129,905	15.37	12	13.95	13.2	15.37
10–14	112,860	13.35	13	15.12	11.5	13.35
15–19	92,698	10.97	6	6.98	9.4	10.97
20–29	150,044	17.75	17	19.77	15.3	17.75
30–39	102,426	12.12	12	13.95	10.4	12.12
40–49	62,072	7.34	5	5.81	6.3	7.34
50–59	33,828	4.00	3	3.49	3.4	4.00
60–69	14,410	1.70	2	2.33	1.5	1.71
70–79	4,577	0.54	0	0.00	0.5	0.54
80–89	938	0.11	0	0.00	0.1	0.11
90–99	109	0.01	0	0.00	0.0	0.01
100+	15	0.00	0	0.00	0.0	0.00
Totals	845,242	99.99	86	100.00	86.0	99.99

TABLE 4.2. Distribution of Euro-American males and females in Illinois in 1850 by Seventh U.S. Census age class (data from DeBow 1854:Tables 30 and 33). N = number of individuals.

Age class	Number of males per 100 females	Males (%)	Females (%)	Males (N)	Females (N)
1–4	96.5	49.11	50.89	69,422	71,938
5–9	95.6	48.88	51.12	63,498	66,407
10–14	92.7	48.11	51.89	54,297	58,563
15–19	97.4	49.34	50.66	45,737	46,961
20–29	88.8	47.03	52.97	70,566	79,478
30–39	79.1	44.17	55.83	45,242	57,184
40–49	80.5	44.60	55.40	27,684	34,388
50–59	76.9	43.47	56.53	14,705	19,123
60–69	80.8	44.69	55.31	6,440	7,970
70–79	81.1	44.79	55.21	2,050	2,527
80–89	86.1	46.27	53.73	434	504
90–99	98.2	49.54	50.46	54	55
100+	50.0	33.33	66.67	5	10

TABLE 4.3. Distribution of males and females in the Donner Party by Seventh U.S. Census age class. N = number of individuals.

Age class	Males (%)	Females (%)	Males (N)	Females (N)
1–4	43.75	56.25	7	9
5–9	66.67	33.33	8	4
10–14	53.85	46.15	7	6
15–19	66.67	33.33	4	2
20–29	64.71	35.29	11	6
30–39	75.00	25.00	9	3
40–49	20.00	80.00	1	4
50–59	100.00	0.00	3	0
60–69	100.00	0.00	2	0
Unknown			1	0
Totals			53	34

TABLE 4.4. Numbers of Euro-American females per 100 Euro-American males in Oregon and California in 1850 (data from DeBow 1854:Table 33).

Age class	Oregon	California	Donner Party
1–9	97.4	92.7	86.7
10–14	96.5	71.6	85.7
15–19	77.5	19.1	50.0
20–29	33.7	3.5	54.6
30–39	40.6	4.5	33.3
40–69	43.4	7.1	66.7

is almost identical to the proportion of Euro-American males in Oregon in 1850 (73 percent). While the sex ratios of the Donner Party were not typical of the population from which that group had been drawn, they were typical of the population toward which it was heading. No wonder survivor Virginia Reed suggested to her cousin in Springfield that she "tell the girls that this is the greatest place for marrying they ever saw."[9]

THE AGE OF DEATH

Some basic information on the fate of the members of the Donner Party is summarized in Table 4.5, which shows the distribution of death in this group

TABLE 4.5. Donner Party members: Sex and survivorship by Seventh U.S. Census age class.

Age class	Males: survived?			Females: survived?			Totals	% Died
	Yes	No	% Died	Yes	No	% Died		
1–4	2	5	71.4	4	5	55.6	16	62.5
5–9	6	2	25.0	4	0	0.0	12	16.7
10–14	5	2	33.3	6	0	0.0	13	15.4
15–19	3	1	25.0	2	0	0.0	6	16.7
20–29	2	9	81.8	5	1	16.7	17	58.8
30–39	3	6	66.7	2	1	33.3	12	58.3
40–49	1	0	00.0	1	3	75.0	5	60.0
50–59	1	2	66.7	0	0	—	3	66.7
60–69	0	2	100.0	0	0	—	2	100.0
Unknown	0	1	100.0	0	0	—	1	100.0
Totals	23	30	56.6	24	10	29.4	87	46.0

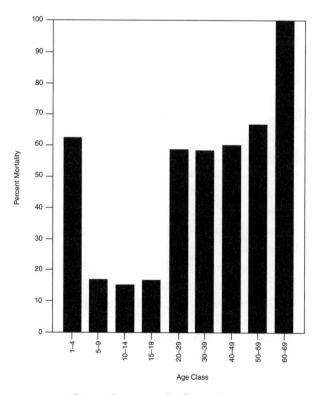

FIGURE 4.1. Donner Party mortality by age class.

by sex and age, using the same age classes used in the Seventh U.S. Census. The last two columns show the total number of people per age class and the percentage of those people who died.

These percentages are plotted in Figure 4.1. As expected, the oldest and youngest members of the group suffered the heaviest mortality, though the situation in which the Donner Party found itself was so horrific that the oldest weren't necessarily very old at all. The lowest mortality rate was for the 31 people between 5 and 19 years old: 16.1 percent. Among those younger than 5, 62.5 percent (10 of 16) died. Among those 20 or older, 61.5 percent (24 of 39) were lost. Of the 10 people 40 or older, only 3—Margaret Breen, Patrick Breen, and James Reed—survived, for a mortality rate of 70 percent. Reed, of course, crossed the Sierra Nevada prior to the forced encampment and thus did not deal with the horrors of that encampment. If we exclude him from the count, then only 2 of those 40 years old or older survived, for a mortality rate of 77.8 percent within that age group.

But is it appropriate to exclude Reed from that calculation? How about William McCutchan, who left the group with Stanton soon after the party had crossed the Bonneville Salt Flats (see Chapter 2)? Or Walter Herron, who chose to leave with Reed while the Donner Party worked its way down the Humboldt?

We have seen that men are far more likely than women to be involved in aggression, violence, and risk-taking behavior. If our interest focuses on the relationship of sex and mortality rates, then Reed's murder of Snyder was a sex-linked trait, given that homicide is far more characteristic of males than females (Chapter 3). The same is true of the risk-taking behavior shown by Herron, McCutchan, and Stanton, all of whom voluntarily left the group long before it was certain that their situation was life-threatening. From the perspective of the situation in which the group found itself at the time these three men left, it was far riskier for them to ride off in pairs, as they did, than it would have been to stay put. This too was male behavior, just as it was for the two forty-niners in Death Valley (Chapter 1). If we are going to assess the relationship between sex and death within the Donner Party, the four men who left must be treated as part of the group, since the very act of leaving was inextricably linked with their sex.

But no matter how we count it, the youngest and oldest fared the worst in the Donner Party, just as our general consideration of human biology led us to expect.

THE SEX OF DEATH

There is, though, far more to what happened to the Donner Party than just age. For a hint of the general pattern, look at the 20–29 year age class in Table 4.5. These are people who were in their physical prime of life, yet over half of them died. The men, however, suffered most of this mortality. Of the 11 men of this age, 9 (81.8 percent) died. Of the 6 women, only 1, or 16.7 percent, died.

In fact, of the 53 males in the Donner Party, 30, or 56.6 percent, died. Of the 34 females, 10, or 29.4 percent, died (Figure 4.2). That is, the male mortality rate was 1.9 times the female mortality rate.[10] In addition, the male mortality rate exceeded that of females in all age classes except for those between 40 and 49 (Table 4.5). The exception itself is interesting, since there was only one male in this age class—James Reed—and he left early. Otherwise, men bore the brunt of death.

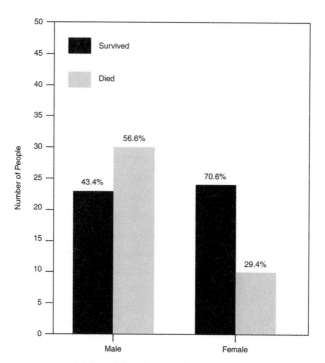

FIGURE 4.2. Male and female mortality rates in the Donner Party.

In calculating these figures, I have included five men who were part of the Donner Party but never actually made it to the Sierra Nevada and thus did not endure the hardships of the forced encampment. These five are Luke Halloran, Mr. Hardcoop, William Pike, John Snyder, and Jacob Wolfinger. My logic here is the same as it was for those who left the group early. Halloran died from disease, Snyder and Wolfinger were murdered, Pike was accidentally shot while preparing to leave the rest of the group, and Hardcoop was forced to walk by Keseberg. In Chapter 2, I referred to Snyder's death as a guy kind of thing. In fact, all five of these deaths were guy kinds of things—disease, aggression, and risk-taking.

Donner Party males, then, died at nearly twice the rate of Donner Party females, an imbalance that Thornton noted in 1849.[11] Even particular episodes within the ordeal show the effect of sex on death. The Forlorn Hope provides an obvious example (see Chapter 2). The stark pattern here drew immediate attention. George McKinstry had traveled Hastings's Cutoff in advance of the Donner Party and was still at Sutter's Fort when the remaining snowshoers were brought in. "Most singular to relate," McKinstry said, in a letter to the *California Star* on February 13, 1847, of "all the females that started, 5 women came in safe, and but two of the men, and one of them was brought in on the back of an Indian. Nine of the men died, and seven of them were eaten by their companions."[12] "That the women stood the hardship better than the men" was, to John Breen, "a curious feature of the disaster."[13]

McKinstry was slightly off in his numbers since, as I discussed in Chapter 2, there were not 11 but 10 men involved in the Forlorn Hope.[14] Of these, 8 died and 7—all but Stanton—were eaten. During this escape attempt, 80 percent of the men died (including 2 homicide victims), but no women did. This was indeed a curious and singular feature of the disaster.

In Chapter 3, we saw that, all other things being equal, males are more likely to die from such things as violence, disease, and risk-taking behavior in general, as well as from cold and famine. Because of this, more Donner Party males than females should have succumbed, and this is exactly what happened.

THE CHRONOLOGY OF DEATH

Earlier I suggested that we might expect males to have died sooner than females, in addition to dying at higher rates (see "Age" in Chapter 3). In fact, they did this as well. I refer here not to the five men who died before the forced encampment but to the pattern of deaths that occurred after that encampment had begun.

To explore this pattern, I need a reasonably accurate chronology of death. The Breen diary is extremely valuable in this regard, since it records the exact dates on which many individuals died. On December 17, for instance, Breen reported that "Bealis died night before last,"[15] making it clear that Baylis Williams, Reed's employee, died on December 15.

Likewise, the Ritchie-Tucker account of the First Relief notes that John Denton was left behind on February 24 and that Ada Keseberg died the next day.[16] The journals Eddy provided for the Forlorn Hope may differ somewhat from version to version (Chapter 2), but they also allow close estimates of the dates of death for those who did not survive this epic ordeal.

In other cases, more approximate dates have to be provided. For instance, Edwin Bryant reports that Keseberg told William Fallon that Tamzene Donner had died two days before the Fourth Relief arrived.[17] Later, however, and away from the bullying and potentially murderous presence of Fallon, Keseberg placed Tamzene's death much earlier, about two weeks after the Third Relief had left. George Stewart estimated the date at around March 27, and I have adopted that estimate here.[18]

The results of tallying all this information are presented in Table 4.6. The forced encampment began on about November 1. The first deaths occurred on or about December 15, six weeks after the encampment had begun. Deaths then continued until the following April, ending with the sad loss of little Elizabeth Graves after her rescue.

Thus tallied, the deaths continued across 108 days. Given this chronology, what does the march of death look like? Figure 4.3 provides the answer. Males, we have already seen, died at almost twice the rate of females. Now we see that they also died sooner. The first 14 deaths, beginning on about December 15 and continuing through January, involved only males. The first female, one-year-old Harriet McCutchan, succumbed on February 2. After that point, both males and females lost their lives.

DEATH TAKES A HOLIDAY

There is an oddity in this sequence. I refer not to the spike of deaths that focused on March 8, which is associated with the massive storm that caused

TABLE 4.6. Donner Party members who died after reaching the Sierra Nevada.

Name	Date	Days to Death*
Donner, Jacob	December 15[a]	1
Williams, Baylis	December 15[a]	1
Reinhardt, Joseph	December 15[a]	1
Shoemaker, Samuel	December 15[a]	1
Smith, James	December 15[a]	1
Stanton, Charles	December 21[b]	7
Antonio	December 25[b]	11
Graves, Franklin	December 25[b]	11
Dolan, Patrick	December 27[b]	13
Murphy, Lemuel	December 28[b]	14
Burger, Charles	December 29[a]	15
Fosdick, Jay	January 5[c]	22
Keseberg, Louis, Jr.	January 24[a]	41
Murphy, John	January 30[a]	47
McCutchan, Harriet	February 2[a]	50
Eddy, Margaret	February 4[a]	52
Eddy, Eleanor	February 7[a]	55
Spitzer, Augustus	February 8[a]	56
Elliot, Milford	February 9[a]	57
Pike, Catherine	February 20[a]	68
Denton, John	February 24[d]	72
Keseberg, Ada	February 25[d]	73
Donner, William Hook	February 28[e]	76
Donner, Lewis	March 7[f]	83
Donner, Isaac	March 8[f]	84
Graves, Elizabeth Cooper	March 8[f]	84
Graves, Franklin, Jr.	March 8[f]	84
Eddy, James	March 8[f]	84
Foster, George	March 8[f]	84
Donner, Elizabeth	March 11[f]	87
Murphy, Levinah	March 20[f]	96
Donner, Samuel	March 20[f]	96
Donner, George	March 26[f]	102
Donner, Tamzene	March 27[f]	103
Graves, Elizabeth	April 1[e, f]	108

* 1 = the day of the first deaths.
Sources: a: Patrick Breen diary (Morgan 1963:310–322; King 1998:50–79); b: W. H. Eddy in J. F. Reed narrative (Morgan 1963:289–301); c: J. Sinclair statement in Bryant (1985:251–255); d: M. D. Ritchie-R. P. Tucker journal (Morgan 1963:331–336); e: Thornton (1986; K. Johnson 1996:14–120); f: Stewart (1960).

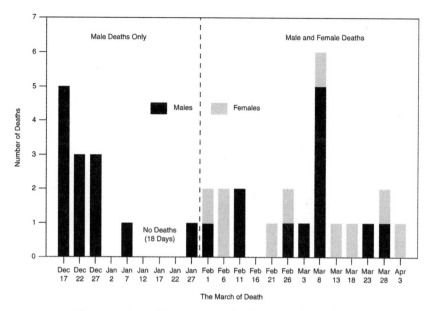

FIGURE 4.3. The chronology of Donner Party deaths among those who reached the Sierra encampment.

such misery at Starved Camp (Chapter 2), but instead to the 18 days during which death apparently took a holiday. From January 6 to January 23, no one died. Before this interlude, only males died. After it, both males and females lost their lives. Of the 14 males who died before the first female death, 12 died during the interval of 22 days or so that began on about December 15 and ended on January 5. During the next 33 days, only 2 more males lost their lives. Why did this 18-day lull in deaths occur, and why did so many males succumb so quickly?

The people who died before the lull are listed in Table 4.7. Not only are all of them male, but 9 of the 12 were between 20 and 35 years old. They were in the physical prime of life, yet not only did they die, but they died first.

Figure 4.4 shows the relationship between age and days-to-death for all of the Donner Party males who reached the Sierra encampment. With only one major, and very telling, exception, this figure shows that the youngest males tended to survive the longest, the oldest ones to die first. The lull in deaths separates an earlier round of male deaths that focused on men who were over 20 years old (11 of the 12 losses) from a later round that focused on males under that age (9 of 13). Statistically, that difference is very significant.[19]

TABLE 4.7. Donner Party deaths before the lull.

Name	Situation	Age
Burger, Charles	Encampment	30
Donner, Jacob	Encampment	56
Williams, Baylis	Encampment	25
Reinhardt, Joseph	Encampment	30
Shoemaker, Samuel	Encampment	25
Smith, James	Encampment	25
Stanton, Charles	Forlorn Hope	35
Antonio	Forlorn Hope	23
Dolan, Patrick	Forlorn Hope	35
Graves, Franklin	Forlorn Hope	57
Fosdick, Jay	Forlorn Hope	23
Murphy, Lemuel	Forlorn Hope	12

The major exception so obvious in Figure 4.4 is 62-year-old George Donner. As I mentioned in Chapter 2, he cut his hand badly in October, a wound that never healed. Once the Donner encampment had been established, he could neither attempt to escape nor fend for himself. His wife, Tamzene, refused to leave with rescuers so she could continue to care for him. According to Keseberg, George Donner died about March 26; Tamzene died the next day. George's wound prohibited him from engaging in high-energy activities. That, along with Tamzene's care, prolonged his life substantially. His brother, Jacob, six years younger (but said to have been in weak health), had been one of the first to die.

Statistical analysis shows the general pattern in Figure 4.4 to be a significant one with or without George Donner: among the males who died, the youngest survived the longest.[20] The average age of the males who died before the lull was 31.4 years. The average age of those who died after it was 15.2 years, George Donner included.

The roles played by age, dependency, and family ties are key to understanding the relationship between age and days-to-death among the Donner Party males and the holiday that death took. I will discuss family ties shortly and now just mention the obvious. Of the 13 males who died during the second episode of death, eight were fully dependent on others for their care. Of these eight, seven were children six years old or younger, while the eighth was George Donner.

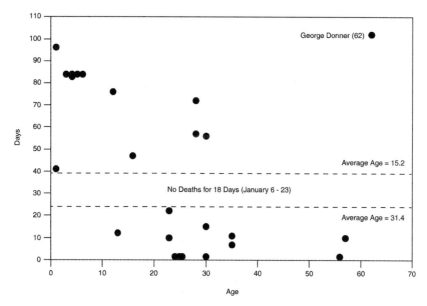

FIGURE 4.4. The relationship between age and days-to-death for Donner Party males who reached the Sierra encampment.

By the time the first bout of death had ended, not many vigorous adult males were left, since these people—males between the ages of 23 and 35— were preferentially removed by the first round of mortality. Unlike the later male deaths, which primarily involved dependents, the earlier round of mortality largely took men who could fend for themselves.

And fend they did. The firsthand accounts make it clear that the Donner Party men bore the brunt of the tremendous physical effort needed to bring the wagons through the Wasatch Range and on whose shoulders the heaviest chores fell in the Sierra Nevada. The trail those men cut through the Wasatch was used in 1847 by Brigham Young and his fellow travelers on their initial trip into the valley of the Great Salt Lake. A member of that group, journalist William Clayton, carefully observed that "the emigrants who passed this way last year must have spent a good deal of time cutting a road through the thickly set timber and heavy brush wood."[21] "The emigrants" were the members of the Donner Party, and it was the men who had done the cutting. "In one place," John Breen later remembered, "all the men in the company worked hard for two weeks, and only advanced thirty miles."[22] In the Wasatch, Eliza Donner Houghton recalled, "our men again took their tools and became roadmakers."[23] Indeed, the main point she makes about the addition of the Graves family to the group is that this addition provided "three fresh men" who were able to speed the completion of the road.[24] Later, at the forced encampment, Elizabeth Cooper Graves asked her son William to not leave with the First Relief since he was needed to cut firewood—which he did, and then left. At the Alder Creek camp, "Noah James ... helped John Baptiste to dig for the carcasses of the cattle. It was weary work ... and at times they searched day after day."[25]

The Donner Party women also participated in essential tasks. However, the tasks that the men performed differed substantially from those performed by the women. Men took on those strength-intensive tasks for which they were biologically best suited and which, not coincidentally, they were fully expected to do. Thus, while Mrs. Graves expected to care for her four small children, she also expected her 17-year-old son to cut firewood for them. The activities of both matched these biologically driven expectations.

Since it was the males who cut the group's way through the Wasatch, retrieved the wagons from the Salt Flats, cut the firewood, probed for snow-entombed cattle, and hunted at the forced encampment, it was also the adult males—especially the prime-aged males—whose energy stores were most rapidly and thoroughly depleted. Since the males were also least biologically fit to cope with the cold, it was not simply the males, but the nondependent adult males who died quickly. Whether behind in the encampment or ahead in the Forlorn Hope, these men died because of their sex and age.

This initial round of death left the survivors bereft of exactly those members of the group whose tasks would have included woodcutting and hunting. Without a full complement of vigorous adult males to perform these tasks, the survivors became far more dependent on rescuers—on physically fit men coming from the west—than they would otherwise have been. Such was the importance of the biologically driven sexual division of labor to the members of the Donner Party.

THE TIMING OF DISTAFF DEATH

If the behavior of the Donner Party females differed from that of the males, and their biological responses to cold and famine differed, we might expect fewer females than males to have died (as we have seen [Figure 4.2]) and that

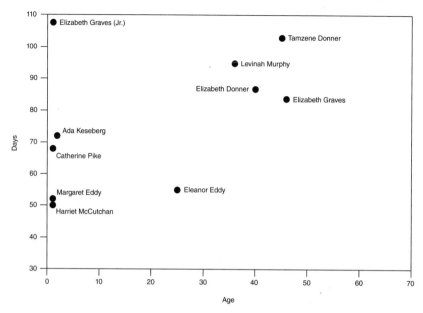

FIGURE 4.5. The relationship between age and days-to-death for Donner Party females who reached the Sierra encampment.

females died later than males (as we have also seen [Figure 4.3]). We might also expect the relationship between age and days-to-death among the females who died to differ from that shown by males.

In fact, it differs dramatically. Figure 4.5 shows the chronology of death for the Donner Party females. Among the males, the youngest lasted longest and the oldest went first. Among the females, however, this relationship is reversed. With the exception of the infant Elizabeth Graves, the youngest females tended to go first, the oldest last. Just as with the males, this relationship is statistically significant,[26] but in the opposite direction.

Of the eight Donner Party women between the ages of 20 and 35, only Eleanor Eddy died, reflecting the greater biological protection that women have against cold and famine, as well as the fact that women participated less than men in heavy physical activities. The survival of these women created the three age groups that are evident in Figure 4.5. First are the five children. Second is Eleanor Eddy. Third are the older, but not very old, women: Levinah Murphy (36), Elizabeth Donner (40), Tamzene Donner (45), and Elizabeth Cooper Graves (46).

The timing of the deaths of the five girls is not distinctly different from those of the boys of the same age.[27] Since this is the case, and since Eleanor Eddy was the only woman between 20 and 35 who lost her life, the positive relationship between age and days-to-death among the females has resulted from the relatively lengthy survivorship of the four older women.

When in life, we might ask, does the biological protection offered by sex to the combined effects of cold and famine begin to decline? I have no answer to that, but perhaps women older than 35 had begun to lose some of that protection. Among those who were to die, the women endured far longer than the men (only the dependent George Donner outlived any of these four women), but ultimately, they too began to lose their lives. It was their ability to survive as long as they did that created the positive relationship between age and days-to-death among the Donner Party females, a pattern that is the reverse of the one that marks the males.

This, though, is only part of the story, since family size played a major role as well.

THE ROLE OF KIN GROUPS

While age and sex go far toward explaining the pattern of mortality seen in the Donner Party, they cannot explain it all. George Donner lived until about March 26; Tamzene Donner, Keseberg tells us, died the next day. Of the 10 Donner Party females who died (see Figure 4.5), only one—Ada Keseberg—came from a family in which a father or husband was still alive and in the Sierra Nevada. Harriet McCutchan's father had crossed early; he participated in the rescue attempts, but he was not in the camps. Margaret Eddy's father (Eleanor's husband) had left with the Forlorn Hope. He soon returned, but it was too late. Catherine Pike's father had been killed at Truckee Meadows. Franklin Graves had died on Christmas Day, a member of the Forlorn Hope, while his wife and most of his children were back in camp. Both Donner husbands died in camp—one early, one late—leaving Elizabeth and Tamzene widowed. Levinah Murphy was a widow when the trip began. All of this suggests that family ties may have influenced survivorship in the Donner Party.

In fact, as Figure 4.6 shows, both the males and females who survived traveled with families that were larger than those who died—an average of 1.3 more people for the males and 0.9 more for the females.

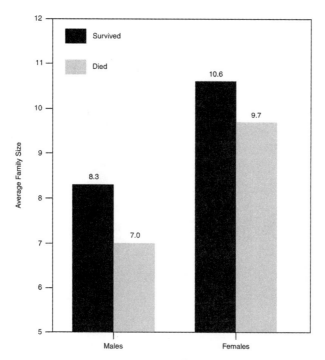

FIGURE 4.6. Donner Party average family sizes, by sex and survivorship.

If we look just at those people between the ages of 5 and 39, those whose ages should have given them some protection against death, we get the results shown in Figure 4.7. Surviving males of this age traveled with families that averaged 2.9 individuals larger than the families of those who died. For the females, the differential is 1.6 individuals.

For both males and females, then, the families of survivors were larger than the families of those who succumbed. Given our understanding of the relationship between the size of social networks and mortality, this outcome is not surprising. It is also not surprising that the males gained more from family ties than did females, just as occurs in contemporary populations (Chapter 3).

When I discussed the life-enhancing effects of marriage, I noted that researchers have focused on three major sets of factors to explain these effects: a reduction in risk-taking behaviors, an increase in economic well-being (including improved nutrition, reduced stress related to economic needs, and increased possibilities for nurturing), and an increase in benefits resulting

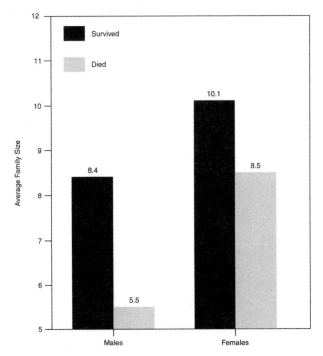

FIGURE 4.7. Donner Party average family sizes, by sex and survivorship, for those between 5 and 39 years of age.

directly from social integration. In disaster settings, these benefits include increased access to information and increased likelihood of assistance.

There is little evidence that any member of the Donner Party reduced risk-taking behaviors. Not only were risky behaviors required just to survive once they reached the encampments, but the behavior of the married Donner Party men who reached California while members of their families remained behind could hardly have been riskier.

William Eddy, for instance, survived the Forlorn Hope. Then, with his wife and children still at the Sierra encampments, he immediately attempted to return with the First Relief. Although he did not make it, he did return with the Third Relief, by which time all of his family had died. William Foster also survived the Forlorn Hope and went with Eddy on the Third Relief, only to learn that his son, George, had died and that his mother-in-law, Levinah Murphy, was in no condition to leave. Foster also played a supporting role in the Fourth Relief; he could not then have known that his mother-in-law had died. Reed and McCutchan failed in their early attempt to return but then led the Second Relief; McCutchan's daughter, Harriet, had died, but Reed got the rest of his family out.

How about the other men who made it out while members of the group were still trapped? Walter Herron, single, had crossed prior to the entrapment and played no further role in the episode. Noah James, single, made it out with the First Relief and did not attempt to return (only to be hung for horse stealing in 1851[28]). Patrick Breen, married, made it out with the Third Relief, via Starved Camp, but his whole family was rescued and he made no attempt to return. Jean-Baptiste Trudeau, single, made it out with the Third Relief and also made no return attempt. The only exception is the remarkable Charles Stanton. Single, he returned anyway and died as a result. He was at the time, and still is, considered a hero.

In these and other ways, what we know of the behavior of the members of the Donner Party shows that family ties increased the willingness of people to take risks on behalf of other members of their families. It also shows that the other two known benefits of marriage and family ties were very much in play. Family members routinely assisted one another, often at great risk to themselves. Not only did married men with family members still at risk return to the encampments, but there is a good deal of evidence that parents hoarded food for their children and some evidence that they provided food to their spouses at expense to themselves. Eleanor Eddy snuck food into her husband's pack before he left with the Forlorn Hope.[29] Margret Reed carefully hid food that she then used to provide a Christmas meal for her children.[30] While assistance also operated across family groups—especially as regards support given to the children of others—it is clear that the bulk of assistance, whether economic (for instance, involving food) or less tangible (for instance, involving nurturance), stayed within family bounds. And perhaps the least tangible of all known benefits of family ties is shown by Tamzene Donner, who stayed behind to tend to her husband and then died the day after he died.

SINGLE MEN AND THE BENEFITS OF MARRIAGE

While those who survived belonged to larger families than those who died, this does not necessarily mean that the larger the family, the greater the chances an individual within that family survived. In fact, in terms of

TABLE 4.8. Single males of the Donner Party.

Name	Survived?	Age
James, Noah	Yes	16
Trudeau, Jean-Baptiste	Yes	16
Antonio	No	23
Halloran, Luke	No	25
Shoemaker, Samuel	No	25
Smith, James	No	25
Snyder, John	No	25
Herron, Walter	Yes	27
Denton, John	No	28
Elliot, Milford	No	28
Burger, Charles	No	30
Reinhardt, Joseph	No	30
Spitzer, Augustus	No	30
Dolan, Patrick	No	35
Stanton, Charles	No	35
Hardcoop, Mr.	No	60

mortality alone, the greatest benefit seems to have been provided by the simple fact of belonging to a family. Conversely, the biggest detriment was to have been a single male.

As we have seen, the Donner Party had far more males (53) than females (34). Of the 53 males, 16 were single men traveling in the absence of relatives; of these, 13 were between 20 and 35 (Table 4.8). There were, in contrast, no single females traveling alone. Only three of the 16 single men survived, for a mortality rate of 81.3 percent. Three of these men (Halloran, Hardcoop, and Snyder) did not make it to the Sierra Nevada, and an additional seven lost their lives before the lull in deaths occurred (Table 4.7; I have not counted Baylis Williams as single, since he traveled with his sister, Eliza).

Table 4.9 shows that single males died in significantly greater numbers than females, all of whom were in family groups.[31] Single males also died in greater numbers than males in family groups[32] and in greater numbers than people in family groups as a whole.[33] All but three of those single males were between 20 and 35 years old. Of these, 92.3 percent died; the only survivor was Walter Herron, who had crossed early with Reed (Table 4.8). Only 42.9 percent of those age-mates who traveled with their families lost their lives.[34] The family benefit is obvious here.

TABLE 4.9. Donner Party survivorship by family status.

Status	Survived	Died	Died (%)
Single males	3	13	81.3
Males in family groups	20	17	45.9
Females in family groups	24	10	29.4
Total in family groups	44	27	38.0

I mentioned that even though those who survived belonged to larger families than those who died, this does not necessarily mean that the larger the family, the greater the survivorship rate. In fact, there appears to be a complex relationship between family size and mortality rates. Table 4.10 shows the survivorship rate for Donner Party members by family size and sex; Figure 4.8 plots the total survivorship (that is, for both males and females) by the size of the families involved. As we know, the smallest "families"—the single males—fared the worst. From here, however, survivorship begins to improve steadily—with the exception of the two families of four people each—reaching a peak with the Reeds and the Breens, and then declines.

In other words, while both the males and females who survived came from families that averaged larger in size than those who died, mortality was least in those families that were neither very small nor very large.

One might think that this is an economic response. The smallest families did not have the resources needed to make it through, while the largest families had to divide their resources across too many mouths. This, though, is extremely unlikely: the very family that lost the most in terms of material goods—the Reeds—survived unscathed. Indeed, Breen's diary makes it quite clear that the Reeds were destitute ("Mrs Graves refusd. to give Mrs. Reid any hides," Breen reported on February 15[35]). Economics does not seem to account for this pattern.

It might also be thought that this is a response to the age of the family members involved. However, there is no significant relationship between the average age of Donner Party families and mortality rates,[36] and none between the size of the family and the average age of its members.[37]

The fact that all of the Breens and all of the Reeds survived has occasioned comment since the tragedy ended.[38] Neither the age of the members nor the economics of the situation would seem to account for this. This

TABLE 4.10. Donner Party survivorship by family size.

Size	Male			Female			Total			Average age
	Survived	Died	Survived (%)	Survived	Died	Survived (%)	Survived	Died	Survived (%)	
1	3	13	18.8	—	—	—	3	13	18.8	28.6
2	0	2	0.0	2	0	100.0	2	2	50.0	*
3	1	0	100.0	1	1	50.0	2	1	66.7	18.7
4	2	2	50.0	1	3	25.0	3	5	37.5	14.4
6	3	0	100.0	3	0	100.0	6	0	100.0	17.7
9	7	0	100.0	2	0	100.0	9	0	100.0	15.9
12	2	3	40.0	5	2	71.4	7	5	58.3	19.3
13	3	4	42.9	4	2	66.7	7	6	53.8	15.5
16	2	6	25.0	6	2	75.0	8	8	50.0	18.6
Totals	23	30	43.4	24	10	70.6	47	40	54.0	

* because Mr. Wolfinger's age is not known, an average age cannot be calculated for families of this size

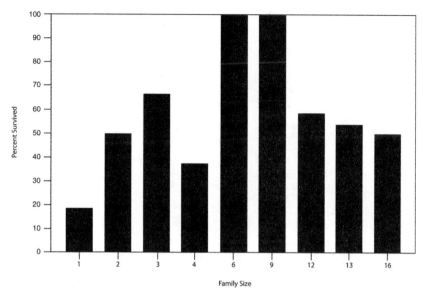

FIGURE 4.8. Donner Party survivorship by family size.

mystery aside, it is abundantly clear that the fact of marriage had considerable protective power and that, as a whole, those who survived traveled with larger family groups than those who did not.

Family Size and Days-to-Death
Within the Donner Party, the youngest males lasted longest and the oldest went first. That situation was reversed for the females, with the youngest tending to go first, the oldest last. Given that there is a relationship between family size and mortality, I can now ask whether the size of the kin group with whom a person traveled impacted the longevity of those who died.

In fact, it did, though the relationships are far more impressive for the females than for the males. The males who were lost during the initial round of deaths were part of family groups that averaged 5.2 people in size. Those males who died during the second round of death traveled with families that averaged 9.9 members. This too is part of the marriage effect. Of the 12 people, all male, who died before the lull, seven were single. In addition, the larger the family to which a male belonged, the longer it took, on average, for him to die if he were going to die.[39]

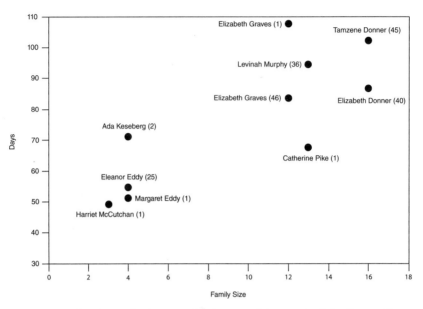

FIGURE 4.9. The relationship between family size and days-to-death for Donner Party females. The numbers in parentheses give the ages of the people involved.

The relationship between family size and days-to-death is far stronger for females[40] (Figure 4.9). There are statistical methods that can help determine the joint impacts of age and family size on days-to-death in this setting. Applying those methods shows that once the contribution of family size has been taken into account, age itself adds little to our ability to explain the pattern displayed by the Donner Party females. This is not the case for the males, for whom both age and family size are significant contributors to days-to-death.[41]

Clearly, family size played an important role in mediating death among both the male and female members of the Donner Party. Survivors among both males and females tended to have larger families than those who died, with this pattern more pronounced for males (16 of whom were traveling alone) than for females (none of whom traveled alone). Among those who did die, those with larger families survived longer than those with smaller ones, though here the effect of family size is far more pronounced for females than it is for males.

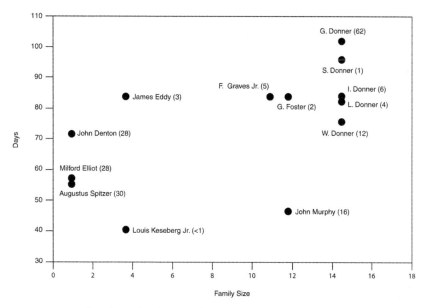

FIGURE 4.10. The relationship between family size and days-to-death for Donner Party males who died during the second round of deaths. The numbers in parentheses give the ages of the people involved.

Why was the impact of family size on days-to-death greater for Donner Party females than for the males? The answer relates to something I have already discussed: the initial round of deaths that carried away 12 people because they were male and because they were, in all but one case (12-year-old Lemuel Murphy), adults. Figure 4.10 shows the relationship between family size and days-to-death for the males who died after the lull ended. The relationship is still not as strong as it is for the females,[42] but family size here plays a more similar role to that seen among the females who succumbed than it does for the males as a whole. Just as for the females, for these males it is family size, and not age, that best explains days-to-death.[43]

Why the shift? The impact of family size on days-to-death was greater for the Donner Party females than it was for the Donner Party males as a whole because the potential advantages to longevity provided by larger families was lost to so many adult males as a result of their age and sex. They were old enough to act like men and lost their lives as a result. Once so many of these men were gone, the patterns of mortality shown by men and women began to look much more similar to one another.

HUMAN BIOLOGY AND THE DONNER PARTY: A SUMMARY

My understanding of the relationship between biology and mortality in human groups led me to three major expectations about the patterns death would take within the Donner Party after the group had become entrapped in the snow.

First, I expected death to fall most heavily on the youngest and oldest members of the group. This is exactly what happened. Among those younger than five, 62.5 percent succumbed. Of those older than 40, 70.0 percent died.

Second, I expected males, both boys and men, to die at higher rates than females, both girls and women. This I expected for two different sets of reasons. Males die at higher rates and have lower life expectancies than females in normal conditions. In addition, considerations of male and female biology, along with the results of experimental studies, led me to expect that the normal sex differentials in mortality and longevity would be exacerbated under conditions of extreme cold and starvation.

This also happened. Males died at nearly twice the rate of females (at 1.93 times the rate, to be exact), and they died at higher rates across nearly all age classes. Males also died sooner than females. Within the Sierra Nevada, the first 14 deaths were exclusively male; not until seven weeks after the first male death did the first female, young Harriet McCutchan, succumb. The earliest male deaths primarily took prime-aged men; once this had happened, death took a break. When it returned some 18 days later, it now took both males and females.

Third, I expected a relationship between the size of a person's support group and the likelihood that person would live or die, and I suspected that among those who did die, those who survived longest would be those who were traveling with larger kin groups.

This too was the case. Both males and females who survived traveled with larger families than those who died. In addition, among those who died, people who traveled with larger kin groups lived longer than those who traveled with smaller ones. This relationship is stronger for the females than for the males, but that is largely because the first round of deaths differentially plucked vigorous adult males. For them, the potential benefits of family affiliation were lost because they behaved like men.

Thus, all three of my major expectations about the pattern of Donner Party deaths are met by what actually happened. We are staring the impact of human biology in the face and seeing the very predictable results that occur when that complex combination of morphology, physiology, and behavior that makes people what they are interacts with a natural disaster caused by cold and famine. Shorn of many of their cultural defenses against freezing temperatures and lack of food, members of the Donner Party died as their biology dictated.

I did not expect some aspects of Donner Party mortality. When I first began to think about what the pattern of mortality within this group should have looked like given what we know about human biology, I thought only of the Donner Party as I had grown up knowing about it: as a group of people stuck in the snow, freezing and starving and eating one another to survive. I did not think about deaths that had occurred before the forced encampments. In fact, I did not even know there had been deaths between the time the Donner Party had taken its final form and the time it had become trapped.

Five deaths occurred during that period. All involved males dying of causes that typically kill more males than females: life-threatening aggression and violence (Hardcoop, Pike, Snyder, and Wolfinger) and disease (Halloran). Even when you don't expect it, there it is.

Finally, while I expected to see a relationship between family size and survivorship, I did not expect to find that survivorship would climb to a peak across family sizes and then decline. Unlike the situation with the five male deaths prior to the Sierra encampment, the cause of this pattern is not evident to me.

WHAT DOES ONE EXAMPLE MEAN?

Psychologist Eleanor Maccoby has done pivotal research on the development of behavioral differences between the sexes. After one of her talks, a distressed young man asked her, "What's good about being male?"[44] I have been asked exactly the same thing after my talks, but I can only recall being asked this by women.

Some of the women in my audiences have seen in my results exactly what I see. They took those results to confirm the major role biology plays in determining who lives and who dies in the kinds of situations in which the Donner Party found itself. Some have gone further than this, suggesting that these results can be taken as an aspect of the biological superiority of women, a not-so-distant echo of "what's good about being male."

Males and females are under very different kinds of biological selective pressures. Differential mortality is one result of the responses to those pressures. The differing amounts and distribution of fat that mark men and women result from the demands of attracting a mate and of pregnancy and lactation. Lessened mortality in situations marked by cold and famine can be seen in part as a fortunate offshoot of female adaptations to successful reproduction. Greater female longevity in this sense is simply a mark of difference.

Some women have also reacted negatively to my argument that the pattern of Donner Party mortality is a function of biology, as opposed to elective or learned behavior.[45] I argue that in the Donner Party context, a bundle of biological traits that includes morphology, physiology, and behavior worked to the benefit of females and to the detriment of males. To me, it is obvious that critically important instances exist in which the behavioral differences between men and women are of biological origins. Hunting and gathering societies provide a famous example, since there are well-understood biological reasons why the men in these groups are so often the hunters and the women the gatherers.[46]

This is also to argue that some very important aspects of sex roles are biological in origin and that, while little girls can be taught to wear blue and little boys to wear pink, it would be far harder to change more significant aspects of human behavior. It might have been the cultural expectation of all Donner Party members that the men would cut the group's way through the Wasatch Range and chop firewood and dig out cattle in the Sierra Nevada, but these expectations follow from human biology.[47] Men may die from the biology of risk and aggression, but they tend to be far better at such things than women are.

However, the Donner Party is just one case, and it is a case that involves a small number of people. Is there not some chance that if we examine other instances of this sort, we would get very different results?

It so happens that there are two other instances of nineteenth-century overland emigrants who encountered severe cold and famine on their way west and who suffered significant mortality as a result. I now turn to these other cases.

CHAPTER 4 NOTES

1. Thornton 1986; K. Johnson 1996.
2. Grayson 1991, 1994a.
3. King 1994, 1998; K. Johnson 1996, 2011a; K. Johnson in Novak and Dixon 2011.
4. For instance, since age class 1–4 had 16.72 percent of the 1850 Illinois population, the comparable Donner Party figure becomes 0.1672(86), or 14.4 people.
5. Chi-square = 3.28, p > 0.10.
6. Chi-square = 6.49, p = 0.01.
7. Unruh 1979.
8. Bagley 2012:vxi. Bagley 2012:242–245 provides an excellent discussion of women on the trail before and immediately after the gold rush.
9. Stewart 1960:222.
10. 56.6/29.4 = 1.93.
11. Thornton 1986:92; K. Johnson 1996:117.
12. Morgan 1963:704.
13. King 1998:207.
14. Morgan 1963:794 also observed that it was 8 of 10 men who died, not 9 of 11.
15. Ibid., 313.
16. Ibid.
17. Bryant 1985:262.
18. Stewart 1960.
19. Chi-square = 9.64, p < 0.01.
20. There is a significant negative correlation between age and days-to-death among Donner Party males. That correlation is stronger without George Donner (Pearson's r = −0.70, p < 0.001) than with him (r = −0.42, p < 0.035) but significant in both cases.
21. Clayton 1921:307; White 1997:176.
22. K. Johnson 1996:142–143.
23. Houghton 1997:35.
24. Ibid., 35.
25. Ibid., 70.
26. r = +0.79, p = 0.01.
27. A runs test shows that the timing of the deaths of the five girls and six boys beneath the age of five is not significantly ordered by sex, p > 0.05.
28. K. Johnson 2011a.
29. Stewart 1960:99.
30. K. Johnson 1996:280; Murphy 1980:37.
31. Chi-square = 11.77, p < 0.01.
32. Chi-square = 5.67, p < 0.02.
33. Chi-square = 9.82, p < 0.01. Although a much higher proportion of males in family groups died than females in family groups, this difference is not significant (chi-square = 2.06, p = 0.15).
34. Chi-square = 5.93, p = 0.015.
35. King 1992:59, 1996:79.
36. r = −0.14, p = 0.758.
37. r = +0.23, p = 0.653; single males were not included in these calculations, nor were families composed of two people, since Mr. Wolfinger's age is unknown.
38. E.g., Stewart 1960; King 1998; Thornton 1986.
39. r = +0.51, p = 0.01.
40. r = +0.81, p < 0.01.
41. Multiple regression shows that, for females, once the effects of family size on days-to-death is taken into account (p = 0.002), incorporating age into the equation does not significantly increase the predictive power of that equation (p = 0.925). For males, both family size (p = 0.010) and age (p = 0.041) are significant predictors of days-to-death.
42. r = +0.59, p = 0.03.
43. Multiple regression shows that for the males who died after the lull, family size is a significant predictor

of days-to-death (p = 0.034), but age is not (p = 0.46).

44. Maccoby 1998:311.

45. E.g., Novak and Dixon 2011.

46. See, for instance, Brown 1970 and Hawkes 1990, 1993.

47. Wood and Eagly 2002, 2012; Eagly and Wood 2009.

5

"THE HEAVENS WEEP"

The Willie Handcart Company

THE HANDCART EXPERIMENT

By 1838, the Mormon community in Missouri was undergoing intense and organized persecution. Church founder Joseph Smith and other church leaders had been imprisoned, and Governor Lilburn W. Boggs—the same Lilburn Boggs we encountered at Fort Laramie in Chapter 2—had declared that "the Mormons must be treated as enemies, and must be exterminated or driven from the State if necessary, for the public peace."[1]

Driven they were, in 1839, to western Illinois, where, under Smith's leadership, the remarkable town of Nauvoo began to rise on the banks of the Mississippi.[2] Although Nauvoo prospered—by 1844, there were some 10,000 people living there—the building of a new and lustrous center did little to stem the hatred that greeted Mormons wherever they went, a hatred now intensified by public knowledge of their practice of plural marriage.[3] In 1844, Joseph Smith and his brother Hyrum were murdered while under arrest in a Carthage, Illinois, jail. One leader gone, another—the powerful Brigham Young—ascended to his place, but this did not change the enmity that those outside the church felt toward church members. Violence against Illinois Mormons continued; in 1845, the state repealed the charter that

MORMONS CROSSING THE PLAINS.

FIGURE 5.1. "Mormons Crossing the Plains": "They travelled on foot, each family drawing a handcart containing household goods, etc. The train presented a novel sight as it moved on over the great overland route to the Pacific." (*Ballou's Pictorial* XI (11–12):177, September 20, 1856; https://archive.org/details/ballouspictorial1112ball).

supported the very existence of Nauvoo, and it became clear that this once prosperous center would have to be abandoned.

That process began early in 1846. Young left in February, with others following during the coming months; by the end of the year, Nauvoo was nearly empty of Saints.[4] The ultimate target was the Great Basin just west of the Rocky Mountains, an area recently described in John C. Frémont's report on his western exploring expedition (see Chapter 2).[5] They spent the winter at what came to be known first as Winter Quarters and then as Florence, now within Omaha, Nebraska.

In April 1847, some 150 people in 73 wagons headed west from Winter Quarters, with Young in the lead. The final stretch of the trip through the Rocky Mountains used the very road cut by the Donner Party the year before. In July, they emerged where a new Zion would soon be born and where Salt Lake City now stands.[6]

It did not take long for the new arrivals to match, and then vastly outdo, their accomplishments at Nauvoo. Salt Lake City thrived, and Mormon colonies were soon established throughout the region. Within a few years, church leaders began giving serious thought to how vast numbers of far-flung and often poor members of the church could be brought west.

The result was the Perpetual Emigrating Fund (PEF), established in 1849.[7] Initially directed toward helping impoverished eastern members

FIGURE 5.2. The Willie Handcart Company in Iowa (from Stenhouse 1873, 315).

of the church come west, it soon focused its efforts on bringing poverty-stricken converts from Europe—in particular, Great Britain and Scandinavia, sites of significant missionizing success by the church since the late 1830s. The funds provided were loans, not grants, and were expected to be paid back, at times with interest.[8]

The plan worked, but by the fall of 1855, the PEF had been dramatically reduced by heavy expenditures, the economic impacts of a bad harvest, and the failure of impoverished emigrants to pay back what they had received.[9] As a result, the church introduced a new method of travel, one that Brigham Young was convinced would be cheaper, easier, and faster than the cumbersome wagon trains that were the standard means of overland conveyance to the west.

Rather than traveling from the railhead to Salt Lake City by ox-drawn wagons, emigrants supported by the fund would now be expected, in the words of European mission president Franklin D. Richards, to "walk and draw their luggage across the plains,"[10] using simple handcarts to convey essential goods (Figures 5.1 and 5.2). The trip would not be easy, but if, as Richards observed, a Muslim could undergo "a long and weary pilgrimage of months and even years"[11] to visit Mecca, then a Mormon could draw a handcart the 1,300 miles from Iowa City, Iowa, to Salt Lake City. As historian Will Bagley has discussed, there were precedents for this, including

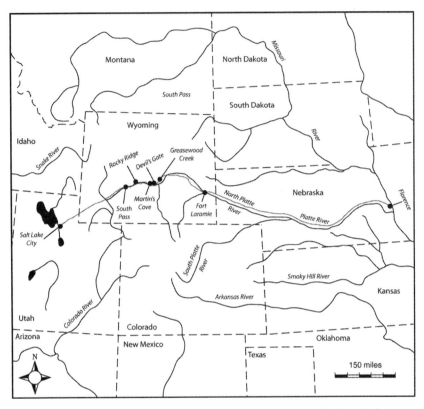

FIGURE 5.3. The handcart trail from Florence, Nebraska, to Salt Lake City, Utah.

men who used handcarts and wheelbarrows to reach, or at least try to reach, California during the gold rush.[12]

Leaving from Liverpool, England, prospective handcarters crossed the ocean to Boston or New York City, then traveled by train to Iowa City, where they received their handcarts. Five people were assigned to each 60-pound cart, which carried 17 pounds of belongings per adult and 10 pounds per child, as well as a small mess kit. Commissary wagons—in 1856, one wagon per 20 handcarts—accompanied each tightly organized group,[13] and rations were apportioned to group members from this central store according to an explicit set of rules. As far as Florence, early handcart groups passed through areas that had been settled by Euro-Americans. Beyond that, they were largely on their own, and the truly challenging part of the journey began (Figure 5.3).

The first two handcart companies left Iowa City on June 9 and June 11, 1856, with 274 and 221 members, respectively. They arrived in Salt Lake City on September 26. The third company, consisting of 320 people, left around June 25 and arrived on October 2. By the time the handcart emigration was terminated in 1860, ten companies had made the trip, bringing some 3,000 European converts to Utah.[14]

The handcart experiment shows Brigham Young to have been right in thinking that these vehicles, these "two-wheeled infernal machines,"[15] could cross the plains less expensively than ox-drawn wagons—as long as expenses were calibrated only in terms of dollars.[16] At its best, the experience was extraordinarily harsh. Even those involved in organizing the scheme were struck by the fact that "it looked too much like hard work for men to perform labor that has hitherto only been considered proper for beasts of draught and burden."[17] To handcarter Elizabeth Sermon, the experience was akin to being a part of "a herd of stock, or something worse."[18] Fellow handcarter Patience Loader "could not see it right at all to want us to do such a humeliating thing to be I said harnest up like cattle and pull a handcart loded up with our beding cooking utencels and our food and clothing."[19]

The experience was cruel at best, but when things went wrong, the handcart experiment was disastrous, causing, in historian David Bigler's words, the "greatest single tragedy in the history of the nation's move west in the nineteenth century."[20] Many Native American groups might question that assessment, as might members of the Donner Party, but no one can question the magnitude of the tragedy that befell two of these companies.

THE WILLIE HANDCART COMPANY: THE TRIP TO SALT LAKE CITY

The third ship to carry would-be handcarters left Liverpool on May 4, 1856.[21] The *Thornton* carried 764 Mormons, 484 of whom were supported by the Perpetual Emigrating Fund. James G. Willie was given charge of this large group, most of whom had come from the British Isles and Scandinavia. Willie, 41 years old at the start of the voyage and just returned from a four-year stint as a missionary in England, the country of his birth, proved to be an effective choice.

The ocean voyage was relatively uneventful, as was the overland trip to Iowa City. The *Thornton* arrived in New York on June 14; by June 26, members of the Fourth, or Willie, Handcart Company had arrived in Iowa City.

Unfortunately, Iowa City was not ready for them. There were no hand-carts and there were no tents. There was not even enough seasoned lumber from which handcarts could be made. The situation became even worse on July 8, when the 600 members of the Fifth, or Martin, Handcart Company began to arrive, taxing scarce resources even more heavily (see Chapter 6).

While the men set about making carts and the women tents, the Fourth Handcart Company was given its full official leadership, all drawn from those who had served as missionaries. James Willie continued as captain. Millen Atwood, Levi Savage, William Woodward, John Chislett, and Johan Ahmanson became captains of the subgroups called Hundreds. Wood-ward's group, Chislett tells us, was mostly Scottish; Ahmanson's, mostly Scandinavian.[22] The rest were mostly English.

It took 19 days before all was ready. On July 15, the Fourth Handcart Company experienced its first taste of what was to come, since on that day they began the 280-mile walk from Iowa City to Florence. When the group left Iowa City, the company consisted of about 500 people, 120 handcarts, 5 wagons, 24 oxen, and 45 beef cattle and milk cows.[23] Chislett tells us that once in use, the handcarts weighed about 160 pounds, a figure he calculated from a cart weight of 60 pounds, plus 17 pounds of luggage per person (recall that 5 people were assigned to each cart), plus the required mess kit.

He also tells us that rations across Iowa were surprisingly low, presum-ably a measure of exactly how unprepared the church was for the flood of people who had arrived that summer. "Our rations," Chislett says, "consisted of ten ounces of flour to each adult per day, and half that amount to children under eight years of age."[24] In addition, they were occasionally given a little rice, sugar, coffee, or bacon. The allowance was so small, Chislett observed, that "any hearty man could eat his daily allowance for breakfast. In fact, some of our men did this, and then worked all day without dinner."[25]

Chislett was not happy about this situation. Whoever had decided on their rations, he suggested, "should drag a hand-cart through the State of Iowa in the month of July on exactly the same amount and quality of fare we had."[26] "Where," he wondered, "was the wisdom in sending forward so many people when the preparations were altogether inadequate for them?"[27]

Some of the company quit along the way, preferring to remain behind than to continue for another 1,000 miles. The rest arrived at Florence on August 11. Here they remained for a week, repairing their already-deteriorating handcarts and tents[28] and wondering whether it was wise to continue west at so late a date. The leaders themselves were divided on this score, some suggesting that they winter in Nebraska and make the trip in the spring. In the end, at a public meeting, they decided to go on.

They left Florence on August 16 and 17. The group was now down to about 440 people, as some decided that Florence was as far as they wished to go, at least for this season. Those who continued had an added burden because the supply wagons could not carry all the supplies. As a result, each cart was required to add a 98-pound bag of flour to its load. The handcarts now weighed as much as 260 pounds.[29]

This was brutally harsh to those pushing and pulling handcarts, but they at least thought their flour would last for nearly 60 days, at a pound per adult per day.[30] Given the calculated distance from Florence to Salt Lake City of 1,031 miles,[31] this means that they thought they had enough flour to get them all the way through if they could average about 18 miles a day. They also expected that additional supplies would be available to them as they came closer to Zion.

Accordingly, rations were raised above the levels that had been provided in Iowa. Each adult would now receive one pound, and each child eight ounces, of flour per day. In addition, fresh beef was occasionally made available and each Hundred had three or four milk cows. The flour on the carts was used first, starting with the carts belonging to the weakest members.[32]

For the first few weeks, thing went reasonably well, save for the fact that the handcarts were continually breaking down, resulting in what historian David Roberts has referred to as an "ordeal by repair."[33] This happened because of the heavy loads they were carrying and because the unlubricated wooden axles were so easily damaged. These problems diminished as the flour was consumed, and the Willie Handcart Company began making about 15 miles a day.

The "light" loads did not last. On the night of September 3, along the Platte River some 270 miles from Florence, "the whole country alive with buffaloes,"[34] their livestock stampeded. Even after three days of searching, 30 remained missing and the group was now left with only two oxen per wagon. There was no choice but to yoke up whatever beef or milk cattle that would stand for it, but even so, they could not pull the loads involved. Each handcart once again received a sack of flour. Almost as bad, the beef cattle and milk cows had become draft animals, removing another source of food.

Hope was provided by a visit from Franklin Richards, his associate Daniel Spencer, and an accompanying party of missionaries. These men were speeding back to Salt Lake City in carriages and light wagons after seeing off the last of the emigrants from Florence. They met the Willie Company along the North Platte on September 12 and left the next morning. In the interim, Richards did his best to boost morale, even "congratulating them on the loss of their cattle which he knew had proved and would prove their salvation if they would hearken to and diligently obey counsel to the letter."[35] He apparently thought that the loss of their cattle was such a good thing that he assisted in the process: Chislett notes that Richards and his group commandeered the company's fattest calf, taking for themselves "what we ourselves so greatly needed."[36] He was, Chislett said, "ashamed for humanity's sake" that they had acted in such a way.[37] The calf, William Woodward added, was killed on the morning of September 13.[38] At least Richards promised to arrange for supplies to be waiting for them at Fort Laramie, some 200 trail miles west.[39]

Willie tells us that his company reached Fort Laramie on September 30, but the provisions that had been promised them by Richards were not to be found.[40] They were now 522 trail miles from Florence and 44 days out, having made only 12 miles a day, far less than they needed given the supplies at hand. Their slowing pace was caused not by the weather, which had held for them, but by the handcarts, which continued to break down.[41]

The slow pace and lack of new provisions meant that rations had to be reduced at the same time that they had to make every effort to travel faster. Daily flour rations fell to 14 ounces for a man, 12 for a woman, 8 for a child, and 4 for an infant. One of the reasons "our people got weak," Woodward noted, "was they had not enough to eat."[42]

As the group moved west along the Platte, a messenger traveling eastward told them that supplies would now be waiting at South Pass. To the extent that hope is edible, this must have helped, but it did nothing to slow the use of their dwindling food supply or speed their passage. On October 14, near Independence Rock, and having come about 170 miles from Fort Laramie, rations had to be reduced again. It was now to be 10.5 ounces of flour per man, 9 per woman, 6 per child, and 3 per infant. There it remained until there was nothing left.[43]

FIGURE 5.4. "The Hand-Cart Emigrants in a Storm" (from Stenhouse 1873, 310).

That was not long. The last flour, Woodward tells us, was issued at the fifth crossing of the Sweetwater, some 90 miles after leaving the Platte.[44] People had begun to fail and die along the upper reaches of the Platte. Now, in mid-October and still along the Sweetwater, the one thing that they had going for them, besides their faith and their remarkable organization, gave way: the weather (Figure 5.4).

Chislett tells us what happened next:

> We had not traveled far up the Sweetwater before the nights, which had gradually been getting colder since we left Laramie, became very severe. The mountains before us, as we approached nearer to them, revealed themselves to view mantled nearly to their base in snow, and tokens of a coming storm were discernable in the clouds which each day seemed to lower around us. In our frequent crossings of the Sweetwater, we had really "a hard road to travel." The water was beautiful to the eye . . . but when we waded it time after time at each ford to get the carts, the women, and the children over, the beautiful stream . . . lost to us its beauty, and the chill which it sent through our systems drove out from our minds all holy and devout aspirations.[45]

In some cases, Chislett noted, people even began to doubt the justice of an overruling Providence. This was especially so since

> *Our seventeen pounds of clothing and bedding* was now altogether insufficient for our comfort. Nearly all suffered more or less at night from cold. Instead of getting up in the morning strong, refreshed, vigorous, and prepared for the hardships of another day of toil, the poor "Saints" were to be seen crawling out from their tents looking haggard, benumbed, and showing an utter lack of that vitality so necessary to our success.[46]

Death, which had come along the upper Platte, now visited with a vengeance. "At first the deaths occurred slowly and irregularly," Chislett observed, "but in a few days at more frequent intervals, until we soon thought it unusual to leave a camp-ground without burying one or more persons."[47] There was little struggle; "life went out as smoothly as a lamp ceases to burn when the oil is gone."[48] As with the Donner Party, each death weakened the whole. Ultimately, Chislett was unable to raise enough men in his Hundred to pitch the tents, and he was amazed that he himself did not die when so many who appeared to be stronger did just that. Then, on October 19, "weather very cold,"[49] they were overtaken by a snowstorm that "the shrill wind blew furiously about us."[50]

BRIGHAM YOUNG RESPONDS

John Chislett would leave the Mormon Church after the ordeal was over. His respect for James Willie and the members of his company shows throughout his narrative. So, however, does his bitterness toward those church officials who allowed such things to happen. Chislett had few kind words for Brigham Young, the author of the handcart experiment. Indeed, Young took criticism from within the church for the difficulties that rolled over the Willie and Martin Companies.[51] The criticism was certainly deserved. The buck had to stop somewhere, and some of Young's later defenses ring hollow—for instance, that to drop while eating or singing must have been a pleasant way to die and that the 1856 "mortality has been much less than attends well fitted animal trains traveling in good season."[52] But it is also true that he acted, and acted decisively, once he learned that the Third Handcart Company, which had arrived on October 2, was not the last of the season.

This happened on October 4, when Richards's group arrived in Salt Lake City. At the time, the Willie Company was a few days west of Fort Laramie, struggling with their reduced rations; the Martin Company was still four days east of the fort.

Young appeared astonished to learn from Richards that some 1,000 handcarters were still on their way and enraged to learn that they had been allowed to leave so late. A month later, on November 2, before either company had made it in, Young's anger, now exacerbated by the suggestion that he was at fault, was clear:

> Here is br. Franklin D. Richards who has but little knowledge of business, except what he has learned in the church; he came into the church when a boy, and all the public business he has been in is the little he has done while in Liverpool, England; and here is br. Daniel Spencer, br. Richards' first counselor and a man of age and experience, and I do not know that I will attach blame to either of them. But if, while at the Missouri River, they had received a hint from any person on this earth, or if even a bird had chirped it in the ears of brs. Richards and Spencer, they would have known better than to rush men, women, and children on to the prairie in the autumn months, on the 3d of September, to travel over a thousand miles. I repeat that if a bird had chirped the inconsistency of such a course in their ears, they would have thought and considered for one moment, and would have stopped those men, women, and children there until another year. If any man, or woman, complains of me or of my Counselors, in regards to the lateness of some of this season's immigration, let the curse of God be on them and blast their substance with mildew and destruction, until their names are forgotten from the earth.[53]

This was a remarkable way of not attaching blame to Richards and Spencer. This was also, as David Roberts has observed, a clever deflecting stroke on Young's part, since "a century and a half later, the blame has stuck where the Prophet flung it."[54] Young's anger was also productive in a different way, as even the apostate Chislett recognized.[55] If there were any fortunate things to come of the timing of the events that were taking place, it is that Richards arrived the day before the beginning of the semiannual conference of the church.

The very evening of Richards's arrival, Young convened a meeting of church officials and other leaders to determine what needed to be done. The next day—October 5, when the conference began—Young was ready with his demands:

> I shall call upon the Bishops this day. I shall not wait until to-morrow, nor until next day, for 60 good mule teams and 12 or 15 wagons. I do not want to send oxen. I want good horses and mules. They are in this Territory, and we must have them; also 12 tons of flour and 40 good teamsters, besides those that drive the teams.[56]

Brigham Young was not to be, and was not, ignored. Daniel Webster Jones, an experienced frontiersman, was one of the good men he had in mind. After Young had made his demands, Jones later recounted, three officials, including Presiding Bishop Edward Hunter, separately told the 26-year-old that they wanted him to make the trip. After the third exhortation, Jones "began to think it was time to decide."[57] Young, he recalled, "seemed moved by a spirit that would admit of no delay."[58]

There were none. The first group of 27 male rescuers left on October 7 under the leadership of George D. Grant, who was, in turn, assisted by William H. Kimball and Robert T. Burton.[59] As if any proof were needed of Young's insistence that all those able to help must help, both Grant and Kimball had been part of Richards's group of returning missionaries. Indeed, of the 13 men in Richards's party, six joined the first rescuers.[60] Three days earlier, they had just arrived in Salt Lake City. Now they were back on the trail heading east. These six, however, did not include Franklin Richards. He who congratulated the Willie Company for losing their cattle and then helped out by taking their fattest calf; he who failed to arrange for the promised supplies at Fort Laramie; and he whose ears failed to hear the chirping bird, stayed behind.

Just as impressive as the speed with which Young had assembled the initial rescuers was the quality of what he had assembled. "A better outfit and one more adapted to the work before us I do not think could have possibly been selected if a week had been spent in fitting up," Jones, the cook for Grant's group, recalled. "We had good teams and provisions in great abundance," he continued. "But best of all, those going were alive to the work and were of the best material possible for the occasion."[61]

The beehive is the great symbol of Mormon industry, but the industry of the rescuers that winter might better be represented by an anthill centered on Salt Lake City, with one trail, full of ants, leading eastward from it. Before October had ended, Young had seen to it that some 250 rescue teams were on the road, though it remains shocking that he saw fit to divert some of these teams to bring in wagons that carried nothing but material items, including his own personal goods.[62] George Grant led the first group of rescuers, and this group was the first to encounter the Willie Company.

"THE HEAVENS WEEP"

"We travelled on in misery and sorrow day after day," wrote Chislett,[63] until, on October 19 (the date is provided by Woodward), a light wagon drove into the snow-covered camp from the west. In it were four men, including Brigham Young's 22-year-old son, Joseph (one of the returning missionaries of October 4), sent ahead by Grant on October 14 in the hope of making contact with the Willie and Martin Companies. They did not stay long. They informed the Willie Company that relief was ahead and left to find the Martin Company. "More welcome messengers never came from the courts of glory" were Chislett's grateful words.[64]

It is not clear when Willie decided it was time for him to take leave of his charges and seek help. According to Chislett, this decision was made after the rescue team's advance party came into camp, but it is possible that the decision was reached before this. The timing is unimportant. What is important is that Willie and Joseph B. Elder rode off into the snow looking for their rescuers. It took them two days, coming into Grant's camp along the headwaters of the Sweetwater on October 20. The next morning, all moved east, joining the Willie Handcart Company and providing it with its first relief on October 21.

Chislett described the scene after Willie and Elder left but before the rescuers arrived:

The scanty allowance of hard bread and poor beef . . . was mostly consumed the first day by the hungry, ravenous, famished souls. We killed more cattle and issued the meat; but, eating it without bread, did not satisfy hunger, and to those who were suffering from dysentery it did more harm than good. This terrible disease increased rapidly amongst us during those three days, and several died from exhaustion. Before we renewed our journey the camp became so offensive and filthy that words would fail to describe its condition, and even common decency forbids the attempt. . . . It was enough to make the heavens weep.

"Such craving hunger," Chislett said, "I never saw before, and may God in his mercy spare me the sight again."[65]

Daniel Jones found the Willie Company "freezing and starving to death" in 10 inches of snow.[66] Nonetheless, the evening of the 21st was one of rejoicing for those who had finally been given real reason for hope.

In the morning, nine more people were buried, and much of Grant's group continued east in their search for the Martin company. William Kimball led the rescuers who remained behind; with them, they had six wagons of supplies. From now until the end of the ordeal, the Fourth Handcart Company was to have continual help.

That does not mean that things became easy. In fact, the Willie Company was about to face what Willie himself called "the most disastrous day on the whole trip."[67] This was the ascent of Rocky Ridge, some five miles of exposed bedrock 25 miles east of South Pass. "Dangerous to wagons, and ought to be crossed with care" was the description in *The Latter-Day Saints' Emigrants' Guide*,[68] but on October 23, the day the Willie Company tried it, it was much worse.

The snow on Rocky Ridge was knee deep that day, Chislett tells us, and a biting northwest wind accompanied the falling snow. People helped one another get their carts up the hill and through the snow: first one cart, then back down for another. The wagons, now burdened with provisions and those who could no longer walk, fell behind, the ox teams worn out. Chislett reached camp at 11:00 p.m., bringing news of all those still behind him. "The boys from the Valley"[69] were immediately sent back, and it was not until five in the morning of the 24th that all who were going to make it, did make it.

This was more than many could bear. There were now so many dead and dying, Chislett said, that they had no choice but to stay where they were for a day. It fell to Chislett to gather up the fallen. In a passage reminiscent of the description of the emotional results of starvation at the Bergen-Belsen concentration camp (Chapter 3), he recalled that by the time he was done, he had collected together, of all ages and both sexes, thirteen corpses, all stiffly frozen. We had a large square hole dug in which we buried these thirteen people, three or four abreast and three deep. When they did not fit in, we put one or two crosswise at the head or feet of the others. We covered them with willows and then with the earth. When we buried these thirteen people some of their relatives refused to attend the services. They manifested an utter indifference about it. The numbness and cold in their physical natures seem to have reached the soul, and to have crushed out natural feeling and affection. . . . Two others died during the day, and we buried them in one grave, making fifteen in all buried on that camp ground.[70]

The few days that had passed since their rescuers had joined them had been unimaginably hard on the Willie Company. A message sent back to Salt Lake City soon after the Rocky Ridge episode pointed out that "men would dig graves for their brethren and before night would die themselves."[71] At least, though, it would get no worse than this.

On his way east, Grant had left both men and provisions at South Pass. The beef, Chislett recalled, was hanging frozen from trees.[72] Once over the pass, not only did the weather improve, but they encountered relief team after relief team. By the time they reached Fort Bridger, on November 2 and 115 miles from their goal, enough help had arrived that the handcarts could be left behind. The deaths had not stopped, but they became fewer in number.

The Willie Company reached Salt Lake City on November 9. Brigham Young, Johan Ahmanson bitterly noted, "did not honor us with a personal visit; presumably he was ashamed to look upon our miserable and wretched condition, the result of his own shortsighted and ill-conceived plan."[73] Nonetheless, Ahmanson also observed that the "Lion of the Lord" had prepared the city for their arrival and everyone who needed help received it immediately.

The *Deseret News* announced their arrival, and with it, a remarkably deceitful interpretation of the handcarters' experience:

Capt. J. G. Willie with the 4th hand-cart company arrived on the 9th inst. . . . After all the hardships of the journey, mainly consequent upon so late a start, the mortality has been far less in br. Willie's company, than in many wagon companies that have started seasonably and with the usual conveniences for the trip. The eminent feasibility of the hand-cart movement had been previously demonstrated; its healthfulness is now proven by the experience of this company, late though they were and in storms, cold, and snow.[74]

How healthful was it? Willie counted 77 deaths between Liverpool and Salt Lake City.[75] Chislett put the number of dead handcarters at 67, or, as he calculated, one-sixth of the total number who had left Florence.[76] And, of course, the Martin Handcart Company was still out there (Chapter 6). The deaths may have been the worst part of it, but no one has even tried to count the number of limbs lost, the number of people disabled.[77] In 1860, the *New York Times* reported that in Salt Lake City, "the awful disasters of the hand-cart expeditions . . . still grate horribly on the memory, the remembrance being kept alive by numerous crippled unfortunates, who were frost-bitten during that time of wretchedness, and who ever and anon intrude upon the sight in the streets of this city and the settlements of the Territory."[78] Late in her life, Elizabeth Sermon told her family that had she not joined the Martin Handcart Company, "you children might not have been made cripples."[79] Patience Loader, in the same company, described a "poor girl eleven years old father and Mother boath did [died] of hunger and cold but there little dughter lived to get to Salt Lake but her poor feet was so frozen that boath had to be amputated above the ankle this poor [girl] was crippled for life."[80]

This was as remarkable a definition of "healthful" as Brigham Young's comforting vision of people happily eating and singing while freezing to death.

THE MEMBERSHIP OF THE WILLIE HANDCART COMPANY

The membership of the Donner Party is well known. This is less true for the Willie Handcart Company, and even less so for the Martin Company (Chapter 6). Leroy and Ann Hafen estimate the number of people involved as 500, most likely taking that figure from William Woodward's 1857 letter to Wilford Woodruff, in which Woodward estimated the size of the company at "about 500 souls."[81] Franklin Richards and Daniel Spencer, in their account of their trip from Florence to Salt Lake City, put the number of people in the company at 404 on September 12, the day they camped with them on the North Platte. They also added that there were 6 wagons, 87 handcarts, 6 yoke of oxen, 32 cows, and 5 mules.[82] In her reconstruction of the Willie Company membership, Susan Black provides a list of 393 people.[83] On the other hand, historians Rebecca Bartholomew and Leonard Arrington put the membership at 440.[84]

Some of the variability in these estimates is explained by the fact that the company varied in size at different stages of the trip. Chislett, for instance, observed that "when we left Iowa City we numbered about five hundred persons. Some few deserted us while passing through Iowa, and some remained at Florence. When we left the latter place we numbered four hundred and twenty, about twenty of whom were independent emigrants with their own wagons, so that our hand-cart company was actually four hundred of this number."[85] Indeed, although the options for escape were fairly limited, some people left after the group had moved beyond Florence. Willie relates that two women decided to stay at Fort Laramie: "Lucinda M. Davenport who immediately married an apostate just arrived from the Valley; and Christine Brown." And, he tells us, two men deserted just before the company arrived at the upper crossing of the Platte, on October 12.[86]

Just as the estimates of the number of people in the Fourth Handcart Company vary, so do the estimates of the number of people who died. Willie, as I have mentioned, put the total number of deaths after leaving Liverpool at 77. The Hafens follow Chislett in recording the number at 67 deaths.[87] Church archivists Melvin Bashore and Linda Haslam list 75 deaths.[88]

Thus, there is no truly secure list of the membership of the Willie Handcart Company, and no definitive list of the members who died. In my previous work on this company,[89] I compiled my own list, with accompanying demographic data, depending heavily on resources made available to me by the LDS Church History Department in Salt Lake City.[90] Since that time, a remarkable amount of research has been done on the membership of both the Willie and Martin Companies.[91] That research has clarified the membership of these companies and the mortalities they sustained at the same time that it has given depth to our understanding of the lives of many of the people involved. I have drawn on these works to build the lists of Willie and Martin Handcart Company members used here along with attendant data on age, sex, family size, and survivorship.[92]

TABLE 5.1. Membership of the Willie Handcart Company west of Florence, NE: Age and sex by Eighth U.S. Census age class.

Age class	Males	Females	Total	Male (%)	Female (%)
1–4	26	22	48	54.2	45.8
5–9	29	29	58	50.0	50.0
10–14	25	27	52	48.1	51.9
15–19	25	29	54	46.3	53.7
20–29	29	44	73	39.7	60.3
30–39	18	37	55	32.7	67.3
40–49	24	29	53	45.3	54.7
50–59	9	14	23	39.1	60.9
60–69	15	6	21	71.4	28.6
70–79	1	1	2	50.0	50.0
Unknown	2	1	3		
Totals	203	239	442	45.9	54.1

My Willie Handcart Company list contains 442 people who proceeded west from Florence, a total that is very close to the number indicated by Bartholomew and Arrington.[93] It is also extremely close to the number implied by the use of the 87 handcarts the Willie Company is said to have had; these suggest 435 people, excluding those in charge. Of these 442 people, 71 are known to have lost their lives.

My list, and the demographic data it contains, is certainly not perfect, but it is the most accurate list of which I am aware. At the same time, however, I am also aware that, as David Bigler suggests, "an accurate count of the number who died will probably never be known because the authorities tried to keep the full horror of the disaster from becoming public, especially in England."[94]

THE DEMOGRAPHIC STRUCTURE OF THE WILLIE HANDCART COMPANY

The Donner Party primarily consisted of families and single men going west to California to better their lives. Some of these families were fairly well-off. The members of the Willie Handcart Company were also heading west to better their lives, but the similarity stops there. Nearly all of these people were poor. Had that not been the case, they would not have been traveling under the Perpetual Emigrating Fund and they would not have pushed and pulled handcarts 1,300 miles.

In addition, the members of the Fourth Handcart Company were not traveling on their own. They were traveling under the auspices of the Mormon Church and had been ever since leaving their homelands. Although church representatives made critical mistakes as regards the Willie and Martin Companies, the handcart companies as a whole were extraordinarily well organized. The Willie and Martin Companies were no exception. Their members were expected to work hard, and they did. They also expected to be provided for and protected, and, up to a point, they were. As a result, the handcart companies contained significant numbers of people who would not otherwise have been crossing the Great Plains, even by wagon. In particular, they had significant numbers of elderly people and single women.

Table 5.1 shows the distribution of Willie Handcart Company members across age and sex categories, using the age classes employed in the 1860 (Eighth) U.S. Census. One of the most remarkable aspects of this distribution involves the relatively large numbers of women between the ages of 20 and 39 who formed part of the Willie Company. In the Donner Party, only 28 percent of those between 20 and 39 were women, and women of this age made up only 9 percent of the group as a whole. Of the 439 people of known age in the Willie Company, 63 percent of those between 20 and 39 were women, and 18.5 percent were women of this age.

In fact, these women were better represented in the Willie Company than they were in Utah at that time. That is the case whether the comparison is to Utah as it was represented in the Seventh (1850) U.S. Census,[95] only three years after the initial Mormon arrival,[96] or to Utah as it was in the Eighth Census, which records the results of a decade of intense emigration.[97] These women are also significantly better represented in the Willie Company than they were in the two states that had, by 1860, provided the majority of U.S.-born inhabitants of Utah: Illinois[98] and New York[99] (see Table 5.2).

The immediate reasons for the abundance of women of this age in the Willie Company are clear. The organization and protection provided by the church created a situation in which women felt secure traveling in the absence of adult male kin. This combined with a general tendency for women to be more likely than men to accept Mormonism in the first place and with an effort by the church "to help all the unmarried girls who are willing to go."[100] As a result, women who would not ordinarily be on the western emigrant trail were there in number.

TABLE 5.2. Female representation by Eighth U.S. Census age class: Illinois, New York, Utah, and Willie Handcart Company (WHC) compared.

Age class	Illinois: 1860	New York: 1860	Utah: 1850	Utah: 1860	WHC
1–4	49.2	49.4	49.6	49.2	45.8
5–9	49.3	49.4	49.0	49.3	50.0
10–14	48.6	49.3	50.1	47.6	51.9
15–19	49.5	52.1	50.3	52.2	53.7
20–29	46.3	53.1	41.3	51.6	60.3
30–39	44.4	49.5	44.0	50.4	67.3
40–49	44.2	47.5	44.0	47.5	54.7
50–59	43.8	48.3	35.4	49.3	60.9
60–69	45.1	49.3	48.5	49.9	28.6
70–79	46.5	50.2	41.5	51.0	50.0

How true this is can be seen if we examine the members of the Willie Company according to the kin groups with which they traveled after leaving Florence (Table 5.3). Of the 68 families (one or two parents plus one or more children) represented, only 41 had both parents. Two had only a father, but an amazing 24—35.3 percent of all the families—had only a mother.

In addition to the 24 single-mother families, 44 women traveled on their own, 6 women traveled with their sisters, and 1 woman traveled with her younger sister and child. That is, there were 75 women in the Willie Company traveling alone, with their sisters, or as the heads of families, representing 17 percent of the group as a whole.

This is, of course, in stark contrast with the Donner Party, with no single women traveling alone and only one family led by a single mother—Levinah Murphy (36), herself a member of the Mormon Church.[101] She, however, had her son John (16) and her two sons-in-law—William Pike (32) and William Foster (31)—with her. In the Willie Company, on the other hand, the 24 families with single mothers included just seven males over the age of 14 and only two over the age of 20: Mary Findley's (59) 26-year-old son, Allen, and Margaret Kirkwood's (47) 22-year-old son, Robert. Otherwise, these women had no related men with them.

Thus, the attraction of the church to women, the protective organization that the church provided, and the church's recruitment efforts all combined to remove the restraints that otherwise deterred women who were unaccompanied by adult male kin from striking out across the plains.

TABLE 5.3. Traveling groups of Willie Handcart Company members who proceeded west from Florence, NE (abbreviations are used in later tables).*

Group type	Number of groups	Number of individuals
Single females (SiF)	44	44
Single males (SiM)	45	45
Mothers only with children (MoCh)	24	86
Fathers only with children (FaCh)	2	5
Mothers and fathers with children (MoFaCh)	41	230
Husband and wife without children (HuWi)	8	16
Mother with sister and child	1	3
Siblings	6	12
Total	171	441

* excludes one individual of unknown family group type (Rose Kay)

Women between 20 and 39 were particularly abundant in the Willie Company because so many of the single mothers were of this age. Among the 86 people in families with single mothers, 17 women and only 2 men were between the ages of 20 and 39 years. In contrast, of the single people traveling without families, 30 women and 24 men were in this age group.

In short, women between 20 and 39 were common in the Willie Company because single mothers led so many of its families, and those families included so many women of this age. Since this was the case, it is appropriate to wonder what happened to the husbands of all those single mothers.

The answer does not lie in polygamy. Since the early 1840s, it had been known to outsiders that the LDS Church sanctioned plural marriage and that church founder Joseph Smith had multiple wives.[102] For the next decade, the church, including its European missionaries, vehemently denied the practice. That all changed in August 1852, when the church announced that "the Latter Day Saints have embraced the doctrine of a plurality of wives, as a part of their religious faith,"[103] and then published Smith's 1843 revelation sanctifying plural marriage.[104] The *Millennial Star*, the church's British proselytizing periodical, published that divine communication on January 1, 1853, after having previously denied any such behavior.[105] The *Star*'s pages now quickly filled with defenses of the newly announced doctrine.[106]

Even so, there is no indication that any of the single mothers in the Willie Company were plural wives. In other words, there is no reason to think that they were married to men who I have counted as the heads of other families in the group or that they were the wives of any of the married leaders of the group. All of these men had been missionaries and, as such, were forbidden by the church "to enter into any alliances with the sisters abroad, or to make any proposals of marriage to them, or to enter into any matrimonial covenants."[107] Some of the women in the Willie Company became plural wives after their arrival in Utah, but none seem to have held this status prior to that point.[108]

Instead, some combination of four other factors must explain the lack of husbands. In at least eight cases, the single mothers at the head of these families were widows.[109] In other instances, wives may have simply left their husbands behind to lead their children to Zion. This was certainly the case for Elizabeth Panting. As her son noted, "my father was very much against the Mormons and threatened to kill my mother if she did not stay away from the Mormons. . . . He finally got so mean, she took her two children . . . and left him."[110]

It is also possible that some husbands had already made the pilgrimage and their families were now following along behind or that women were taking their children to Zion with the understanding that their husbands would join them later.

No matter what the explanation, this very distinctive aspect of Willie Company membership had an important impact on the outcome of the ordeal, as we shall see.

COMPARING MORTALITY IN THE DONNER PARTY AND THE WILLIE HANDCART COMPANY

For all the reasons discussed in earlier chapters, we expect that deaths in the Willie Handcart Company would have fallen most heavily on the oldest and youngest and on the males. We should also expect that married people did better than those who were single and that the size of an emigrant's kin group played a role in determining his or her fate. The ordeals suffered by the Donner Party and the Willie Company, however, differed in some very important ways, and we should expect these differences to have played a role in determining the outcome as well.

The members of the Donner Party were exposed to cold and famine for as long as six months. The members of the Willie Company were never well fed and they traveled "in misery and sorrow day after day" long before extreme cold hit them.[111] However, their exposure to the cold lasted no more than about three weeks—between October 19 and their arrival in Salt Lake City on November 9—and, as we have seen, they had assistance for much of that time.

On the other hand, although the members of the Donner Party did their share of walking, they did not attempt to walk 1,300 miles across the plains, over the Continental Divide, and through the Wasatch Range while pushing and pulling their belongings in a wooden cart. To make things even worse, children in handcart companies were often carried by their parents or added as passengers to the carts, thus increasing the energy costs incurred by those who cared for those children. We might expect this mode of travel to have significant implications for mortality patterns within the Willie Company.

As with the Donner Party men, the Willie Company men were expected to—and did—engage in energy-intensive tasks from which the women were largely exempt. Chislett is quite explicit about this, telling us that the men had to "stand guard at night, wade the streams repeatedly by day to get the women and children across, erect tents, and do many duties which women could not do."[112]

However, the Willie Company women performed far more heavy labor than their counterparts in the Donner Party. Women not only pushed and pulled handcarts, they also routinely carried their infants as they walked.[113] The 45 single men in the Willie Company were distributed to the women who needed help, but so many women traveled in the absence of related men that there were not enough single men to go around. As a result, Chislett tells us, "several carts were drawn by young girls exclusively."[114] At times, if a woman lost her male workmate during the trip, she was on her own. Chislett, for instance, tells the depressing story of "old man James" (he was 48) who, after struggling to get his handcart up Rocky Ridge, could push no more (Figure 5.5). His wife and two daughters took over for him, but he soon died.

Compared to the women in the Donner Party, the women in the Willie Handcart Company performed substantially greater amounts of heavy labor. As a result, there is every reason to believe that the work-induced sex differential in energy expenditure was far less among the members of the Willie Company than among the members of the Donner Party.

FIGURE 5.5. "The Old Man James" on Rocky Ridge (from Stenhouse 1873, 329).

The Willie Company differed from the Donner Party in another critical way. The foodstuffs available to members of the Donner Party moved readily within family groups but far less readily between them. Things could not have been more different for the Willie Company, where food was apportioned to almost everyone from a central store according to a strict and explicit set of rules. There is no question that rank had its privileges among the handcarters, with company captains and leaders of the Hundreds having access to foodstuffs denied the rank-and-file.[115] In addition, some people were able to purchase food items at Fort Laramie and some could hunt. Nonetheless, there appear to have been no significant differentials in access to food among the vast majority of company members. How much those people received depended only on their age and sex. Indeed, it was this, as well as the mode of travel itself, that makes the handcart episode unique as a civilian enterprise.

There are also some unmeasurable but certainly significant differences between the Donner Party and the Willie (and Martin) Handcart Company. Wagon trains generally lacked strong leadership and consisted of modules that could readily become independent of one another. As a result, they would routinely rupture along fault lines generated by internal disputes. The Mormon Church, on the other hand, was, and is, exquisitely organized, and that organization extended to the handcart companies. Compared to the Donner Party, the handcart companies had both sufficiently strong leadership and sufficiently tight organization to overcome the squabbling that seems to have characterized the handcart experience as much as it characterized the experience of other overlanders. In addition, the handcart companies consisted of modules (individual sets of handcarters) that could not survive in the absence of the group as a whole once they left areas settled by Euro-Americans.

Religion also played a role. The Donner Party included devoutly religious people, but the handcarters were tied together not only by devoutness but by dedication to a common religion and the strong belief that God was on their collective side. Diary after diary, reminiscence after reminiscence, makes this clear. Ann Rowley, traveling with her eight children, recalled that, in mid-October,

> Night was coming and there was no food for the evening meal. I asked for God's help as I always did. I got on my knees, remembering two hard sea biscuits that were still in my trunk. They had been left over from the sea voyage. They were not large and were so hard they couldn't be broken. Surely that was not enough to feed 8 people. But 5 loaves and 2 fishes were not enough to feed 5,000 people either, but through a miracle, Jesus had done it. So, with God's help, nothing is impossible. I found the biscuits and put them in a dutch oven and covered them with water and asked for God's blessing. Then I put the lid on the pan and set it on the coals. When I took off the lid a little later, I found the pan filled with food. I kneeled with my family and thanked God for his goodness.[116]

There can be no doubt that shared religious devotion and the social coherence provided by the remarkable organization of the handcart companies made a significant difference, even if the magnitude of that difference cannot be measured.

In short, while we should expect the general patterns of mortality in the Willie Company to be similar to those seen in the Donner Party, we should not expect them to be identical. Insofar as they differ, however, they should differ in ways that follow from the experiences of the groups themselves.

MORTALITY IN THE WILLIE HANDCART COMPANY

Of the 442 members of the Willie Handcart Company known to have continued on from Florence, 71, or 16.1 percent, died.[117] By comparison, of the
87 members of the Donner Party, 40, or 46.0 percent, died. That is, the
mortality rate in the Donner Party was nearly three times that in the Willie
Company. This difference follows directly from the fact that the Donner
Party was exposed to cold and famine for so much longer than the Willie Company. Even with this lower mortality rate, however, we should still
expect to see the old, the young, and males to bear the brunt of death.

MORTALITY AND AGE

Table 5.4 provides the basic data we need on age, sex, and survivorship for
the Willie Company members who traveled west from Florence. The mortality rates by age class (from the last column in Table 5.4) are shown in
Figure 5.6. Clearly, the highest mortality rates mark the oldest members
of the company. Of the 99 adults who were at least 40 years old, 43, or 43.4
percent, lost their lives. Only 28 people younger than 40, or 8.2 percent,

TABLE 5.4. Mortality, by Eighth U.S. Census age class, of Willie Handcart Company
members who proceeded west from Florence, NE.*

Age class	Males: survived?			Females: survived?			Totals	% Died
	Yes	No	% Died	Yes	No	% Died		
1–4	23	3	11.5	22	0	0.0	48	6.3
5–9	24	5	17.2	28	1	3.4	58	10.3
10–14	22	3	12.0	24	3	11.1	52	11.5
15–19	24	1	4.0	28	1	3.4	54	3.7
20–29	26	3	10.3	42	2	4.5	73	6.8
30–39	16	2	11.1	33	4	10.8	55	10.9
40–49	11	13	54.2	26	3	10.3	53	30.2
50–59	4	5	55.6	11	3	21.4	23	34.8
60–69	0	15	100.0	4	2	33.3	21	81.0
70–79	0	1	100.0	0	1	100.0	2	100.0
Unknown	2	0		1	0		3	
Totals	152	51	25.1	219	20	8.4	442	16.1

* excludes individuals of unknown ages (Nancy Stewart, Carsten Jenson, Christen Jorgenson)

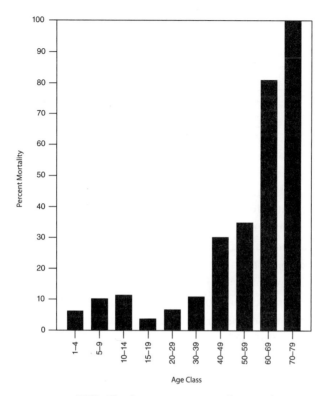

FIGURE 5.6. Willie Handcart company mortality rates by Eighth U.S. Census age class.

succumbed. People 40 years old or older died at more than five times the rate of those younger than them.

The heavy mortality of older people in the Willie Company is similar to what we have seen for the Donner Party. However, unlike the Donner Party, the mortality rate for the youngest members of the Willie Company (those less than five years of age) does not differ significantly from the rates for the other age classes below 40.[118]

The reasons for this difference are clear. In the Donner Party, people younger than five did not begin to die until around January 24 (see Table 4.6 and Figures 4.4 and 4.5). This was some ten weeks after the forced encampment had begun and some five weeks after the first deaths had occurred. As long as there were resources available, parents were able to protect their children, both in the Donner Party and in the Willie Handcart Company.

TABLE 5.5. Willie Handcart Company: Average ages of survivors and non-survivors by sex. N = number of individuals.

	Male (N)	Female (N)
Survived	18.5 (150)	23.5 (218)
Died	41.0 (51)	37.0 (20)
Difference	22.5	13.5

In the Donner Party, those resources were outstripped by the magnitude of the disaster that befell them, and the youngest died. The Willie Company, on the other hand, received help from Salt Lake City in sufficient time to prevent this from happening, and the youngest died at rates no greater than those seen among others less than 40 years old.

With the exception of the youngest members of the group, the general relationship between mortality rate and age in the Willie Company is similar to that in the Donner Party. Death struck most heavily at the older members of both groups, both male and female, while acting more kindly to those who were younger. The Willie Company males who died averaged 22.5 years older than those who survived; the females who were lost averaged 13.5 years older (Table 5.5).

SURVIVORSHIP AND SEX

As we have seen, 56.6 percent of Donner Party males and 29.4 percent of Donner Party females lost their lives. The male mortality rate in this group was 1.9 times the female mortality rate.

The males in the Willie Handcart Company did not do well either. After leaving Florence, 25.1 percent of the males lost their lives compared to only 8.4 percent of the females (Figure 5.7). Not only is this difference highly significant,[119] but the ratio of male to female mortality in the Willie Company is even higher than it is in the Donner Party: 3.0. In both groups, then, males died at far higher rates than females did.

Donner Party males died at greater rates than females across nearly all age classes (Table 4.5). The Willie Handcart Company shows a similar, but less pronounced pattern (Figure 5.8). Here male mortality outstrips female mortality in every age class with any survivors, and male deaths

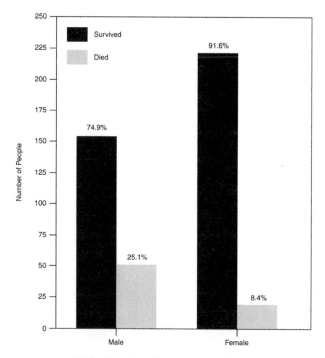

FIGURE 5.7. Willie Handcart Company mortality rates by sex.

were overwhelmingly dominant among people over 39 years old. In fact, 69.4 percent of the Willie Company men 40 years or older died, but only 22.0 percent of the women of this age succumbed. At 48, "old man James" may not have been very old from our perspective, but he was certainly old given the situation in which he found himself (Figure 5.5).

The odds that a Willie Company male under 40 years of age would die are 2.0 times the odds that a female member of this age would die. This difference is in the direction that we would expect—greater odds of male than female mortality under the age of 40—but it does not differ significantly from what we would get by flipping a coin.[120] This differs from the situation in the Donner Party, where the odds that a male Donner Party member under 40 would die are 3.9 times the odds that a female member of this age would die, a difference that is very significant.[121]

In both cases, then, males younger than 40 died at higher rates than females. In the Donner Party, the difference is very significant, but in the Willie Handcart Company, it is not significant at all. This contrast reflects

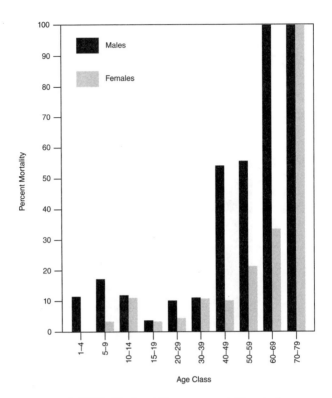

FIGURE 5.8. Willie Handcart Company mortality rates by age
class and sex.

the far shorter ordeal suffered by the Willie Company and the lessened
male-female differential in energy expenditure in this group. It did not
hurt that the younger Willie Company men did not have to cut their way
through the Wasatch Range.

The same kind of analysis can be applied to the Willie Company members who were at least 40 years old (there were only 10 people of this age in
the Donner Party, nearly all of whom died, so a similar approach is of little
value here). If we do that, we discover a number of things. First, we find that
the odds of male and female deaths do not change significantly across age
classes for people who were at least 40.[122] Second, we find a huge difference
in the odds that men and women of this age would die. In this case, the odds
that a man 40 or older died in the Willie Company are 10.3 times the odds
that a woman of this age died, a difference that is very significant.[123]

SURVIVORSHIP AND FAMILY MEMBERSHIP

We have seen that there are significant relationships between family size and survivorship in the Donner Party. Perhaps most impressively, marriage provided important advantages to the men in this party. Of the 16 single men in the Donner Party, 13 died. Of these 13, 10 were gone before the lull in deaths occurred. Just as important, 12 of the 14 (85.7 percent) single Donner Party men between 20 and 35 years old lost their lives, but only 3 of the 7 (42.8 percent) married men of this age died. That is, of the 21 men between 20 and 35, mortality among those who were single was 2.0 times higher than that among those who were married, a difference that is significant.[124]

We have also seen that there is a strong relationship between mortality rates and family size among those members of the Donner Party who traveled with their families. Up to a point (a family size of nine), the larger the kin group, the higher the survivorship. With the exception of the decline in survivorship for the largest Donner Party families, all of this conforms to the expectations that I drew from a general understanding of the relationship between human mortality and family ties. Are there similar relationships in the Willie Handcart Company?

The simplest way to examine the relationship between family size and mortality for the 441 people whose family membership is known is by tallying the average family size of those who lived and those who died. Doing that shows that males who survived traveled with families that averaged 5.0 members, while those who died traveled with families that averaged 3.7 members. For females, the corresponding numbers are 4.7 and 3.6 people, respectively.

We would expect these differences if larger families conferred protection against death. A look at the people involved, however, shows that this relationship is, in part, caused by their ages. Older people—both males and females—tended to travel with smaller families.[125] And since older people are at a severe disadvantage in settings marked by cold and famine, this fact, not the protection provided by larger families, may have caused smaller families in the Willie Company to have higher mortality rates.

This possibility can also be examined by asking what combinations of age, sex, and family size best predict survivorship across all the members of the Willie Company. If we do that, we find that age and sex together predict survivorship but that adding family size to the equation does not improve our ability to explain who lived and who died in this group.[126]

TABLE 5.6. Average group size, age, and mortality by group type: Willie Handcart Company members who proceeded west from Florence, NE. *N* = number of individuals (see Table 5.3 for group membership and abbreviations).*

Group type	Average size	Average age			Mortality (%)
		Survivors (*N*)	Non-survivors (*N*)	Group (*N*)	
MoFaCh	5.6	18.9 (194)	31.1 (36)	20.8 (230)	15.7
MoCh	3.6	20.6 (80)	23.3 (6)	20.8 (86)	7.0
FaCh	2.5	27.0 (3)	62.5 (2)	41.2 (5)	40.0
HuWi	2.0	43.9 (8)	56.0 (8)	49.9 (16)	50.0
Siblings	2.0	22.7 (12)	—	22.7 (12)	0.0
Single	1.0	26.7 (67)	52.7 (19)	32.4 (86)	22.1

* excludes three individuals of unknown age (Nancy Stewart, Carsten Jenson, Christen Jorgenson), one individual of unknown family group type (Rose Kay), and one mother-sister-child family (Ann, Hannah, and Charles Herbert)

This is quite different from what we saw in the Donner Party. Nonetheless, family membership did have a very important impact on mortality in the Willie Company. It is just harder to see because the family structures in the Willie Company were so different from those within the Donner Party and because of their differing mode of transportation.

As I have discussed, nearly all the members of the Donner Party traveled as single men, as husbands and wives without children, or as members of families with mothers and fathers present. The only exceptions were Eliza and Baylis Williams, who were brother and sister (and employed by the Reeds), and the widowed Levinah Murphy, who traveled with her large family, including two sons-in-law.

The situation in the Willie Handcart Company was far more complex. There were eight distinctly different kinds of "traveling groups," each differing from the other in average size, average age, and mortality rate.

As Table 5.3 shows, the Willie Company was composed of men traveling alone (45), women traveling alone (44), siblings (12), mothers traveling with their children (86), fathers traveling with their offspring (5), mothers and fathers with their children (230), husbands and wives without children (16), and a mother with her child and sister (3). This situation could hardly have been more different from the Donner Party and is, as I have discussed, accounted for by the fact that people had placed their faith in the LDS Church. The church would, and to some extent did, protect them. As a result, single women and women traveling with children—people who

TABLE 5.7. Average group size, age, and mortality by group type: Willie Handcart Company females who proceeded west from Florence, NE. *N* = number of individuals (see Table 5.3 for group membership and abbreviations).*

Group type	Average size	Average age			Mortality (%)
		Survivors (*N*)	Non-survivors (*N*)	Group (*N*)	
MoFaCh	5.6	20.2 (105)	25.9 (9)	20.6 (114)	7.9
MoCh	3.6	24.7 (56)	40.7 (3)	25.5 (59)	5.1
FaCh	2.5	27.0 (3)	—	27.0 (3)	0.0
HuWi	2.0	47.3 (6)	57.0 (2)	49.8 (8)	25.0
Siblings	2.0	23.6 (8)	—	23.6 (8)	0.0
Single	1.0	26.5 (37)	45.2 (6)	29.1 (43)	14.0

* excludes one individual of unknown age (Nancy Stewart), one individual of unknown family type (Rose Kay), and two members of the mother-sister-child family (Ann and Hannah Herbert).

TABLE 5.8. Average group size, age, and mortality by group type: Willie Handcart Company males who proceeded west from Florence, NE. *N* = number of individuals (see Table 5.3 for group membership and abbreviations).*

Group type	Average size	Average age			Male mortality (%)
		Survivors (*N*)	Non-survivors (*N*)	Group (*N*)	
MoFaCh	5.6	17.5 (89)	32.8 (27)	21.1 (116)	23.3
MoCh	3.6	11.1 (24)	6.0 (3)	10.5 (27)	11.1
FaCh	2.5	—	62.5 (2)	62.5 (2)	100.0
HuWi	2.0	33.5 (2)	55.7 (6)	50.1 (8)	75.0
Siblings	2.1	20.8 (4)	—	20.8 (4)	0.0
Single	1.0	26.9 (30)	56.2 (13)	35.7 (43)	30.2

* excludes one individual of unknown age (Carsten Jenson) and one member of the mother-sister-child family (Charles Herbert)

generally avoided the western emigrant trail—felt fewer qualms about a trip that they would otherwise have seen as far too dangerous.

We expect that male mortality would tend to be higher than female mortality across the various kinds of traveling groups, and that is indeed the case (see Tables 5.6–5.8 and Figure 5.9). With the exception of siblings, who suffered no losses, male mortality was higher than female mortality in all of these groups. It is also not surprising that for both males and females, the surviving members of a given traveling group tended to be younger than those who died.

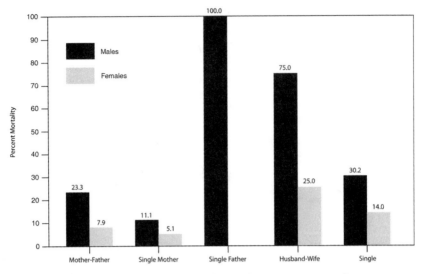

FIGURE 5.9. Mortality rates by sex and Willie Handcart Company traveling group.

TABLE 5.9. Willie Handcart Company mortality rates by traveling group.*

Group type	Survived	Died	Totals	Mortality (%)
Single females	38	6	44	13.6
Single males	32	13	45	28.9
Mothers only with children	80	6	86	7.0
Fathers only with children	3	2	5	40.0
Mothers and fathers with children	194	36	230	15.7
Husband and wife without children	8	8	16	50.0
Siblings	12	0	12	0
Mother with sister and child	3	0	3	0
Totals	370	71	441	16.1

* excludes one individual of unknown family group type (Rose Kay)

What is remarkable, however, is the low level of mortality suffered by people in single-mother families (Tables 5.6 and 5.9). Total mortality in these families was only 7.0 percent, well below that for all other sizeable traveling groups that included children. The mortality rate in mother-father families, for instance, was 2.2 times greater, a difference that is statistically significant.[127]

Why did the single-mother families of the Willie Handcart Company have such a low mortality rate? There are two reasons for this, one of which is obvious. Because these families lacked fathers, they also lacked the most vulnerable subpopulation within the company: older males. In fact, of the 27 males in these families, only 7 were older than 15 and only 2 were older than 20; the oldest, Allen Findlay, was 26. None of these men died (Table 5.10). Mother-father families, on the other hand, had 38 men over 29, of whom 17 (44.8 percent) died (Table 5.11). Because single-mother families lacked older males, this group suffered lower mortality rates than the traveling groups that had them.

This lowered mortality rate came in part at the expense of the single men whose labor was, as I discussed, distributed across the single-mother groups. Having access to labor provided by unrelated men kept the mortality rate lower than it otherwise would have been within the families who benefited in this way. It may also help account for the very high mortality rate suffered by single men (28.9 percent; see Tables 5.9 and 5.12), assuming that these men ended up doing more energy-intensive labor than they otherwise would have done.

It is impossible to know which men were associated with any given single-mother family. Indeed, since there were more single men (45) than there were single-mother families (24), and since single men were also assigned to help single women (44), there is no way of knowing which men

TABLE 5.10. Mortality by age class in single-mother families in the Willie Handcart Company.

Age class	Males		Females	
	Survived	Died	Survived	Died
1–4	3	1	5	0
5–9	8	1	12	0
10–14	6	1	4	0
15–19	5	0	6	0
20–29	2	0	10	1
30–39	0	0	5	1
40–49	0	0	7	0
50–59	0	0	5	0
60–69	0	0	2	1
70–79	0	0	0	0
Unknown	0	0	0	0
Totals	24	3	56	3

TABLE 5.11. Mortality by age class in mother-father families in the Willie Handcart Company.

Age class	Males		Females	
	Survived	Died	Survived	Died
1–4	19	2	17	0
5–9	16	4	16	1
10–14	16	2	19	3
15–19	11	1	13	1
20–29	6	1	8	0
30–39	9	2	14	2
40–49	9	9	13	0
50–59	3	4	4	2
60–69	0	2	1	0
70–79	0	0	0	0
Unknown	0	0	0	0
Totals	89	27	105	9

TABLE 5.12. Age distribution and survivorship of single men in the Willie Handcart Company.

Age class	Survived	Died	Total
1–4	0	0	0
5–9	0	0	0
10–14	0	0	0
15–19	6	0	6
20–29	15	2	17
30–39	7	0	7
40–49	1	1	2
50–59	1	1	2
60–69	0	8	8
70–79	0	1	1
Unknown	2	0	2
Totals	32	13	45

were associated with such families at all. There is also no way of knowing whether all single-mother families who needed help even had such a male. This is because Chislett tells us that only "young men" were so assigned.[128] Given that he refers to 48-year-old William James as an "old man," it seems safe to assume that the men involved did not include the 11 who were 50 or older, 10 of whom died (Table 5.12), and we know that it did not include 42-year-old James Willie himself.

This leaves 31 single men of known age, 3 of whom died (Table 5.12). If we treat these 31 as part of the single-mother group, then there were 117 (86 plus 31) people in this group, of whom 9 (6 in single-mother families plus 3 single men), or 7.7 percent, died. This mortality rate is still lower than that suffered by most other traveling groups and is significantly lower than that which struck all other sizeable traveling groups that included children[129] (Tables 5.6 and 5.9).

In most cases, the differences in mortality rates between single-mother families and the other kinds of traveling groups are clearly due to differences in the age and sex structures of these groups. The 40 percent mortality rate suffered by single-father families resulted from the fact that the two fathers involved were 60 and 65 years old, both of whom died. Among the eight members of husband-wife pairs who died, three of the men were 63 or older while Elizabeth Ingra was 74.

It takes no great insight to attribute the higher mortality rates in these groups to the age and sex of the people involved. It is also no surprise that mortality among single men was far higher than that shown by single-mother families. Such higher mortality is exactly what we expect with single men.

What still seems odd is that the mortality rate among mother-father families was more than twice that in single-mother families (Tables 5.6 and 5.9), even including mortality among the single males who may have been assigned to help them. Mother-father family mortality remains higher even if we eliminate the nine males in these families who were 50 years old or older, of whom six died. Doing this provides a mortality rate of 13.6 percent, still higher than the 7.7 percent mortality suffered by single-mother families and their possible single male helpers, though it is not significantly higher.[130]

What might account for the higher mortality in mother-father families? The answer seems to be provided by John Chislett, among many others. Sometimes, Chislett observed,

> when the little children had walked as far as they could, their fathers would take them on their carts, and thus increase the load that was already becoming too heavy as the day advanced. But what will parents not do to benefit their children in time of trouble?

TABLE 5.13. Numbers of young children in mother-father and single-mother families in the Willie Handcart Company and associated ratios.

Family type	Number of children under the age of:						
	11[a]	10	9	8	7	6	5
Single mother	31	30	23	20	18	13	9
Mother-father	86	75	68	59	51	44	38
	Ratios of the number of children to numbers of family groups						
	11[b]	10	9	8	7	6	5
Single mother (24 families)	1.29	1.25	0.96	0.83	0.75	0.54	0.38
Mother-father (41 families)	2.10	1.83	1.66	1.44	1.24	1.07	0.93
	Differential in numbers of children						
	11[c]	10	9	8	7	6	5
Mother-father/Single mother	1.63	1.46	1.73	1.73	1.65	1.98	2.45

[a] Single-mother families had 31 children under 11; mother-father families had 86 children of this age.
[b] The 31 children under 11 in single-mother families were distributed across 24 families; 31/24= 1.29. The corresponding ratio for mother-father families is 86/41 = 2.10.
[c] 2.10/1. 29 = 1.63, meaning that mother-father families were caring for 1.63 times the number of children under 11 than were being cared for by single-mother families.

> The most affecting scene, however, was to see a mother carrying her child at the breast, mile after mile, until nearly exhausted.[131]

Exhausted children, Chislett and others tell us, were often carried or transported in handcarts.[132] The more children a family had, the greater the amount of energy adult family members expended to transport those children. Because adults received the same amount of food no matter how much energy they were expending (when food was available at all), adults whose families contained greater numbers of young children may have been at higher risk of dying than adults whose families contained fewer numbers of such children. Perhaps, then, mother-father families were at greater risk because they had more young children than single-mother families.

It is not possible to know the age at which children were young enough to require being carried or placed in handcarts on a routine basis. Indeed, at times, adults had to be transported in the carts. I assumed that children over 10 were not routinely transported in this way and counted the number of

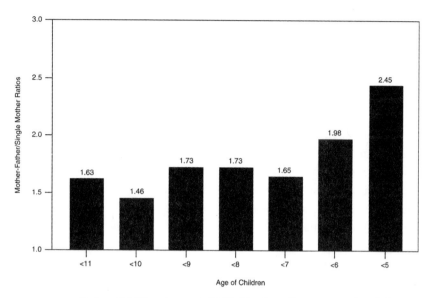

FIGURE 5.10. Ratios of children by age in Willie Handcart Company mother-father and single-mother families.

children 10 years old or younger in single-mother and mother-father families. I used these numbers to calculate the ratios of children by age in these two family types. The results are provided in Table 5.13 and plotted in Figure 5.10.

Those results tell us that adults in mother-father families were caring for many more young children than were their counterparts in single-mother families. The values range from a minimum of 1.46 times more (for children under 10) to a maximum of 2.45 times more (for children under 5). This is what we would expect if the greater mortality in mother-father families is explained by the fact that such families had greater numbers of children than single-mother families.

It appears, then, that single-mother families suffered lower mortality than other kinds of Willie Company traveling groups for a number of reasons. First, and most obviously, they lacked large numbers of vulnerable older men. Second, these families were provided with the labor of single younger men. That reduced mortality within single-mother families at the same time it likely increased mortality among single men. Third, single-mother families contained fewer younger children than mother-father families. As a result, they incurred lower childcare costs than did their fully parented—and so more vulnerable—counterparts. All these conditions combined to create a mortality rate that, for the Willie Handcart Company, was exceptionally low.

SEX, FAMILY SIZE, AND THE CHRONOLOGY OF DEATH

In the Donner Party, males tended to die sooner than females. This was not the case in the Willie Handcart Company. Figure 5.11 shows the chronology of death for the 68 members of the company whose date of death is known with reasonable accuracy. The many deaths that occurred between October 19 and October 26—11 females and 20 males—marks the fateful combination of a massive winter storm and the exhaustion of food stores. Things would have been even worse had rescuers not begun to reach the emigrants on October 21.

Although males died in greater numbers during this episode, just as they did during the entire journey, there is no significant relationship between sex, age, or family size and the chronology of death within the Willie Handcart Company.[133] Age, sex, and family size helped determine who

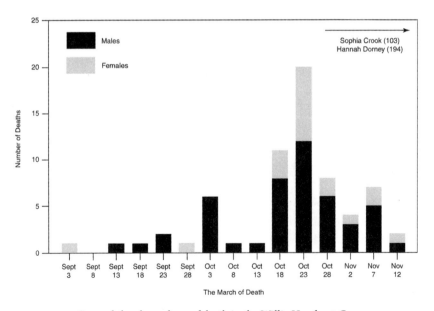

FIGURE 5.11. Sex and the chronology of death in the Willie Handcart Company.

lived and who died, but so many people were overwhelmed in such a short period of time that these factors did not influence how long it took for those doomed individuals to lose their lives.

THE WILLIE HANDCART COMPANY: A SUMMARY

The expectations about human mortality under conditions of cold and famine that I derived from an understanding of human biology were strongly met by the Donner Party. The oldest and youngest suffered the highest mortality, nearly twice as many males as females died, and, up to a point, larger families conferred some degree of protection against death.

The results of my analysis of the Willie Handcart Company are very much in line with what we saw for the Donner Party, given that the two experiences differed in significant ways—given, that is, that the sufferings of the Willie Company did not last nearly as long as those of the Donner Party, that people had equal access to food as long as there was food, and that the members of the Willie Company traveled with handcarts.

As in the Donner Party, the oldest members of the Willie Company underwent heavy attrition—44 percent of people 40 or older lost their lives. Unlike the Donner Party, however, the youngest members of the Willie Company—those under five—did not die at rates significantly higher than those at which people under 40 died. This difference follows from the fact that the Willie Company hardships did not last so long as to prevent people from providing their children with the resources they needed to survive. The Donner Party was not so fortunate.

As with the Donner Party, males were at a serious disadvantage in the Willie Company: three times as many males as females lost their lives. In the Willie Company, the odds of a male less than 40 years old dying were 2.0 times the odds of a female of this age dying. Among those at least 40, the odds of a man dying were 10.3 times the odds of a woman dying. Male frailty in these circumstances is written all over the histories of both the Donner Party and the Willie Handcart Company.

Things are more complex as regards the relationship between mortality and family size in the Willie Company. Many different kinds of traveling groups were represented in this company, a reflection of the faith that these people had in their church. These groups varied from single males and single females, on one hand, to single-mother and more traditional mother-father families, on the other. The highest death rates tended to mark those groups whose members were older. Single-father families, for instance, suffered 40 percent mortality, and husband-wife pairs suffered 50 percent mortality; these two groups had average ages of 41.2 and 49.9 years, respectively (Table 5.6). What emerges most forcefully from the relationship between mortality and kin group type in the Willie Company, however, is the very low mortality suffered by single-mother families. Those families did well because they lacked older males and because the women involved lost less energy to childcare and, in particular, to transporting their children across the landscape.

CHAPTER 5 NOTES

1. Arrington and Bitton 1992. The brief history of the Willie Handcart Company that follows depends heavily on Hafen and Hafen 1992; Bartholomew and Arrington 1993; Olsen 2006; Roberts 2008; Bagley 2009, 2014; and on the primary literature cited below.
2. Nauvoo is still there and worth the visit (www.historicnauvoo.net).
3. The practice of plural marriage at Nauvoo was to be kept secret but word got out, as I discuss later in this chapter.
4. Arrington and Bitton 1992.
5. Frémont 1845.
6. Arrington and Bitton 1992.
7. B. Young et al. 1849[1997].
8. Taylor 1855; Bagley 2009, 2014; Turner 2012.
9. Arrington 1958; Arrington and Bitton 1992; Bagley 2009, 2014; Turner 2012.
10. Hafen and Hafen 1992:35.
11. Ibid., 34.
12. Bagley 2009, 2012:259–263.
13. Arrington and Bitton 1992; Carter 1995.
14. Hafen and Hafen 1992; Carter 1995; Bagley 2009, 2014.
15. Amhanson 1984:33.
16. Olsen (2006:29) notes that a wagon and oxen team would have cost around $300, compared to $10 for a handcart with wooden wheels.
17. Taylor 1855.
18. Camm 1892.
19. Petree 2006:57.
20. Bigler 1998:118.
21. Turner 1996; Olsen 2006. Hafen and Hafen (1992) and Christy (1997–1998) give the date as May 3. Given that the ship left around 3:00 a.m., the difference does not matter (Turner 1996:2).
22. Chislett 1873. Ahmanson (1984:29) said that he had been asked "to escort the indigent Danes with their train of handcarts, since I was the only one of them who had any competence in English."
23. Woodward 1857; Hafen and Hafen 1992.
24. Chislett 1873:316.
25. Ibid.
26. Ibid.
27. Ibid.
28. Woodward 1857.
29. This figure is very close to the 300 pounds that was initially projected

as the total weight of a handcart
and the goods it carried. See Taylor
1855.

30. Woodward 1857.
31. Kimball 1983; Christy 1997–1998.
32. Woodward 1857; Chislett 1873.
33. Roberts 2008:97.
34. Chislett 1873:318.
35. Woodward 1856:September 12.
36. Chislett 1873:319.
37. Ibid. Fanny Stenhouse (1875:218)
tells an even harsher version of
this story, related in a letter supposedly written to her from "Mary
Burton." Ronald W. Walker (1974)
observed that this letter was most
likely written by John Chislett or
taken from Chislett (1873), a point
made by Hubert Howe Bancroft
(1889) nearly a century earlier.
It is no coincidence that Chislett (1873) appears in *The Rocky
Mountain Saints* (1873), authored
by T. B. H. Stenhouse, Fanny's
husband.
38. Woodward 1856.
39. Kimball 1983.
40. Willie 1856. Roberts (2008) points
out that Richards's failure to provide the promised provisions has
never been adequately explained.
41. Woodward 1857.
42. Ibid.
43. Ibid.; the mileage comes from Kimball 1983.
44. Woodward 1857.
45. Chislett 1873:320.
46. Ibid. (emphasis in original).
47. Ibid., 321.
48. Ibid.
49. Woodward 1856.
50. Chislett 1873:322.
51. Kimball 1856.
52. B. Young 1856c; Bagley 2009:95.
This letter was also published in
the *Millennial Star* (B. Young 1857),

bringing deceptively good news to
potential emigrants; see also end-
note 94 herein.
53. B. Young 1856b.
54. Roberts 2008:326.
55. Chislett 1873:331.
56. B. Young 1856a.
57. Jones 1890:62.
58. Ibid.
59. Ibid.; Bartholomew and Arrington
1993.
60. The six were James Ferguson,
George Grant, William Kimball,
Chauncey Webb, Cyrus Wheelock,
and Joseph Young, Brigham Young's
eldest son (Hafen and Hafen
1992:101, 127; Olsen 2006:122).
61. Jones 1890:63.
62. Woodruff 1856; Bagley 2009:87–91,
2014:179–181.
63. Chislett 1873:322.
64. Ibid., 322.
65. Ibid., 324.
66. Jones 1890:64.
67. Willie 1856.
68. Kimball 1983:72.
69. Chislett 1873:329.
70. Ibid., 329 (emphasis in original).
71. Woodruff 1856.
72. Chislett 1873:330.
73. Ahmanson 1984:35.
74. Arrivals 1856.
75. Willie 1856.
76. Chislett 1873:331
77. See Roberts 2008:317–320 for a discussion of this issue; the reading is
not pleasant.
78. From Utah 1860.
79. Camm 1892.
80. Petree 2006:80. Petree notes that
Patience Loader may be describing
the fate of Ellen Pucell, who also
lost both of her parents during the
journey. See Olsen 2006:425.
81. Hafen and Hafen 1992; Woodward
1857.

82. Richards and Spencer 1856.
83. Black 1980.
84. Bartholomew and Arrington 1993.
85. Chislett 1873:331.
86. Willie 1856.
87. Hafen and Hafen 1992.
88. Bashore and Haslam n.d.
89. Grayson 1996.
90. Those resources include Black 1980; Jensen n.d.; and Riverton Wyoming Stake n.d. See also Madsen 1998. For the list I initially compiled, used as the basis of Grayson 1996, see Grayson 1994b.
91. Turner 1996; Olsen 2006; Allphin 2012; Olsen and Allphin 2013; Church of Jesus Christ of Latter-day Saints 2015a, 2015b.
92. These lists are available at http://hdl.handle.net/1773/34984. Bashore et al. (2014) provide age, sex, and survivorship data for the members of the Willie and Martin Companies as part of a list of about 56,000 people who emigrated to Salt Lake City between 1847 and 1868 (http://statistics.byu.edu/news). I have not consulted this compilation, which appeared after the analyses presented here had been completed and does not include the full set of demographic information I have analyzed. Although the authors present no detailed analysis of handcart company mortality, they report a mortality rate of "about 16.5%" for the Willie and Martin Companies combined (Bashore et al. 2014:121). The data I have compiled provide a combined mortality rate of 17.4 percent—close but not identical. Parts of the analysis of Bashore and colleagues run closely parallel to that in Grayson 1996, including the comparative use of U.S. Census data from 1850 and 1860, but the authors do not cite that paper. This is perplexing, since my paper attracted significant media attention (e.g., Brody 1996), and I provided Bashore with a copy of it as soon as it appeared.
93. Bartholomew and Arrington 1993.
94. Bigler 1998:118. The *Millennial Star* reported that many members of the Martin Company arrived "with frozen fingers, feet, and hands" but attributed this to "an unusual severity of weather, even for these mountains at this season" (Woodruff 1857). Similarly, the *Star* reported that within that company, "about fifty-six out of six hundred had died upon the Plains, up to that date [October 28]" but added that "those who had died were mostly old people" (J. A. Young 1857). Counterbalancing these hedged statements, the *Star* observed that "the immigration will all reach comfortable quarters for the winter, and that too with far less mortality than has often attended companies amply supplied with all the customary facilities for crossing the Plains" (Companies Yet on the Plains 1857) and repeated Brigham Young's deceptive assertion that "the mortality has been much less than often attends well fitted animal trains, travelling in good season" (B. Young 1857).
95. DeBow 1854.
96. Chi-square = 22.08, p < 0.001.
97. Kennedy 1864; chi-square = 7.54, p < 0.01.
98. Chi-square = 16.35, p < 0.001.
99. Chi-square = 7.10, p < 0.01.
100. Arrington and Bitton 1992; F. Stenhouse 1875:199.
101. Dorius 1997.

102. For instance, John C. Bennett was Joseph Smith's handpicked mayor of Nauvoo from 1841 to early 1842, when he had a bitter falling out with Smith. Bennett left Nauvoo and quickly "outed" Smith's sexual proclivities. "Joseph Smith," he observed in the *Sangamo Journal* of July 8, 1842, was "the great Mormon seducer, one who has seduced not only hundreds of single and married females, but more than the great Solomon, attempted to seduce Miss Nancy Rigdon, the eldest daughter of Sidney Rigdon, to submit to his hellish purposes, and become one of his *clandestine* wives under the new dispensation" (Bennett 1842; emphasis in original). See also the discussions of celestial marriage in the 1844 issues of the *Warsaw Message* (renamed the *Warsaw Signal*), published in nearby Warsaw, Illinois (e.g., Buckey's Lamentations for the Want of More Wives, February 7, 1844, and Why Oppose the Mormons, April 24, 1844, Uncle Dale's Readings in Early Mormon History (Newspapers of Illinois), http://www.sidneyrigdon.com/dbroadhu/IL/sign1844.htm). Smith denied these and multiple other accusations of polygamy, but the cat was out of the polygamous bag (Hallwas and Launius 1995:part III; Turner 2012). As I noted at the beginning of this chapter, polygamy was just one of the activities that led to the anti-Mormon actions that caused the abandonment of Nauvoo and the 1847 emigration to the Great Salt Lake area (Arrington and Bitton 1992; Hallwas and Launius 1995; Turner 2012).

103. O. Pratt in Minutes of Conference 1852:14.

104. Minutes of Conference 1852:25–27.

105. See, for instance, The Latter-Day Saints 1841; John C. Bennett 1842; Letter from an Englishman 1844; Smith 1850; Kane 1851; and Snow 1852.

106. See, for instance, Jaques 1853; A Word with Our Opponents 1853; and Celestial Marriage in Deseret 1853. In 1850, the *Millennial Star* had a circulation between 5,000 and 6,000. By April 1852, that figure had climbed to 23,000 (Weekly Issue of the Star 1852). There followed an "unaccountable falling off in the circulation," down to about 6,000 by the end of 1856 ("Stars" and "Journals" for 1857 1856:729). One wonders whether the unaccountable can be accounted for by the public admittance of polygamy after so many years of deceit, in a journal whose very prospectus promised "a Periodical devoted entirely to the great work of the spread of truth" (Pratt 1840:1).

107. F. Stenhouse 1875:202. F. Stenhouse (1875:522) tells us that an exception was made for Orson Pratt, given permission by Brigham Young to marry a "young girl" in Liverpool, whom he then brought to Utah with him.

108. For instance, Edmund Ellsworth, who led the First Handcart Company (see Roberts 2008), married Brigham Young's eldest daughter, Elizabeth, in 1842, then married Mary Ann Dudley in 1852. His handcart company arrived in Salt Lake City on September 26, 1856. About a month later, he took First Handcart Company members Mary Ann Bates and Mary Ann

Jones as his third and fourth wives (Hafen and Hafen 1992:57). See also Bagley 2009:73 and The Church of Jesus Christ of Latter-day Saints, Mormon Pioneer Overland Travel, 1847–1868: Edmund Ellsworth Company (1856), https://history.lds.org/overlandtravels/companies/111/edmund-ellsworth-company, last modified September 1, 2016.

109. Allphin 2012.
110. Ibid., 101.
111. Chislett 1873:322.
112. Ibid., 320.
113. Ibid.; Carter 1995.
114. Chislett 1873:315.
115. Elizabeth Sermon, for instance, observed that a Martin Company reduction in rations meant "starvation to us but not so to the Captains. By our going around camp at night where cooking pots of some of the Captains could be seen, they looked pretty full and smelled quite savory. In fact, the Captains fed well while we drank ours in porridge for I could not make bread with the small allowance of flour" (Camm 1892).
116. Allphin 2012:116; Olsen and Allphin 2013:142.
117. See note 92 herein for access to the raw data from which these numbers are drawn.
118. Chi-square = 3.52, p = 0.62.
119. Chi-square = 22.85, p < 0.001.
120. In the Willie Company, 152 males were younger than 40, of whom 17, or 0.1118 (17/152), died; 135, or 0.8882 (135/152) survived. That is, the odds that a male under 40 died are 0.1118/0.8882, or 0.1259. Of the 188 Willie Company females under the age of 40, 11, or 0.0585, died; 177, or 0.9415, survived. That is, the odds of a Willie Company female younger than 40 dying are 0.0585/0.9415, or 0.0621. Dividing 0.1259 by 0.0621 gives us 2.03. This value does not differ significantly from an odds ratio of 1.0 (p > 0.05). Other analyses provide very similar results. The survivorship of males and females under 40 does not differ significantly across age classes (Mantel-Haenszel homogeneity chi-square = 2.43, p > 0.10). In addition, bivariate logistic regression of sex against mortality for those under 40 provides a p value of 0.08.
121. In the Donner Party, 25 of the 46 males under 40, or 0.5435, succumbed (Table 4.5), while 7 of the 30 females of this age, or 0.2333, suffered a similar fate. So the odds of a Donner Party male of this age dying are 0.5435/0.4565, or 1.191. For females, the odds are 0.2333/0.7667, or 0.3043. The ratio of these odds (1.191/0.3403) is 3.91 (p < 0.01).
122. Mantel-Haenszel homogeneity chi-square = 1.72, p > 0.10.
123. In the Willie Company, 49 men were at least 40. Of these, 34, or 0.6939, succumbed; 15, or 0.3061, survived. Among the women, 9 of 50, or 0.1800, died; 41 of 50, or 0.8200, survived. That is, the odds that a man 40 or older died are 0.6939/0.3061, or 2.2669; the comparable odds for a woman are 0.1800/0.8200, or 0.2195. The ratio of these odds, 2.2669/0.2195, is an impressive 10.33 (p < 0.01).
124. Chi-square = 4.20, p = 0.04.
125. For males, Spearman's rho between age and family size is = −0.38, p < 0.001; for females, that value is −0.38, p < 0.001.
126. Multivariate logistic regression, with mortality as the dependent variable and age (p < 0.001), sex (p < 0.001), and family size (p = 0.38) as independent variables.

127. Chi-square = 4.09, p = 0.04.
128. Chislett 1873:315.
129. Chi-square = 4.68, p = 0.03.
130. Chi-square = 2.59, p = 0.10.
131. Chislett 1873:315.
132. Observations of this sort are common in handcart company diaries and reminiscences. See, for instance, Allphin 2012:51, 53, 81, 111 and Olsen and Allphin 2013:27, 128.
133. For the relationship between age and days-to-death in bivariate logistic regression, p = 0.14. For age and days-to-death in linear regression, r = +0.20 (p = 0.11); for family size, r = +0.05, p = 0.71.

6

"CRUEL BEYOND LANGUAGE"

The Martin Handcart Company

THE MARTIN HANDCART COMPANY: THE TRIP ACROSS

The *Thornton*, carrying those who became members of the Willie Handcart Company, left Liverpool on May 4, 1856, headed for New York City. The *Horizon*, carrying those who were to compose the heart of the Fifth, or Martin, Handcart Company, left the same port three weeks later—on May 25—bound for Boston. By July 9, the roughly 600 people who would soon follow 37-year-old Edward Martin to Zion were all in Iowa City.[1]

Here, they encountered not only the Willie Company, which had arrived two weeks before, but also the same problems that the earlier company was having in gearing up for the trip. Handcarts and other supplies were not ready for them, and the same scramble resulting from the Willie Company's arrival was now replayed for a larger group under even more trying conditions. The Willie Company left Iowa City July 15. The Martin Company followed around July 28 and reached Florence on August 22, four days after Willie's group had left. They moved out from their campground east of Florence on August 25, now nine days behind the Willie Company.[2] Two church-associated wagon trains traveled in concert with, but separately from, them. Led by W. B. Hodgett and J. A. Hunt, these two trains had about 400 emigrants between them.

The organization of the Martin Company was the same as that of the Willie Company, as was the quality of their handcarts. Those in the Martin Company were, in the words of company historian John Jaques, "poor ones . . . the squeaking of the wheels through lack of sufficient grease could often be 'heard a mile.'"[3] Much time was spent repairing them, a situation made worse by the fact that Martin Company members transported loads at least as burdensome as those of the Willie Company. On leaving Florence, Jaques noted,

> the loads on the handcarts were greater than ever before, most carts having 100 pounds of flour, besides ordinary baggage. The tents were also carried on the carts. The company was provisioned sixty days, a daily ration of one pound of flour per head, with about half a pound for children.[4]

Those heavy burdens became a point of contention between Martin and some company members. Elizabeth Sermon, for instance, was dealing with a failing husband (he would die in November) and four children, the oldest of whom was nine. She decided she could not also deal with 100 pounds of flour on her cart when her family did not have enough for themselves. "I told Captain Martin if I and my children could not eat some of it, I would not draw it any further, as it is my duty to look after my husband and family first."[5] She and several others then continued without that burden.

In a letter written from Florence on September 3, Franklin Richards, target of both Brigham Young's and John Chislett's wrath (see Chapter 5), predicted that the later handcart companies "may experience some cold."[6] In early September, Richards had no way of knowing how bad it would get. As we have seen for the Willie Company, "some cold" turned out to be a significant understatement. The Willie Company first encountered severe cold along the Sweetwater River on October 19, with some four inches of snow on the ground the next morning. The Martin Company, making their last crossing of the Platte River, was hit by the same storm on the same day. October 19, Jaques reported, was "bitter cold":

> Winter came on all at once, and that was the first day of it. The river was wide, the current strong, the water exceedingly cold and up to the wagon beds in the deepest parts, and the bed of the river

was covered with cobble stones. Some of the men carried some of the women over on their backs or in their arms, but others of the women tied up their skirts and waded through, like heroines as they were, and as they had done through many other rivers and creeks. The company was barely over, when snow, hail and sleet began to fall, accompanied by a piercing north wind, and camp was made on this side of the river.[7]

The next day—the day the rescuers reached the Willie Company on the Sweetwater—the Martin Company moved another 10 miles through the snow, but, Jaques says, "the teams and so many of the people were so far given out"[8] that the decision was made to stay where they were with hopes that things would improve.

They had left Florence with 60 days' rations. Those 60 days had expired on crossing the Platte, some 650 miles west of Florence and 380 miles east of Salt Lake City.[9] They had seen it coming, just as the Willie Company had. Jaques tells us that the first reduction in daily rations came soon after they left Fort Laramie—from 16 ounces of flour a day to 12; soon, it was 8.[10]

On October 17, just before the Platte crossing, they took another drastic step:

Owing to the growing weakness of emigrants and teams, the baggage including bedding and cooking utensils, was reduced to 10 pounds per head, children under 8 years, 5 pounds. Good blankets and other bedding and clothing were burned, as they could not be carried further, though needed more than ever, for there was yet 400 miles of winter to go through.[11]

And now, stranded just west of the Platte, with much of their baggage in ashes some 30 miles back, their rations were reduced again—to four ounces of flour a day—and remained at this level until rescuers arrived.[12] They killed many of their cattle here, but the animals were in such poor shape that the additional food did not help much.

So many of the people were ailing, Jaques observed on October 21, that they could go no further. Many, in fact, had given out long before this. Eliza Openshaw (20) became ill on September 7 and was transported in a handcart until her death on October 18. Charles Edmonds (56) and Robert Walsh

(5) died on September 13; Lydia Hartle (71) on September 17; Robert Pierce (31) and Ann Gregory (63) the next day; Charles Woodcock (52) two days later; and Joseph Akres (24) two days after that.[13] Once begun, the deaths continued until the ordeal finally ended. "It was," Langley Bailey (18) said, "not any trouble to die."[14]

Parallel in the heavy burdens they hauled, in the cruel weather they encountered, in the exhaustion of their supplies, and in losing members to death, the Willie and Martin Handcart Companies also became parallel in their dependence on rescuers. Had help not come, few would have survived. Even so, Elizabeth Sermon recalled, "it was a miracle any of us lived."[15]

THE MARTIN COMPANY RESCUE

George Grant's rescue team had reached the Willie Company on October 21. They knew that many others were still on the trail somewhere to the east, but they had no idea where they might be and assumed they were closer than they actually were. The challenge was to locate them, then do all they could to get them in.

Finding the Fifth Handcart Company was the job of the rescuers who had been sent ahead by Grant on October 14 (Chapter 5). After contacting the Willie Company on October 19, this forward group continued eastward to search for the others. Providing material support to the company once found was the task of Grant's rescue team and those that Grant assumed were following behind them from Salt Lake City.

Leaving William Kimball and six wagons with the Willie Company, Grant led the rest of his men, and eight wagons, eastward in the expectation that they would meet the forward team on its way back with the information they required. On October 22, they made 17 miles, "snow growing deeper and deeper all the way"[16]—so deep, in fact, that they could not move at all the next day. Nonetheless, by October 26, they had reached Devil's Gate (Figure 5.3), "perpendicular rocks 400 feet high" through which the Sweetwater passed[17] and, in the words of rescuer Harvey Cluff, the site of "a small stocade and a few log houses."[18]

They had yet to find the Martin Company, but they did find the rescuers who had been sent ahead. They had failed in their mission and were waiting here for further orders. Cluff tells us what happened next:

Deliberations on the uncertainty as to the best course to persue in our dialema resulted in selecting two good horsemen who were to ride as rapidly as horses could endure. Four days was the extent of time they were to be gone. If the emigrants were not found within that length of time the two men were to return and the conclusion would be that the companies had gone into winter quarters. The return of the two horsemen at night of the forth day brought the news that the companies were on the uper crossing of the Platt River, sixty-five miles away. Ah! then there was hurrying to and froe! and on the following day, every team but one, and all the men but ten started out on force march.[19]

There were actually three, not two, members of this express team, one of whom was Daniel Jones, whom we have already met in the context of the Willie rescue. It did not take the men long to accomplish their goal, since they found the Martin Company on October 28. "This company," Jones reported, "was in almost as bad a condition as the first one. Their provisions were about exhausted and many of them worn out and sick. When we rode in . . . many declared we were angels from heaven."[20]

To John Jaques, October 28 was a "red letter day."[21] The company now knew that help was nearby. The express rode off to find the Hunt wagon train, some 15 miles east, and the revitalized Martin Company began moving again on October 29.

As the express returned westward from its rendezvous with Hunt, it encountered the Martin Company on the road. Jones was appalled by what he saw:

We continued on, overtaking the hand-cart company ascending a long muddy hill. A condition of distress here met my eyes that I never saw before or since. The train was strung out three or four miles. There were old men pulling or tugging their carts, sometimes loaded with a sick wife or children—women pulling along sick husbands—little children six to eight years old struggling through the mud and snow. As night came on the mud would freeze on their clothes and feet.[22]

The express spent that evening with the group, then sped off in the morning, covering the 35 miles to Devil's Gate by seven that night. On the morning of October 31, as the rescuers were on their way east, the Martin Company continued its struggle west. That evening, they all met at Grease-wood Creek, 16 trail miles from Devil's Gate.[23] The Martin Company finally had the help it needed. The rescuers, led by Grant, had brought six wagons of supplies, including sufficient flour for the daily rations to once again reach a pound a day. This was, Jaques reported, "the beginning of better days."[24] By November 2, all were at Devil's Gate.

From the bottom of the abyss things did look better. From the rescuers' perspective, however, the situation was bleak, as Grant explained in a letter sent to Brigham Young from Devil's Gate:

> It is not of much use for me to attempt to give a description of the situation of these people, for this you will learn from your son Joseph A. and br. Garr, who are the bearers of this express; but you can imagine between five and six hundred men, women and children, worn down by drawing hand carts through snow and mud; fainting by the way side; falling, chilled by the cold; children crying, their limbs stiffened by cold, their feet bleeding and some of them bare to snow and frost. The night is almost too much for the stoutest of us; but we go on doing all we can, not doubting nor despairing. Our company is too small to help much, it is only a drop in the bucket, as it were, in comparison to what is needed. I think that not over one-third of br. Martin's company is able to walk. This you may think is extravagant, but it is nevertheless true . . . a great many are like children and do not help themselves much, nor realize what is before them.[25]

Devil's Gate presented yet another challenge. First, the weather was atrocious: "snow deep, very cold," rescuer Robert T. Burton reported on November 2, with over a foot of snow on the ground.[26] Second, the Hunt and Hodgett wagon trains arrived not long after the Martin Company, meaning that over 1,000 people were now amassed in these narrow confines. In response, on November 4—"cold continued very severe," Burton noted[27]—the Martin Company moved some three miles to a spot now known as Martin's Cove. Getting there required crossing the icy Sweetwater, which, though only a few feet deep, was some 100 feet across. When confronted with the crossing, Patience Loader was not alone in being unable to hold back her tears.[28]

The rescuers had every expectation that assistance from Salt Lake City would have reached them by now and were "at a loss to know why others had not come on to our assistance."[29] In fact, others had tried, but they had encountered snow deeper than that which had initially confronted Grant's team. Failing to find their quarry, these rescuers concluded that all must be dead and turned back. "Cowardly in the extreme" was Jones's later assessment of this decision.[30]

It was not until November 9, a week after the Martin Company had arrived at Devil's Gate and the very day that the Willie Company reached Zion, that all got under way again. There were two reasons for this delay. First was the weather: "Thermometer 11 degrees below zero . . . so cold the people could not travel," Burton noted on November 6.[31] Second, the rescuers simply did not know what to do. "Many were dying from exposure and want of food," Jones observed, the men "failing and dying faster than the women and children."[32] There were so few rescuers and so many to be rescued, and the consequences of a bad decision so potentially disastrous, that it took several days of considering the options to reach their wise decision.

Once the decision had been made, however, it did not take long for them to carry it out. They would cache all the goods at Devil's Gate, except for the bare minimum needed to support their escape. The emptied wagons would be used to transport as many as possible of those too weak to walk. They would abandon as many handcarts as they could. They would continue to "ask the Lord to turn away the storm, so that the people might live."[33] Then they would get out of there.

The rescuers felt that they could not risk leaving the cached contents of the wagons unprotected, so it was also decided to leave behind a crew until those goods could be retrieved. Rescuer Daniel Jones supported the idea fully, but he supported it thinking that since he was the groups' best cook, he would be the last man to be asked to stay. He was wrong in this thought. Not only was he asked to stay, but he was also to choose the men to stay with him. "I had a great mind to tell him I wanted Captains Grant and Burton," Jones recalled, but did not do so.[34] Jones did not see Salt Lake City again until the following spring, but he and his 19 companions all survived what proved to be a vicious winter. "God bless him for what he has done," Brigham Young and George Grant wrote later.[35]

The Martin Company pulled out at 11:00 a.m. on Sunday, November 9, "a fine, warm morning."[36] Less than half of those who were weak enough to merit wagon transportation could be so transported,[37] and some were still pulling handcarts. "There was," Jaques said, "considerable crying of women and children, and perhaps a few of the men, whom the wagons could not accommodate with a ride."[38]

Two days later, apparently at the junction of what was then called Bitter Cottonwood Creek with the Sweetwater,[39] 23 miles west of Devil's Gate, the Martin Company was settling in for the evening when Ephraim Hanks rode into camp. Hanks had come from Salt Lake City as one of the rescuers sent out after Grant's group had left. When the others decided to turn back, he continued on. Now, with two horses loaded with the meat of a bison he had killed 12 miles back, he encountered the Martin Company:

> The sight that met my gaze as I entered camp can never be erased from my memory. The starved forms and haggard contenances of the poor sufferers, as they moved about slowly, shivering with cold, to prepare their scanty evening meal was enough to touch the stoutest heart.[40]

Fortunately, more rescuers were soon to arrive. Four wagons, Burton recorded, were met on November 12; more again on the 16th and 18th. The arrivals on the 18th were particularly important, since Hosea Stout, who was part of this third group, tells us that some 30 wagons were involved.[41] The weather had not improved, and the people were "a sad sight . . . thinly clad poor and worn out with hunger & fatigue trudging along in this dreary country facing a severe snow storm and the wind blowing hard in their face,"[42] but there were now enough wagons for everyone to ride. This was good timing, since they all ascended Rocky Ridge on November 18, that place of such horror for the Willie Company nearly a month before.[43]

From here they averaged over 20 miles a day, routinely meeting supply wagons on the way. On November 30, they arrived in Salt Lake City, where, on Brigham Young's orders, they were immediately distributed to families that could properly care for them.

The experience, John Jaques later wrote, had been "cruel to a degree far beyond the power of language to express":[44]

> Worn down by the labors and fatigues of the journey, and pinched
> by hunger and cold, the manliness of tall, healthy, strong men

would gradually disappear, until they would grow fretful, peevish, childish and puerile, acting sometimes as if they were scarcely accountable beings. In the progress of the journey it was not difficult to tell who was going to die within two or three weeks. The gaunt form, hollow eyes, and sunken countenance, discolored to a weather-beaten sallow, with the gradual weakening of the mental faculties, plainly forboded the coming and not far distant dissolution, though the faces and limbs of some were swelled or bloated.[45]

There were times, he said, when he would have scarcely cared had he died himself.

THE MEMBERSHIP OF THE MARTIN HANDCART COMPANY

The list I have compiled of the membership of the Martin Handcart Company, and the fates of those members, depends on many of the same sources I used for the Willie Company (Chapter 5).[46] As with the Willie Company, I have focused entirely on those people who are known to have proceeded west from Florence, Nebraska. My list contains 618 Martin Company members who made the trek westward from Florence. Of these, my list suggests, 113 died.[47]

How do these results compare to statements made by eyewitnesses? As with the Willie Company, the answer depends on the particular estimate that is being compared. Franklin Richards and Daniel Spencer reported that when they encountered the Martin Company on their trip from Florence to Salt Lake City on September 7 (see Chapter 5), Martin had with him "some 576 persons, 146 hand-carts, 7 wagons, 6 mules and horses, and 50 cows and beef cattle."[48] My tally is substantially larger than theirs, though both tallies are less than those implied by the number of handcarts. John Jaques estimated the size of the company when it left Iowa City at "about 600 persons," as did Daniel Jones.[49] Given that not all of those who went west from Iowa City also continued beyond Florence, my tally exceeds these estimates as well, though not by much. It does not, however, exceed the estimate of Martin Company member Josiah Rogerson, 15 at the time. He put the membership at Florence as 622 or 623, virtually identical to the number on my list.[50]

In 1878, Jaques estimated the number of Martin Company deaths at about 100.[51] The next year, Rogerson observed that "with regard to the number of deaths in the company from Winter Quarters [Florence], till our arrival in Salt Lake, I could not say they were less than 150, and I believe more, though one of our leaders says 102, yet I know it is set down by many who survived at 200 or more."[52] Much later, in 1913, Rogerson worked with LDS Church historians to estimate that "between 135 and, possibly, 150" members of the company had died.[53] It is not clear whether this figure was also restricted to those who left Florence. If so, and if that figure is accurate, then my list has fallen significantly short. On the other hand, Susan A. Madsen lists 29 people who are known to have died prior to the Florence departure. Combined with the 113 fatalities on my list, that provides a total of 142 losses, a figure that coincides with Rogerson's.[54]

It is unlikely that I have a complete list of Martin Company members who died west of Florence. As historian Howard A. Christy has noted, we may never have such a list.[55] As a result, the mortality for this part of the trip may have been greater than the 18.3 percent that I have calculated (see below). However, even if my list is incomplete, there is no reason to think that it is biased for or against males or females or any particular age class and no reason to think that it is not representative of all fatalities.

THE DEMOGRAPHIC STRUCTURE OF THE MARTIN HANDCART COMPANY

The Willie Company was marked by the fact that it contained significant numbers of elderly people and women traveling in the absence of related men. This, I pointed out, resulted from the fact that all expected to be protected and provided for by the church. The Martin Company was no different.

Table 6.1 shows the distribution of the Martin Company members who continued west from Florence by sex and by Eighth U.S. Census (1860) age class. In many ways, this distribution is very similar to that which marks the Willie Company (Table 5.1).

Figure 6.1 shows the distribution of people by age class for both companies (the data are in Tables 5.1, 6.1, and 6.2) and makes it clear that the age structures of these two groups were very much alike once they left Florence. In fact, the only significant difference between these distributions involves men between 60 and 69 years of age. These men are far better represented in the Willie Company than they are in Martin's group.[56]

TABLE 6.1. Membership of the Martin Handcart Company west of Florence, NE: Age and sex by Eighth U.S. Census age class.

Age class	Males	Females	Total	Male (%)	Female (%)
1–4	35	35	70	50.0	50.0
5–9	43	41	84	51.2	48.8
10–14	33	37	70	47.1	52.9
15–19	36	38	74	48.6	51.4
20–29	41	62	103	39.8	60.2
30–39	30	50	80	37.5	62.5
40–49	30	36	66	45.5	54.5
50–59	22	29	51	43.1	56.9
60–69	4	8	12	33.3	66.7
70–79	4	3	7	57.1	42.9
Unknown	1	0	1		
Totals	279	339	618	45.1	54.9

TABLE 6.2. Age and sex by Eighth U.S. Census age class: Martin and Willie Handcart Companies compared.

Age class	Martin Handcart Company		Willie Handcart Company	
	In age class (%)	Female (%)	In age class (%)	Female (%)
1–4	11.3	50.0	10.9	45.8
5–9	13.6	48.8	13.2	50.0
10–14	11.3	52.9	11.8	51.9
15–19	12.0	51.4	12.3	53.7
20–29	16.7	60.2	16.6	60.3
30–39	13.0	62.5	12.5	67.3
40–49	10.7	54.5	12.1	54.7
50–59	8.3	56.9	5.2	60.9
60–69	1.9	66.7	4.8	28.6
70–79	1.1	42.9	0.5	50.0

To Rogerson, the Martin Company contained "the most aged and infirm—the cleanings up of the season's emigration."[57] If that were the case, and those people continued beyond Florence, it would seem that those between 60 and 69 years old should be better represented in the Martin Company than in the Willie Company. This may represent a problem with my membership list.

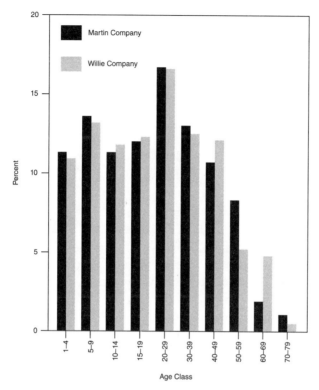

FIGURE 6.1. Martin and Willie Handcart Companies' membership by Eighth U.S. Census age class.

However, it may also represent the fact that some of the oldest members of the Martin Company had either left the group or died before the departure from Florence. In addition, Rogerson was writing 60 years after the fact. While he had assistance from church historians in estimating the number of people who died, his report about the large numbers of "the most aged and infirm" was simply his recollection, a recollection perhaps deeply influenced by how a 15-year-old—then or now—perceives his elders.

The Willie and Martin Companies were also alike in being composed of a multiplicity of "traveling groups" (Table 6.3). Just as with the Willie Company, single-mother families were common in the Martin group. Of 102 families (one or more parents with at least one child), 37.3 percent were led by a single mother, almost identical to the 36.8 percent in the Willie Company. There were also 42 women traveling alone and 9 in all-female

TABLE 6.3. Traveling groups of Martin Handcart Company members who proceeded west from Florence, NE (abbreviations are used in later tables).

Group type	Number of groups	Number of individuals
Single females (SiF)	42	42
Single males (SiM)	37	37
Mothers only with children (MoCh)	38	134
Fathers only with children (FaCh)*	4	9
Mothers and fathers with children (MoFaCh)	60	343
Husband and wife without children (HuWi)	16	32
Husband, wife, and sibling (HuWiSi)	2	6
Siblings	7	15
Total	206	618

* includes one grandfather-granddaughter pair (Jonathan Stone and his granddaughter, whose first name is not known)

sets of siblings. As a result, 14.4 percent of the Martin Company consisted of women traveling alone or as heads of families, very close to the 17 percent of such women in the Willie Company.

The membership of these two handcart companies was thus strikingly similar in some very important ways. With the exception of men between 60 and 69 years of age, members were similar in age structure and sex composition by age class; they were also similar in the nature and composition of their traveling groups.

They did, however, differ in the amount of time they were exposed to cold and famine. "Weather very cold," William Woodward noted in the Willie Company journal for October 19, the same day John Jaques observed that "winter came on all at once" for the Martin Company.[58] The Willie Company arrived in Salt Lake City 22 days later; the Martin Company, 43 days later. In addition, rescuers met the Willie Company on October 21 but did not meet the Martin Company until October 31. Finally, all of the members of the Willie Company abandoned their handcarts on November 2; for the Martin Company, this did not occur until November 18.

On the other hand, even though the Martin Company was on its own and exposed to severe cold far longer than the Willie Company, their energy expenditure during some of those days was reduced by the two extended periods they spent in camp. These occurred between October 23 and 29, while camped along the Platte River, and between November 4 and 9, while at Martin's Cove. Equally important is the fact that while Willie's group ran out of food, Martin's company did not. Jaques tells us that the last reduction in rations—to four ounces of flour—was "the extremity of their privations as to food,"[59] while Daniel Jones notes that when the rescuers arrived, Martin Company rations were "about exhausted,"[60] not that they were exhausted.

In short, the Martin Company was exposed for a longer period of time than the Willie Company, but for about 10 days of that time, members of the Martin Company remained in camp and were never completely out of food. The results of some of these similarities and differences in terms of mortality will soon be clear.

MORTALITY AND AGE

Basic data on age, sex, and survivorship for the Martin Handcart Company members who went west from Florence are provided in Table 6.4. We have come to expect that high mortality rates will characterize the older members of the Martin Company, and Figure 6.2 shows that this is what happened. The age-class mortality rates that mark the Martin Company were, in general, quite similar to those in the Willie Company, with the oldest members of both groups suffering the highest mortality (Figure 6.3). Exposed to the cold far longer, mortality among the very youngest members of the Martin Company—those younger than five—was three times higher than it was in the Willie Company (18.6 percent versus 6.3 percent), though this difference is not statistically significant.[61] Mortality among those 40 years of age or older was slightly higher in the Willie Company (43.4 percent) than in the Martin Company (36.6 percent), but this difference is also not significant.[62]

In the Donner Party disaster, children under the age of five did not begin to die until they had been trapped in the Sierra Nevada for well over two months. Neither handcart company was exposed to such severe conditions for so long. Just as with the Willie Company, members of the Martin Company were able to provide their children with the resources they needed to keep their mortality rates well beneath the horrendous figures that marked the Donner Party. The behavior of David Blair (46), described

TABLE 6.4. Mortality, by Eighth U.S. Census age class, of Martin Handcart Company members who proceeded west from Florence, NE.

Age class	Males: survived?			Females: survived?			Totals	Died (%)
	Yes	No	Died (%)	Yes	No	Died (%)		
1–4	28	7	20.0	29	6	17.1	70	18.6
5–9	38	5	11.6	40	1	2.4	84	7.1
10–14	29	4	12.1	35	2	5.4	70	8.6
15–19	28	8	22.2	37	1	2.6	74	12.2
20–29	30	11	26.8	59	3	4.8	103	13.6
30–39	20	10	33.3	44	6	12.0	80	20.0
40–49	21	9	30.0	33	3	8.3	66	18.2
50–59	7	15	68.2	22	7	24.1	51	43.1
60–69	2	2	50.0	2	6	75.0	12	66.7
70–79	0	4	100.0	0	3	100.0	7	100.0
Unknown	1	0	—	0	0		1	
Totals	204	75	26.9	301	38	11.2	618	18.3

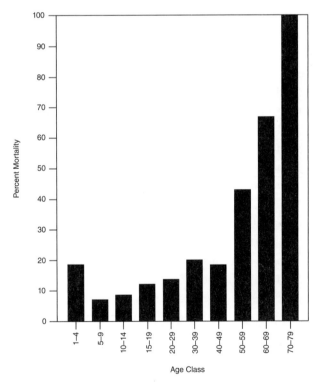

FIGURE 6.2. Martin Handcart Company mortality rates by Eighth U.S. Census age class.

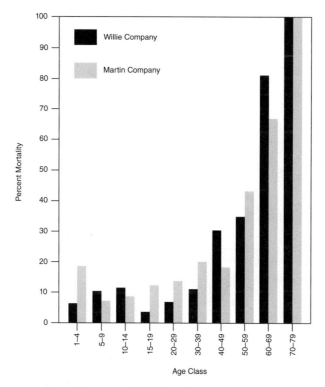

FIGURE 6.3. Martin and Willie Handcart Companies' mortality rates compared by age class.

by Patience Loader, shows the kinds of sacrifices that parents made on behalf of their children:

> I remember well poor Brother Blair. He was a fine, tall man, had been one of Queen Victoria's life guards in London. He had a wife and four children. He made a cover for his cart and he put his four children on the cart. He pulled his cart alone, his wife helped by pushing behind. The poor man was so weak and worn down that he fell several times that day but he still kept his dear little children on the cart all day. This man had so much love for his wife and children that instead of eating his morsel of food himself he would give it to his children. Poor man, he pulled the cart as long as he could, then he died and his wife and children had to do the best

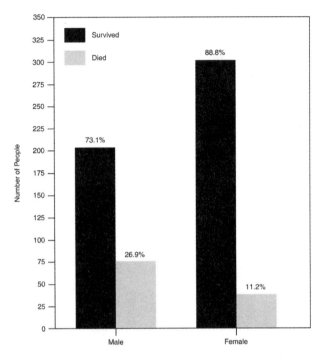

FIGURE 6.4. Martin Handcart Company mortality rates by sex.

they could without his help. The children got frozen. Some parts of their bodies were all sores, but they got to Salt Lake City alive.[63]

The shorter duration of the horrors suffered by the Willie and Martin Handcart Companies, coupled with resources that parents gave their children, help account for the fact that mortality rates among the youngest members of these companies were far lower than the 63 percent mortality suffered by their age-mates in the Donner Party.

SURVIVORSHIP AND SEX

In the Donner Party, males died at a rate 1.93 times higher than did females. The comparable figure for the Willie Company is 3.00. It is no surprise that male deaths also predominated in the Martin Company. After leaving Florence, 26.9 percent of the males but only 11.2 percent of the females lost their lives (Figure 6.4). In this group, males died at 2.40 times the rate at which

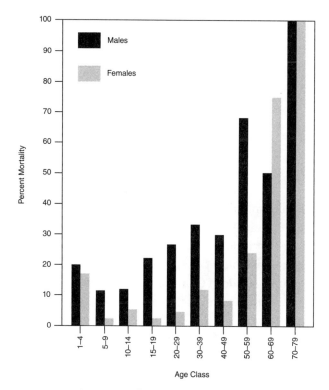

FIGURE 6.5. Martin Handcart Company mortality rates by age class and sex.

females died. And, much as in the Willie Company, Martin Company male death rates were greater than female death rates across nearly all age classes (Figure 6.5). Indeed, the male mortality rate is at least twice the female rate in seven of those classes. The only exceptions are for the youngest (1–4 years old) and oldest (60–79 years old) members of the group.

As with the Willie Company, the odds that Martin Company males and females under 40 years old would survive the ordeal do not differ across age classes.[64] In general, while both age and sex are significant predictors of mortality in the Martin Company as a whole, only sex played a role for those under the age of 40.[65] This is the same situation that marked the Willie Company.

In the Willie Company, the odds of a male member of the group under 40 dying were 2.0 times the odds that a female member of this age would die. That difference, we have seen, was in the expected direction but not

TABLE 6.5. Martin Handcart Company: Average ages of survivors and non-survivors by sex. N = number of individuals.

	Male (N)	Female (N)
Survived	19.5 (203)	23.6 (301)
Died	32.9 (75)	37.7 (38)
Difference	13.4	14.1

statistically significant. In the Martin Company, the odds that a male under 40 would die are 3.3 times the odds that a female member of this age would die, a difference that is quite significant, just as it was in the Donner Party (for which the comparable ratio was 3.9).[66]

Among Martin Handcart Company members 40 years of age and older, the odds that men died were 2.95 times the odds that women of this age were lost, a difference that is also significant.[67] It is, however, much less than the odds differential for the Willie Company members of this age. Here, the odds of men 40 or older dying were 10.3 times those of women of this age dying.

The reason for this difference between the two companies is simple: the Willie Company had more elderly men than the Martin Company did after the groups left Florence. Of the 201 Willie males of known age, 16 (8.0 percent) were at least 60, compared to 8 (2.9 percent) in the Martin Company. All 16 of the older men in the Willie Company were lost, compared to 6 in the Martin Company. That is, differences in the age structures of these two groups seem to account for the lower mortality rate for older males in the Martin Company.

SOME CONCLUSIONS ABOUT SURVIVORSHIP, AGE, AND SEX

In short, mortality rates were far higher for males in the Martin Company than for females across nearly all age classes. In addition, death struck most heavily at very young and older individuals. The males who died averaged 13.4 years older than those who survived; the females who died averaged 14.1 years older than those who lived (Table 6.5). All this matches what we have already seen for the Donner Party and the Willie Handcart Company.

Given this, we can now ask what role the size of support groups played in determining who lived and who died in the Martin Handcart Company.

SURVIVORSHIP AND FAMILY MEMBERSHIP

In Chapter 5, I noted the important relationships between the nature of the family group with which a Willie Handcart Company member traveled and whether that person lived or died. Much the same is true for the Martin Company. And, as with the Willie Company, these connections are not immediately evident.

In fact, looking only at the relationship between average family size and survivorship would suggest no connection between these two things. Males who survived traveled with families that averaged only 0.7 people more than those who died; among females, survivors traveled with families that averaged 0.4 people less than those who died. If we ask what combinations of age, sex, and family size best predict survivorship across the members of the Martin Company, we find that, as with the Willie Company, age and sex together accurately predict who lived and who died but that family size does not significantly increase the accuracy of these predictions beyond this point.[68]

Of course, this does not mean that families did not matter. As Table 6.6 shows, mortality rates differed substantially across the various Martin Company traveling groups, just as with the Willie Company. In fact, the

TABLE 6.6. Martin Handcart Company mortality rates by traveling group.

Group type	Survived	Died	Totals	Mortality (%)
Single females	38	4	42	9.5
Single males	19	18	37	48.6
Mothers only with children	126	8	134	6.0
Fathers only with children*	5	4	9	44.4
Mothers and fathers with children	275	68	343	19.8
Husband and wife without children	26	6	32	18.8
Husband, wife, and sibling	6	0	6	0.0
Siblings	10	5	15	33.3
Totals:	505	113	618	18.3

*includes one grandfather-granddaughter pair (Jonathan Stone and his granddaughter, whose first name is not known)

TABLE 6.7. Average group size, age, and mortality by group type: Martin Handcart Company members who proceeded west from Florence, NE. N = number of individuals (see Table 6.3 for group membership and abbreviations).

Group type	Average size	Average age			Mortality (%)
		Survivors (N)	Non-survivors (N)	Group	
MoFaCh	5.7	18.2 (275)	31.2 (68)	20.8	19.8
MoCh*	3.5	22.7 (125)	34.3 (8)	23.4	6.0
FaCh	2.3	25.2 (5)	24.8 (4)	25.0	44.4
HuWi	2.0	33.1 (26)	50.2 (6)	36.3	18.8
HuWiSi	3.0	22.8 (6)	—	22.8	0.0
Siblings	2.1	21.2 (10)	37.8 (5)	26.7	33.3
Single	1.0	33.3 (57)	41.6 (22)	35.6	27.8

* excludes one individual of unknown age (James Thomas)

TABLE 6.8. Average group size, age, and mortality by group type: Martin Handcart Company females who proceeded west from Florence, NE. N = number of individuals (see Table 6.3 for group membership and abbreviations).

Group type	Average size	Average age			Mortality (%)
		Survivors (N)	Non-survivors (N)	Group	
MoFaCh	5.7	18.4 (151)	32.1 (25)	20.4	14.2
MoCh	3.5	27.4 (84)	46.5 (4)	28.3	4.5
FaCh	2.3	14.5 (2)	10.0 (1)	13.0	33.3
HuWi	2.0	31.3 (14)	59.5 (2)	34.8	12.5
HuWiSi	3.0	20.8 (4)	—	20.8	0.0
Siblings	2.1	21.8 (8)	61.0 (2)	29.6	20.0
Single	1.0	34.4 (38)	48.8 (4)	35.8	9.5

mortality rates for the three major kinds of family groups—mother-father, single father, and single mother—in the two companies are statistically identical to one another. In both cases, the single-mother families have by far the lowest mortality rate of all family groups.

Mortality rate patterns in the Martin Company replicate the Willie experience in other ways as well. Male death rates outstripped those of females in all traveling group types visited by death (Tables 6.7–6.9). In addition, with only two exceptions—the single-father groups (nine people), and the two sets of husband, wives, and siblings (six people, all of whom survived)—the

TABLE 6.9. Average group size, age, and mortality by group type: Martin Handcart Company males who proceeded west from Florence, NE. N = number of individuals (see Table 6.3 for group membership and abbreviations).

Group type	Average size	Average age			Mortality (%)
		Survivors (N)	Non-survivors (N)	Group	
MoFaCh	5.7	17.9 (124)	30.7 (43)	21.2	25.7
MoCh*	3.5	13.0 (41)	22.0 (4)	13.8	8.9
FaCh	2.3	32.3 (3)	29.7 (3)	31.0	50.0
HuWi	2.0	35.3 (12)	45.5 (4)	37.8	25.0
HuWiSi	3.0	27.0 (2)	—	27.0	0.0
Siblings	2.1	19.0 (2)	22.3 (3)	21.0	60.0
Single	1.0	30.9 (19)	40.0 (18)	35.4	47.9

* excludes one individual of unknown age (James Thomas)

average age of both the males and females who died in each kind of traveling group were higher than the average ages of those who survived in that group.

In the Willie Company, mother-father families had a mortality rate (15.7 percent) over twice that suffered by single-mother families (7.0 percent). Even when we add in the single men who may have been assigned to assist single-mother families, the mortality rate in those families remained far lower than that shown by mother-father families. While Willie Company single-mother families had a lower mortality rate in part because they had no older males, they did have older women, and even these people died at a significantly lower rate than older women in mother-father families. The reason for this, I suggested, was that single-mother families had far fewer younger children to care for and thus spent far less energy carrying them or transporting them in handcarts.

The Martin Company experience could hardly be more parallel. Mother-father families in this group had a mortality rate of 19.8 percent, over three times higher than that of single-mother families (6.0 percent). While single-mother families had only 2 men older than 29, mother-father families had 57 men of this age, 26 of whom (45.6 percent) died (see Tables 6.10 and 6.11). As in the Willie Company, single-mother mortality rates were reduced, in part, because these families had almost no older males.

What of the older women in the two family types? Martin Company mother-father families had 54 women who were at least 30 years old, 15 of whom (27.8 percent) died. The single-mother families had 40 women of

TABLE 6.10. Mortality by age class in single-mother families in the Martin Handcart Company.

Age class	Males		Females	
	Survived	Died	Survived	Died
1–4	3	0	5	0
5–9	10	0	7	0
10–14	12	1	8	0
15–19	11	2	14	0
20–29	4	0	13	1
30–39	1	1	15	0
40–49	0	0	10	1
50–59	0	0	12	1
60–69	0	0	0	1
70–79	0	0	0	0
Unknown	1	0	0	0
Totals	42	4	84	4

TABLE 6.11. Mortality by age class in mother-father families in the Martin Handcart Company.

Age class	Males		Females	
	Survived	Died	Survived	Died
1–4	25	7	24	6
5–9	27	4	33	1
10–14	16	3	23	1
15–19	12	2	12	1
20–29	13	1	20	1
30–39	13	8	21	6
40–49	12	7	14	1
50–59	4	9	4	4
60–69	2	1	0	1
70–79	0	1	0	3
Totals	124	43	151	25

this age, only 3 of whom (7.5 percent) died. Again, there is something more going on here than the lack of older people in the single-mother families.

It makes little difference if we add to the single-mother families those men who may have been assigned to help them. There were 28 single men in

TABLE 6.12. Age distribution and survivorship of single males in the Martin Handcart Company.

Age class	Survived	Died	Total
1–4	0	0	0
5–9	0	0	0
10–14	1	0	1
15–19	3	3	6
20–29	5	5	10
30–39	4	1	5
40–49	5	2	7
50–59	1	4	5
60–69	0	1	1
70–79	0	2	2
Totals	19	18	37

the Martin Company between 15 and 49 years old, excluding Martin himself (Table 6.12). Of these, 11 died. If we add these people to the single-mother families, there would have been 162 people (134 in the single-mother families plus 28 single males) in the group, 19 of whom died. The resultant mortality rate (11.7 percent) is higher than that for the same set of people in the Willie Company (7.7 percent) but remains lower than that for any other sizeable traveling group in the Martin Company. It is also significantly lower than the mortality rate for the mother-father families (19.8 percent).[69] Only if we exclude men in mother-father families who were at least 50 years old do those rates become comparable.[70] As with the Willie Company, mother-father families were at a disadvantage, in part because they had greater numbers of older men.

There is yet another parallel with the Willie Company. In the Willie Company, parents transported their children who could not walk. Since mother-father families had far more of these children than did single-mother families, people in those families spent far more energy caring for their young than individuals in single-mother families did and suffered higher mortality as a result (Chapter 5).

Parents also routinely transported their young children in the Martin Company. Company member Elizabeth Sermon provides an example:

My eldest boy [John, 9] had the mountain fever, and we had to haul him on the cart. . . . One day we started him out before the carts

TABLE 6.13. Numbers of young children in mother-father and single-mother families in the Martin Handcart Company and associated ratios.

Family type	Number of children under the age of:						
	11[a]	10	9	8	7	6	5
Single mother	29	25	21	18	14	11	8
Mother-father	137	127	116	103	91	82	62
	Ratios of the number of children to numbers of family groups						
	11[b]	10	9	8	7	6	5
Single mother (38 families)	0.76	0.66	0.55	0.47	0.37	0.29	0.21
Mother-father (60 families)	2.28	2.12	1.93	1.72	1.52	1.37	1.03
	Differential in numbers of children						
	11[c]	10	9	8	7	6	5
	3.00	3.21	3.51	3.66	4.11	4.72	4.90

[a] Single-mother families had 29 children under 11; mother-father families had 137 children of this age.
[b] The 29 children under 11 in single-mother families were distributed across 38 families; 29/38= .76. The corresponding ratio for mother-father families is 137/60 = 2.28.
[c] 2.28/.76 = 3.00, meaning that mother-father families were caring for 3 times the number of children under 11 than were being cared for by single-mother families.

started in the morning to walk with the aged and sick, but we had not gone far on our journey when we found him lying by the roadside unable to go any further. I picked him up and put him on my back and drawed my cart as well as I could, but could not manage far so I put him in the Cart which made children [John, 9; Robert, 5; Marian 3] and my baggage, my failing husband [Joseph, 54], besides our regular load. The Captain put a young man to help me pull for a short time. My other son, Henry, at 7 years old, walked the entire 1300 miles with the exception of a few miles.[71]

As a result, Martin Company mother-father families may have been at greater risk than single-mother families because they had greater numbers of young children who had to be transported.

Table 6.13 and Figure 6.6 show that this was the case. Women in mother-father families were caring for 3.0 times the number of children less than 11 years old than were women in single-mother families and 4.9 times the

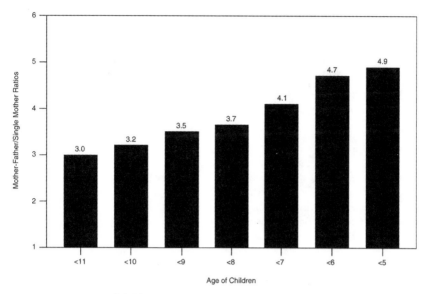

FIGURE 6.6. Ratios of children by age in Martin Handcart Company mother-father and single-mother families.

number who were under 5 years old. The higher mortality suffered by Martin Company mother-father families, compared to that suffered by single-mother families, follows from this fact, just as it did for the Willie Company.

ONE LONG TORTURE

As we have come to expect, Martin Company males died at far higher rates than females, and the old died at far higher rates than the young.[72] Family size by itself played little detectable role in determining who lived and who died—the handcart company members were provisioned from a central store and were under strong central supervision—but the nature of the kin groups with which people traveled did play a major role. Mother-father families in the Martin Company suffered far higher mortality than the single-mother families with whom they traveled because of the uneven distribution of the very young in these families, the huge energy costs associated with moving handcarts across the plains and over the Rocky Mountains, and because the mother-father families included greater numbers of older men. This is precisely what we saw for the Willie Company.

Mormon historian Juanita Brooks has correctly described the entirety of the handcart experience as "one long torture."[73] For those who endured the experience at its worst, freezing and starving during the winter of 1856—the result of "some misguided scheme and speculations, which will, some day, have to be atoned for"[74]—it was a torture whose outcome was heavily dictated by sex, age, and family ties.

CHAPTER 6 NOTES

1. The brief history of the Martin Handcart Company in this chapter depends heavily on Hafen and Hafen 1992; Bartholomew and Arrington 1993; Olsen 2006; Roberts 2008; Bagley 2009, 2014; as well as the primary literature cited below.
2. Olsen 2006. For slightly different departure dates, see Hafen and Hafen 1992 and Christy 1997–1998.
3. Bell 1978:119.
4. Turner 1996:106.
5. Ibid., 215; Camm 1892.
6. Bell 1978:125.
7. Ibid., 144. See also Rogerson 1907e.
8. Bell 1978:147.
9. Kimball 1983.
10. Bell 1978:142; Rogerson 1907d.
11. Ibid., 144.
12. Ibid., 147.
13. These dates are collated in Allphin 2012.
14. Ibid., 162.
15. Ibid., 303; Camm 1892.
16. Burton 1856.
17. Kimball 1983:70, from W. Clayton's *The Latter-Day Saints' Emigrants' Guide* (1848).
18. Hafen and Hafen 1992:234.
19. Ibid., 235.
20. Jones 1890:66.
21. Bell 1978:148.
22. Jones 1890:68.
23. Bell 1978:150; Jaques 1878b.
24. Turner 1996:122.
25. Grant 1856.
26. Burton 1856.
27. Ibid.
28. Bartholomew and Arrington 1993.
29. Jones 1890:69.
30. Ibid., 74.
31. Burton 1856.
32. Jones 1890:69.
33. Burton 1856.
34. Jones 1890:72.
35. Ibid., 114.
36. Burton 1856.
37. Brooks 1964:606.
38. Bell 1978:166.
39. Bartholomew and Arrington 1993.
40. Hanks 1856.
41. Brooks 1964:606.
42. Ibid.
43. Bell 1978:169; Jaques 1878c.
44. Bell 1978:179.
45. Ibid., 171.
46. Black 1980; Turner 1996; Madsen 1998; Allphin 2012; and, especially, Church of Jesus Christ of Latter-day Saints 2015a.
47. The full list is available at http://hdl.handle.net/1773/34984. See also Chapter 5, note 92.
48. Richards and Spencer 1856. This meeting is also reported by Jaques 1878a and Rogerson 1907b.
49. Bell 1978:118; Jones 1890:69.
50. Rogerson 1913.
51. Jaques 1878c.

52. Rogerson 1879.
53. Rogerson 1913.
54. Madsen 1998.
55. Christy 1997–1998: 51, 72.
56. The overall distributions of Willie and Martin Handcart Company members into Eighth U.S. Census age classes do not differ significantly from one another (chi-square = 11.97, p = 0.22). Analysis of single cell adjusted residuals (Everitt 1977) shows all to be insignificant at p = 0.05, except for people between 60 and 69 years of age. Compared to the Willie Handcart Company, people of that age are significantly underrepresented in the Martin Company (Martin Company adjusted residual = −2.61, p < 0.01). In addition, there are no significant differences between these companies in the distribution of females across age classes (chi-square = 2.46, p = 0.98), with no single cell adjusted residual approaching significance (p > 0.10). For males, all but one of the single cell adjusted residuals are insignificant at p = 0.10; the single exception is for males between the ages of 60 and 69, who are significantly underrepresented in the Martin Company (adjusted residual = −3.33, p < 0.001).
57. Rogerson 1907a. This statement is repeated in Rogerson 1914.
58. Willie 1856; Bell 1978: 144.
59. Turner 1996:120; Jaques 1878b.
60. Jones 1890:66.
61. Chi-square = 3.69, p = 0.06.
62. Chi-square = 1.32, p > 0.10.
63. Bell 1978:150.
64. Mantel-Haenszel chi-square = 4.99, p > 0.10.
65. Multivariate logistic regression for the group as a whole, with mortality as the dependent variable and age (p < 0.001) and sex (p < 0.001) as the independent variables; multivariate logistic regression for those under 40, with mortality as the dependent variable and age (p = 0.13) and sex (p < 0.001) as the independent variables.
66. Given that 45 of the 218 Martin Company males who were younger than 40 died, the odds of a member of this subset of members dying are 0.2064/0.7936, or 0.2601. Of 263 females of this age, 19 died, so the corresponding figures for females are 0.0722/0.9278, or 0.0778. Dividing .02601 by 0.0778 gives us 3.34 (p < 0.001).
67. Of the 60 Martin Company men 40 or older, 30 (0.5000) succumbed, compared to 19 of 76 (0.2533) women of this age. That is, the odds of a man this age dying are 0.5000/0.5000, or 1.0000. For women of this age, the odds of dying are 0.2533/0.7467, or 0.3392; 1.0000/0.3392 = 2.95 (p < .01).
68. Multivariate logistic regression with mortality as the dependent variable and sex (p < 0.001), age (p < 0.001), and family size (p = 0.16) as the dependent variables.
69. Chi-square = 5.06, p = 0.03.
70. Chi-square = 1.31, p = 0.25.
71. Camm 1892. The term *mountain fever* was commonly applied to any illness accompanied by fever; some instances may be related to Colorado tick fever, transmitted by the western North American *Dermacentor andersoni* (Bagley 2012; http://www.cdc.gov /coloradotickfever/). For other examples of Martin Company children being transported in carts, see the comments by Langley Bailey

(Allphin 2012:161), Sarah Crossley (Allphin 2012:194), Patience Loader (Bell 1978:150), and Josiah Rogerson (1907f). Elizabeth Sermon's children all survived, as did she, but her husband did not, a fate shared with many others in similar family settings. This includes "poor Brother Blair," whose misery was so well described by Loader earlier in this chapter.

72. In Chapters 4 and 5, I examined the relationship between age, sex, family size, and the chronology of death for the Donner Party and the Willie Handcart Company. I was able to do this because I had reasonably accurate dates of death for the vast majority of those who lost their lives. For the Martin Company, I have equivalent data for only 66 of the 113 people who died and so have not examined this issue for them.

73. Brooks 1964:601.

74. Camm 1892.

7

GENDERED DEATH?

Psychologist Julia Wallace once asked some 500 midwestern university students why they thought women live longer than men.[1] The five most common responses are summarized in Table 7.1. How do these notions stack up against what we have seen happen to the Donner, Willie, and Martin groups?

Not very well. These students make the very common, and very understandable, error of failing to understand how deeply human biology runs.

Let me begin by eliminating the one item on the list that is simply incorrect. Even though 14.6 percent of the respondents—12 percent of the women and 19 percent of the men—in Wallace's sample thought that American women lead less stressful lives than American men, exactly the opposite is true. Women in general report far higher levels of stress than men do from a diverse variety of causes.[2]

For different reasons, I also do not need to consider the belief that women take better care of their health than men do. Least important, some of the likely components of this option—Wallace mentioned eating better, exercising more, and seeing physicians more often—do not pertain to the situations I have examined here. More to the point, "taking better care of yourself" is no different from "taking fewer risks," which also appears on the list. If a certain set of behaviors is seen as having negative health consequences for longevity, then performing those behaviors is risky, and

TABLE 7.1. The opinions of 493 midwestern college students on the causes of the sex differential in human longevity: The five most common responses (Wallace 1996).

Cause	Responses (%)
Women take better care of their health	24.9
Men engage in riskier behavior	21.7
Women undergo less stress	14.6
Biology favors women	14.6
Men have more physically demanding jobs	14.0

eliminating them from one's behavioral repertoire is risk reducing. Smoking, for instance, is a very risky behavior that is shown more often by men than women.[3] Conversely, visiting a physician for preventive health care or in response to perceived illness is risk-reducing behavior that increases longevity and marks women more than men.[4]

We are now left with three folk opinions: men perform jobs that require more physical labor, men engage in more risky behavior (including riskier jobs), and men are biologically prone to earlier deaths. All three of these opinions are correct, but these students made a distinction between biology and behavior that is illusory. All three opinions refer to the same thing.

Men clearly performed more physical labor than women in the emigrant groups I have examined here. As we have seen, Donner Party males engaged in higher levels of physical activity than Donner Party females. We have also seen that while the activity levels of handcart company men and women were more similar to one another than they were in the Donner Party, handcart company men still engaged in higher levels of physical activity than their female counterparts.

Patience Loader, for instance, tells us that "since our dear father died, it had fallen on me and my sister, Maria, to get most of the wood,"[5] implying that men were expected to do that job. Camping just west of Devil's Gate, John Jaques relates that "some of the men were so weak that it took them an hour or two to clear the places for their tents."[6] "I could not," John Chislett recalled, "raise enough men to pitch a tent."[7] Willie Company member Jens Nielson remembered that after four of the men in his tent died, "I had to ask some of the largest and strongest women to help me raise the tents and it looked like we should all die."[8] Men were also charged with standing guard at night[9] and herding cattle when there were cattle to herd, and they often carried women and children across streams.[10] The extra energy costs associated with such activities increased the mortality rate suffered by males compared to that suffered by females. In fact, Josiah Rogerson found standing guard to be so physically demanding that he thought this task helped explain why more Martin Company men than women died.[11] In that sense, these people provide support for the popular notion that male mortality rates are higher than female rates because males more routinely engage in physically demanding tasks.

Of course, there was a good reason that the men in these groups engaged in higher levels of strength-related activities than women did. Men tend to be better at them because men tend to be bigger and stronger than women—not because they learned to be but for reasons that are biological, just as Alice H. Eagly and Wendy Wood's biosocial theory observes (Chapter 3). As the men in these groups began to weaken and die, the women took over the tasks they could do—Patience and her sister cut and hauled wood, for instance, and the "largest and strongest women" put up tents—but most women could not do these things as well as most men could. Chislett may have overstated the case when he said that the men in his company performed "many duties which women could not do,"[12] but he would have gotten to the biological core had he instead said "which women tended not to do as proficiently."

So, of the five options provided by Wallace's students, we are left with risk and biology. Men, those students correctly observed, engage in riskier behavior than women, and their willingness to do this may shorten their lives. However, we have already seen that this difference seems to have evolved in our deep past as a result of competition among individuals to maximize the number of successful offspring they leave behind. These differences are deeply embedded in our biology.

In this context, it is worth taking a closer look at why William Manly and John Rogers did what they did in 1849. These were the men, mentioned in Chapter 1, who rode some 270 miles in 26 days to find help for their traveling companions stuck in Death Valley. Manly (29 years old) was a friend of the Bennett family and Rogers (24 or 25) was a friend of Manly; both were single. It was Asabel Bennett's suggestion that "two of our youngest, strongest men"[13] head out to seek help while the rest remained behind. Bennett, at 36, was no oldster, but he was traveling with his wife, Sarah (25), and three children, all of whom were under 10. Bennett suggested that he and Manly go, but Rogers was ultimately selected to accompany Manly.[14]

One might think that it would be just as risky to stay in Death Valley as it was to leave, but it was not. All recognized that Manly and Rogers might not survive. Those left behind were to wait 18 days and then leave if the two had not returned. Indeed, some members of the stranded group did decide to leave, and all but one—Richard Culverwell (48)—made it to safety.

The greater risks were taken by two young men who had strong bonds of friendship to each other, a strong tie to the Bennett family, and no kin left behind. As usual in such groups, no single women could have been selected. Three women were present, but all were caring for children under 10, so we are not surprised that none of them emerged as a possibility. In fact, what would have been surprising would have been the very presence of single women in this group (see Chapter 5).

Risk-averse behavior and childcare responsibilities aside, there is another reason why women of the appropriate age would have not been the best choice to make the run for help. Men tend to have far better abilities at long-distance spatial navigation than women do, a difference found in other species of mammals as well. Edward Clint and his colleagues estimated the cross-species male advantage at about 30 percent. As they note, the "male advantage in spatial tasks in humans and rodents is among the most robust and well-documented cases of cognitive sexual dimorphism."[15] Importantly, these differences are innate, not learned.[16] Men and women also tend to have different navigational strategies. Men tend to orient themselves with distances and directions, women by using landmarks.[17] While most women have better abilities than men to remember the location of objects once seen—think "male refrigerator blindness"[18]—most men are far better at navigating novel landscapes. There are several competing hypotheses as to why this is the case,[19] but that very fact is what is of importance here. In Death Valley in 1849, risk-taking males, with their better navigational abilities, represented the best biological option open to the stranded emigrants in their selection of those who were to seek help.

The Donner Party provides a parallel example. In early September, two men—the single Charles Stanton (35) and the married William McCutchan (30)—left the group to seek help (Chapter 2). Much later and mired in snow, the party was buoyed by the fact that Stanton had returned and provided them with the secure knowledge that rescue attempts were being made from the other side.

Accordingly, it was, at first, less risky to remain in camp and far riskier to try to leave. No surprise, then, that the first attempt to escape, on about November 12, involved 13 men but only 2 women. The second attempt, some nine days later, involved 16 men and 6 women. The third and final attempt—the Forlorn Hope—began on December 16, the day after people started dying in camp. This group consisted of 10 men and 5 women. That is, as the risks incurred by staying rose and those incurred by leaving declined, the proportion of women who tried to walk out increased from 13 percent to 27 percent to 33 percent.[20]

Just as Wallace's students said, men engage in more intense physical labor than women and take greater risks than women. But it is a mistake to distinguish such things from biology. It is true that "biology favors women" when it comes to longevity, but an important part of that advantage stems from gendered behaviors that are very much biological in origin.

DECONTEXTUALIZED TRAGEDIES

Anthropologists Shannon Novak and Kelly Dixon do not admire this conclusion. In fact, they don't admire my emigrant research at all. They find that I have conflated sex and gender so thoroughly that my work "fails to take into account the biocultural influences on physiology and cultural repertoires of both men and women."[21] As a result, "individuals have been decontextualized in time and space."[22] To them, I have failed to take into account the "biocultural construction of the body," "failed to distinguish between the biological body, the performed body, and the categorized body."[23]

I probably have failed to distinguish between biological, performed, and categorized bodies, since I am not certain what these terms mean. I can, however, respond to the critique that I have decontextualized the unfortunate people who went through the triple tragedies at the heart of this book, since Novak and Dixon are clear what they mean by *decontextualization*. They mean that I have ignored the fact that members of the Donner Party came from particular cultural backgrounds and that these backgrounds determined how they behaved and how and why they died. That is, they argue that I am wrong in concluding that human biology is behind the mortality patterns that are so starkly displayed by the Donner Party tragedy because those patterns follow not from human biology but from learned behavior.

The example they provide comes from Tamzene Donner. As I have discussed, she refused to leave her injured husband and then died a day after he did. According to Novak and Dixon, Tamzene died because she was "an ideal Victorian wife and mother."[24] That is, she died because of learned behavior.

In particular, they observe that

> the duality of gender roles in the first half of the nineteenth century became codified in public discourse and reified in separate spheres. Civility, education, and morality were seen as intrinsically female concerns to be nurtured by wives and mothers within the home. The domestic sphere became an idealized haven from corrupt forces of the market, as well as a sanctuary for companionate marriage.

Once on the trail, they continue,

> travelers negotiated new physical and social landscapes, though the activities and the space they occupied remained gendered. Women, in general, were responsible for the hearth and meals, care of the children, and bringing an air of civility to the mobile community. Men performed the heavy labor of the daily traverse, negotiated goods and supplies, and maintained defense of livestock and family. Leisure time for bourgeois women circulated around literary activities . . . while the men used big game hunting to negotiate rank and solidify fraternal bonds.[25]

When Novak and Dixon refer to gendered activities, they don't mean activities preferentially performed by men and women because their biology makes them better at it. They mean activities that are preferentially performed by men and women because the specific culture within which they were raised has trained them to accept that these are the things they should do. They seem to believe that women were the primary caretakers of kids only because they were taught to do so and that men performed the heavy labor only because that was what they were taught they should do. Novak and Dixon seem to believe that the Donner Party men hunted to "negotiate rank and solidify fraternal bonds" as opposed to hunting because everyone was starving to death. The implication is that had the Donner Party come from a very different cultural context, the men might have taken care of the children and the women might have cut the trail through the Wasatch Range.

They are welcome to believe this, though they would be hard put to find any cultural context in which it would have occurred. They are welcome to believe that men performed the heavy labor only because they had been taught to do so, but then they might have to argue that men were also taught to have far greater muscle mass than women.[26] They are welcome to believe that the men hunted only because they had been taught to do so, but then they would have to explain why men hunt and women gather in almost all foraging societies, and why there are such strong relationships between these behaviors and human reproductive biology (see Chapters 3 and 4). They are welcome to believe that males have learned to be better at spatial orientation than females, but then they would have to explain why this difference has been confirmed for people in 35 countries and seven different ethnic groups, why this difference emerges as one of the prime psychological differences between males and females in general, and why boy rats and girl rats show the same cognitive difference.[27]

Novak and Dixon are probably correct in saying that women were expected to "bring an air of civility" to the Donner Party setting. Indeed, Donner Party member William Eddy was impressed by the fact that "the difficulties, dangers, and misfortunes which frequently seemed to prostrate the men, called forth the energies of the gentler sex, and gave to them a sublime elevation of character, which enabled them to abide the most withering blasts of adversity with unshaken firmness."[28] In 1849, Peter Decker's experiences on the gold rush trail led him to observe that "women seem to undergo the hardships of this journey with uncommon philosophy."[29] But to defend their belief that there is no biological basis to the provision of such psychic glue (Chapter 1), Novak and Dixon would have to explain why the tend-and-befriend response to stress, powerfully described by Shelley Taylor and her colleagues, is so widespread among women, and why both women and female rats release greater amounts of oxytocin—the affiliation hormone—under stress than men and male rats do (Chapter 3).[30]

But let us grant them all these things. Let us grant them that women could have learned to have greater body mass and less body fat, that men could have learned to shed less heat when exposed to cold, and so on. Even if we did this, we would still have to contend with the fact that the 87 people in the Donner Party came from remarkably disparate backgrounds. Those people, Will Bagley reminds us, included "Irish, English, Belgian, and German emigrants, infants and elders; and Catholics, Protestants, Mormons, and perhaps an Austrian Jew," as well as Mexican and French frontiersmen.[31] Could people from these remarkably varied backgrounds really have shared the same learned beliefs? And if so, could those beliefs also have been shared by the 1,100 or so members of the Willie and Martin Handcart Companies, people from very different backgrounds whose patterns of mortality were so similar to those of the Donner Party?

Cultural differences were certainly of great importance in determining the outcomes of these three tragedies. There was no set of genes that dictated that people push and pull handcarts some 1,300 miles across the heart of North America. There was no set of genes that created the exceptional organizational abilities of members of the Church of Jesus Christ of Latter-day Saints, abilities that saw to it that mortality within the Willie and Martin Companies was not far higher than it was. It is also true that the construction of gender roles is a very complex affair, that the psychological differences between men and women are far less than is often thought, and that the overlap in the physical capabilities possessed by men and women is substantial.[32]

However, the division of labor among the members of the Donner Party was determined by their biological sex, no matter what kinds of nuances their upbringing might have brought to their behavior in this realm. As Eagly and Wood have argued (Chapter 3), gendered behaviors of this sort follow from biology. Cultures generalize from those differences to determine norms of proper gendered behavior.

I do not expect Novak and Dixon to accept any of this. After all, Dixon also thinks that "because the Donner Party was snowbound for less than five months, the entrapment of these individuals lacks the longevity to serve as a study of either physiological or structural adaptation."[33] This an astonishing statement; it would be even in the absence of decades of research showing how quickly such physiological responses as vasoconstriction, changes in metabolic rate, and shivering can occur in response to cold.[34]

Substantial cultural differences separated the Donner Party from the Willie and Martin Handcart Companies, but the patterns of mortality within those groups are well explained by the very human biology of the people they contained, even as their learned behaviors differed substantially.

GOOD ADVICE?

Shortly after I first wrote about the Donner Party,[35] a reporter for *Outside* magazine asked me what my advice would be to someone going into the mountains on their own during the northern winter. My answer was that it would help to be a healthy woman between 20 and 29 years old.

How good was this advice given the three groups I have studied here? Table 7.2 provides a composite view of the fates of these groups combined. Figure 7.1 plots the mortality results.

In general, what we see in this figure is what we have come to expect to see. Death rates were highest for the very youngest, then declined, then began an inexorable rise that continued until the point where no one survived. In every age class save one, male death rates were higher than those for females, and the sole exception is for those 70 or older, none of whom survived. Excluding that class, the age class mortality rates for males range from 1.3 times that of females for the youngest travelers, to 5.3 times the female rate for those between 15 and 29, and 5.6 times that rate for those between 5 and 9. As a whole, the male mortality rate was 2.6 times that of females (Table 7.3).

My suggestion to *Outside* magazine was not bad. Women between 20 and 29 suffered a 5.3 percent mortality rate, the third lowest of all age class specific rates. The two lower rates were for women between 15 and 19 and girls between 5 and 9, both about 2.8 percent.[36] Given that girls are not likely to have survived at this rate without family support, my advice was good enough. Unless, of course, you get stuck and you need brawny, aggressive risk-taking males to help bail you out and, in so doing, increase your chances of making it out while decreasing theirs.

CONCLUSIONS

There is no need to summarize all that we have seen in this traversal of the fates of the three unfortunate mid-nineteenth-century overland emigrant

TABLE 7.2. Combined mortality rates for the Donner Party and Willie and Martin Handcart Companies.

Age class	Males				Females			
	Survived	Died	Total	Mortality rate (%)	Survived	Died	Total	Mortality rate (%)
1–4	53	15	68	22.1	55	11	66	16.7
5–9	68	12	80	15.0	72	2	74	2.7
10–14	56	9	65	13.8	65	5	70	7.1
15–19	55	10	65	15.4	67	2	69	2.9
20–29	58	23	81	28.4	106	6	112	5.4
30–39	39	18	57	31.6	79	11	90	12.2
40–49	33	22	55	40.0	60	9	69	13.0
50–59	12	22	34	64.7	33	10	43	23.3
60–69	2	19	21	90.5	6	8	14	57.1
70–79	0	5	5	100.0	0	4	4	100.0
Unknown	3	1	4	—	1	0	1	—
Totals	379	156	535	29.2	544	68	612	11.1

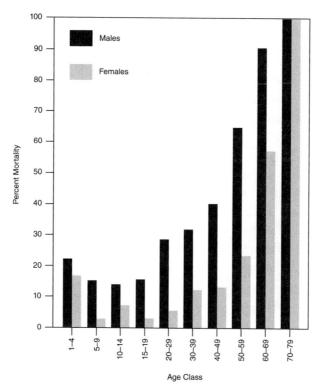

FIGURE 7.1. Mortality rates by age class and sex for the combined membership of the Donner Party and Willie and Martin Handcart Companies.

TABLE 7.3. Mortality rates by sex and age class for the Donner Party and Willie and Martin Handcart Companies combined. N = number of individuals.

| Age class | Mortality rate | | Ratio |
	Male	Female	
1–4 (N = 134)	22.1	16.7	1.3
5–9 (N = 154)	15.0	2.7	5.6
10–14 (N = 135)	13.8	7.1	1.9
15–19 (N = 134)	15.4	2.9	5.3
20–29 (N = 193)	28.4	5.4	5.3
30–39 (N = 147)	31.6	12.2	2.6
40–49 (N = 124)	40.0	13.0	3.1
50–59 (N = 77)	64.7	23.3	2.8
60–69 (N = 35)	90.5	57.1	1.6
70–79 (N = 9)	100.0	100.0	1.0
Total	29.2	11.1	2.6

groups analyzed here. Sex, age, and family structure account extremely well for the general pattern of mortality suffered by these groups. Even the changing proportions of Donner Party women who attempted to walk out in the absence of rescuers is accounted for by biologically driven propensities to take or avoid risk.

People are cultural beings, buffered from environmental assault by complex learned behaviors that provide us—no matter who "us" is—with shelter, food, social contacts, and all those other things that help us survive and reproduce successfully. What we have seen here is what happens when our cultural mechanisms for dealing with certain kinds of assaults—famine and extreme cold—are reduced to the extent that our main protection becomes what our very bodies can provide within contexts structured by social relationships. Human biology takes over, and the results are remarkably predictable.

CHAPTER 7 NOTES

1. Wallace 1996. See Emslie and Hunt 2008 for a more recent qualitative approach to the same issue; the responses given by Emslie and Hunt's subjects share many similarities with those examined by Wallace, including the possibility that males suffer greater stress, have more physically demanding jobs, take poorer care of their health, and are biologically weaker than women.
2. Verbrugge 1985; Mataud 2004; McLean and Anderson 2009; McLean et al. 2011; Cohen and Janicki-Deverts 2012.
3. For the United States, see Jamal et al. 2014; for the world as a whole, see World Bank 2015.
4. Bertakis et al. 2000; Galdas, Cheater, and Marshall 2005. For more nuanced analyses of this phenomenon, see Hunt et al. 2011 and Wang et al. 2013.
5. Bell 1978:152.
6. Ibid., 154.
7. Chislett 1873:321.
8. Allphin 2012:92.

9. Rogerson 1879, 1907c.
10. Allphin 2012:197.
11. Rogerson (1879) was clear on the possible impacts of guarding on the Martin Handcart Company men: "if less night guarding had been done, from Laramie to the Devils Gate, and even from Iowa City to Winter Quarters, and from Winter Quarters to the Devils Gate, the death list, would not have been so great by several, large able bodied men, who seemed at the Commencement of the Journey, able to endure anything. After a man had pulled a hand Cart 20–25-and 30 miles in a day, to go, and tramp around on guard from sundown till midnight, every other night, and sometimes oftener, is more than mortal bone and Sinew Cand [can] stand, and the fact that more men died than women, attests what I have above written" (underlining in original; for more on night guarding, see Rogerson 1907c).
12. Chislett 1873:320.

13. Manly 1977:150.
14. Ibid.; Lingenfelter 1986; Johnson and Johnson 1987.
15. Clint et al. 2012:292. See also Moffat, Hampson, and Hatzipantelis 1998:73.
16. McBurney, Gaulin, Devineni, and Adams 1997; Grön et al. 2000; Silverman, Choi, and Peters 2007; Ngun et al. 2011.
17. Dabbs et al. 1998; Grön et al. 2000; Silverman, Choi, and Peters 2007.
18. Male refrigerator blindness refers to the inability of many males to see things staring them in the face in a refrigerator and, as a result, needing female help to fund such things as milk and eggs. See, for instance, Macnab and Bennett 2005.
19. Clint et al. 2012.
20. During the first escape attempt, males were significantly better represented in the escape party than they were among those who stayed behind, and females were significantly better represented among those who stayed behind (chi-square = 5.05, p = 0.025). During the next two attempts, the ratios of men to women in the escape parties did not differ significantly from those ratios among those who stayed behind (for the November 21 attempt, chi-square = 1.72, p = 0.19; for the Forlorn Hope, chi-square = 0.50, p = 0.48). My count for the Forlorn Hope does not include Charles Burger and William Murphy, who returned to camp the same day the group left.
21. Novak and Dixon 2011:7.
22. Ibid.
23. Ibid., 26.
24. Ibid., 10.
25. Ibid., 7–10.
26. Miller et al. 1993; Arendt 1994; Lassek and Gaulin 2009.

27. Hyde 2005; Silverman, Choi, and Peters 2007. For a curious denial, see Fausto-Sterling 2012:35.
28. Thornton 1986: 29; Johnson 1996:54.
29. Bagley 2012:224.
30. Taylor et al. 2000.
31. Bagley 2010:122.
32. E.g., Hyde 2005, Fausto-Sterling 2012.
33. Dixon 2011:104.
34. See Chapter 3, but also such papers as Tikuisis, Bell, and Jacobs 1991; Aoki et al. 2003; Taniguchi et al. 2011; and Castellani and Young 2016. The research in this area is almost inexhaustibly rich.
35. Grayson 1991.
36. The higher rate for girls between the ages of 10 and 14 is curious but may not be meaningful. It does not occur in the Donner Party but marks both the Willie and Martin Companies. It is curious because it appears in both of these companies and because mortality in human populations does not generally show this spike (Figure 3.5). It may not be meaningful because of the very small sample size involved: 5 mortalities among the 64 girls of this age in the two parties combined. In addition, female mortality in the 10–14 age class is not significantly higher than that in either the 5–9 age class (chi-square = 1.66; p = 0.20) or in the 15–19 age class (chi-square = 1.51, p = 0.22). On the other hand, there is evidence that premenarcheal girls are at a thermoregulatory disadvantage when compared to boys of the same age and to young menarcheal women, perhaps a result of different vasoconstrictive responses and body surface area-to-mass ratios (Klentrou et al. 2004).

LITERATURE CITED

UNATTRIBUTED AUTHORSHIP (CITED IN TEXT BY REFERENCE TITLE)

Arrivals. 1856. *Deseret News*, November 12. Electronic document, https://history.lds.org/overlandtravel/sources/8828/arrivals-deseret-news-weekly-12-nov-1856-285.

A Word with Our Opponents. 1853. *Millennial Star* 15(17):257–260.

Celestial Marriage in Deseret. 1853. *Millennial Star* 15(14):214–216.

From Utah.; Arrival of Judge Kinnev—The Mormon Conference—Mormon Feeling towards the States—Brigham Young's Plans Miscellaneous News. The Exodus of Negroes from the South. 1860. *New York Times*, November 8. Electronic document, http://www.nytimes.com/1860/11/08/news/utah-arrival-judge-kinnev-mormon-conference-mormon-feeling-towards-states.html?pagewanted=all.

History of Sangamon County, Illinois. 1881. Inter-State Publishing, Chicago.

John C. Bennett. 1842. *Millennial Star* 3(6):103–109.

Letter from an Englishman. 1844. *Millennial Star* 4(10):153–155.

Minutes of Conference: A Special Conference of the Elders of the Church of Jesus Christ of Latter-Day-Saints Assembled in the Tabernacle, Great Salt Lake City, August 28th, 1852, 10 o'clock, a.m., Pursuant to Public Notice. 1852. *Deseret News Extra*, September 14. Electronic document, http://hdl.handle.net/2027/njp.32101074862515.

"Stars" and "Journals" for 1857. 1856. *Millennial Star* 18(46):729–730.

The Companies Yet on the Plains. 1857. *Millennial Star* 19(12):186–187.

The Latter-day Saints. 1841. *Millennial Star* 2(8):123.

Weekly Issue of the Star. 1852. *Millennial Star* 14(9):137.

ATTRIBUTED AUTHORSHIP (CITED IN TEXT BY AUTHOR)

Ahmanson, J. 1984. *Secret History: A Translation of* Vor Tids Muhamed, translated by G. L. Archer. Moody Press, Chicago.

Allphin, J. S. 2012. *Tell My Story, Too*. 8th ed. Tell My Story Publishing, Kaysville, UT.

Andrews, T. F. 1968. The controversial Hastings overland guide: A reassessment. *Pacific Historical Review* 37:21–34.

Andrews, T. F. 1971. *The Controversial Career of Lansford Warren Hastings: Pioneer California Promoter and Emigrant Guide*. Ph.D. dissertation, University of Southern California, Los Angeles.

Andrews, T. F. 1973. Lansford W. Hastings and the promotion of the Salt Lake Desert cutoff: A reappraisal. *Western Historical Quarterly* 4:133–150.

Aoki, K., D. P. Stephens, A. R. Saad, and J. M. Johnson. 2003. Cutaneous vasoconstrictor response to whole body skin cooling is altered by time of day. *Journal of Applied Physiology* 94:930–934.

Archer, J. 2009. Does sexual selection explain human sex differences in aggression? *Behavioral and Brain Sciences* 32:249–311.

Arendt, E. A. 1994. Orthopaedic issues for active and athletic women. *Clinics in Sports Medicine* 13:483–503.

Arrington, L. J. 1958. *Great Basin Kingdom: An Economic History of the Latter-day Saints.* Harvard University Press, Cambridge.

Arrington, L. J., and D. Bitton. 1992. *The Mormon Experience: A History of the Latter-day Saints.* 2nd ed. University of Illinois Press, Urbana.

Austad, S. N. 2006. Why women live longer than men: Sex differences in longevity. *Gender Medicine* 3(2):79–92.

Austad, S. N. 2011. Sex differences in longevity and aging. In *Handbook of the Biology of Aging*, edited by E. J. Masoro and S. N. Austad, pp. 479–495. 7th ed. Academic Press, San Diego.

Austad, S. N. 2015. The human prenatal sex ratio: A major surprise. *Proceedings of the National Academy of Sciences* 112:4839–4840.

Bae, K. A., N. Y. An, Y. W. Kwon, C. Kim, C. S. Yoon, S. C. Park, and C. K. Kim. 2003. Muscle fibre size and capillarity in Korean diving women. *Acta Physiologica Scandinavia* 179:167–172.

Bagley, W. 2009. "One long funeral march": A revisionist's view of the Mormon handcart disasters. *Journal of Mormon History* 35:50–115.

Bagley, W. 2010. *So Rugged and Mountainous: Blazing the Trails to Oregon and California, 1812–1848.* University of Oklahoma Press, Norman.

Bagley, W. 2012. *With Golden Visions Bright before Them: Trails to the Mining West, 1849–1852.* University of Oklahoma Press, Norman.

Bagley, W. 2014. *South Pass: Gateway to a Continent.* University of Oklahoma Press, Norman.

Baker, M. D., Jr., and J. K. Maner. 2008. Risk-taking as a situationally sensitive male mating strategy. *Evolution and Human Behavior* 29:391–395.

Baker, M. D., Jr., and J. K. Maner. 2009. Male risk-taking as a context-sensitive signaling device. *Journal of Experimental Social Psychology* 45:1136–1139.

Bancroft, H. H. 1886. *History of the Pacific States of North America*, Vol. XXI. *California*, Vol. IV: 1840–1845. A. L. Bancroft, San Francisco.

Bancroft, H. H. 1889. *The Works of Hubert Howe Bancroft*, Vol. XXVI. *History of Utah: 1540–1886.* History Company, San Francisco.

Barrett, E. L. B., and D. S. Richardson. 2011. Sex differences in telomeres and lifespan. *Aging Cell* 10:913–921.

Bartelink, M. L., A. De Wit, H. Wollersheim, A. Theeuwes, and T. Thien. 1993. Skin vascular reactivity in healthy subjects: Influence of hormonal status. *Journal of Applied Physiology* 74:727–732.

Bartholomew, R., and L. J. Arrington. 1993. *Rescue of the 1856 Handcart Companies.* Revised ed. Charles Redd Center for Western Studies, Brigham Young University, Provo.

Bashore, M. L., and L. Haslam. n.d. *1856, James G. Willie Company: Company Members who Died on the Trek to Utah*. Manuscript on file at the History Department Library, Church of Jesus Christ of Latter-day Saints, Salt Lake City.

Bashore, M. L., H. D. Tolley, and the BYU Pioneer Mortality Team. 2014. Mortality on the Mormon Trail, 1847–1868. *BYU Studies Quarterly* 53(4):109–123.

Becker, S. W., and A. H. Eagly. 2004. The heroism of women and men. *American Psychologist* 59:163–178.

Beekman, M., et al. (40 authors). 2013. Genome-wide linkage analysis for human longevity: Genetics of Healthy Aging study. *Aging Cell* 12:184–193.

Bell, S. J. 1978. *Life History and Writings of John Jaques*. Ricks College Press, Rexburg, ID.

Bennett, J. C. 1842. Astounding Disclosures! Letters from Gen. Bennett. *Sangamo Journal* 10(46), 8 July. Electronic document, http://www.sidneyrigdon.com/dbroadhu/IL/sang1842.htm#0114.

Bergen G., L. H. Chen, M. Warner, and L. A. Fingerhut. 2008. *Injury in the United States: 2007 Chartbook*. National Center for Health Statistics, Hyattsville, Maryland. Electronic document, http://www.cdc.gov/nchs/data/misc/injury2007.pdf.

Berkman, L. F. 1984. Assessing the physical health effects of social networks and social support. *Annual Review of Public Health* 5:413–432.

Berkman, L. F., and S. L. Syme. 1979. Social networks, host resistance, and mortality: A nine-year follow-up study of Alameda County residents. *American Journal of Epidemiology* 109:186–204.

Berko, J., D. D. Ingram, S. Saha, and J. D. Parker. 2014. Deaths attributed to heat, cold, and other weather events in the United States, 2006–2010. *National Health Statistics Reports* 76:1–15.

Bertakis, K. D., R. Azari, L. J. Helms, E. J. Callahan, and J. A. Robbins. 2000. Gender differences in the utilization of health care services. *Journal of Family Practice* 49:147–152.

Betz, M. J..and S. Enerbäck. 2015. Human brown adipose tissue: What we have learned so far. *Diabetes* 64:2352–2360.

Bigler, D. L. 1998. *Forgotten Kingdom: The Mormon Theocracy in the American West, 1847–1896*. Arthur H. Clark, Spokane.

Black, S. L. W. 1980. *Members of the Willie and Martin Handcart Companies of 1856: A Sesquicentennial Remembrance*. Manuscript on file at the History Department Library, Church of Jesus Christ of Latter-day Saints, Salt Lake City.

Bliege Bird, R., and E. A. Smith. 2005. Signaling theory, strategic interaction, and symbolic capitol. *Current Anthropology* 46:221–248.

Bloor, I. D., and M. E. Symonds. 2014. Sexual dimorphism in white and brown adipose tissue with obesity and inflammation. *Hormones and Behavior* 66:95–103.

Bogue, D. J. 1969. *Principles of Demography*. Wiley, New York.

Brannigan, D., I. R. Rogers, I. Jacobs, A. Montgomery, A. Williams, and N. Khangure. 2009. Hypothermia is a significant medical risk of mass participation long-distance open water swimming. *Wilderness and Environmental Medicine* 20:14–18.

Brody, J. E. 1996. Sex and the Survival of the Fittest: Calamities are a Disaster for Men. *New York Times*, 24 April.

Brooks, J., ed. 1964. *On the Mormon Frontier: The Diary of Hosea Stout, 1844–1861*, Vol. 2: 1848–1861. University of Utah Press, Salt Lake City.

Brown, D. J. 2009. *The Indifferent Stars Above: The Harrowing Saga of the Donner Party.* HarperLuxe, New York.

Brown, J. H., and A. K. Lee. 1969. Bergmann's rule and climatic adaptation in woodrats (*Neotoma*). *Evolution* 23:329–338.

Brown, J. K. 1970. A note on the division of labor by sex. *American Anthropologist* 72:1073–1078.

Bryant, E. 1985. *What I Saw in California.* Facsimile reprint of the 1848 edition. University of Nebraska Press, Lincoln.

Burbank, V. K. 1987. Female aggression in cross-cultural perspective. *Behavior Science Research* 21:70–100.

Burbank, V. K. 1994. *Fighting Women: Anger and Aggression in Aboriginal Australia.* University of California Press, Berkeley.

Burse, R. L. 1979. Sex differences in human thermoregulatory response to heat and cold stress. *Human Factors* 21:687–699.

Burton, R. T. 1856. Camp Journal of Capt. Robert T. Burton's Relief Train. Journal History of the Church, November 30, 1856. Manuscript on file at the History Department Library, Church of Jesus Christ of Latter-day Saints, Salt Lake City (hereafter Journal History, date).

Camm, E. W. [Elizabeth Sermon]. 1892. Letter, San Francisco, California, to "My Dear Children," March 16. Electronic document, https://history.lds.org/overlandtravels /sources/7527/camm-elizabeth-whittear-sermon-letter-san-francisco-california-to -my-dear-children-1892-march-16.

Camp, C. L., ed. 1960. *James Clyman, Frontiersman.* Champoeg Press, Portland.

Campbell, A. 1993. *Men, Women, and Aggression.* Basic Books, New York.

Carey, C. H. 1932. Historical note. In *The Emigrants' Guide to Oregon and California,* by L. W. Hastings, pp. vii–xxii. Princeton University Press, Princeton.

Caro, T. M., and D. W. Sellen. 1990. The reproductive advantages of fat in women. *Ethology and Sociobiology* 11:51–66.

Carter, L. 1995. The Mormon handcart companies. *Overland Journal* 13:2–18.

Castellani, J. W., and A. J. Young. 2016. Human physiological responses to cold exposure: Acute responses and acclimatization to prolonged exposure. *Autonomic Neuroscience: Basic and Clinical* 196:63–74.

Celi, F. S., T. N. Le, and B. Ni. 2015. Physiology and relevance of human adaptive thermogenesis response. *Trends in Endocrinology & Metabolism* 26: 238–247.

Centers for Disease Control and Prevention. 1985. Perspectives in disease prevention and health promotion hypothermia-associated deaths—United States, 1968–1980. *Morbidity and Mortality Weekly Report* 34(50):753–754.

Chaffin, T. 2002. *Pathfinder: John Charles Frémont and the Course of American Empire.* Hill and Wang, New York.

Chen, K. Y., et al. (11 authors). 2013. Brown fat activation mediates cold-induced thermogenesis in adult humans in response to a mild decrease in ambient temperature. *Journal of Clinical Endocrinology & Metabolism* 98(7):E1218–E1223.

Chen, Y.-F., C.-Y. Wu, C.-H. Kao, and R.-F. Tsai. 2010. Longevity and lifespan control in mammals: Lessons from the mouse. *Ageing Research Reviews* 9 (Supplement):S28–S35.

Chislett, J. 1873. Mr. Chislett's narrative. In *The Rocky Mountain Saints,* by T. B. H. Stenhouse, pp. 312–332. Appleton, New York.

Christy, H. A. 1997–1998. Weather, disaster, and responsibility: An essay on the Willie and Martin Handcart story. *BYU Studies* 37:7–74.

Chung, W.-H., R.-L. Dao, L.-K. Dhen, and S.-L. Hung. 2010. The role of genetic variants in human longevity. *Ageing Research Reviews* 9 (Supplement):S67–S78.

Clayton, W. 1921. *William Clayton's Journal: A Daily Record of the Journey of the Original Company of "Mormon" Pioneers from Nauvoo, Illinois, to the Valley of the Great Salt Lake.* Deseret News, Salt Lake City. Electronic document, https://archive.org /details/williamclaytonsjooclay.

Clayton, W. 1983. *The Latter-day Saints' Emigrants' Guide,* edited by S. B. Kimball. Patrice Press, St. Louis.

Clint, E. K., E. Sober, T. Garland, Jr., and J. S. Rhodes. 2012. Male superiority in spatial navigation: Adaptation or side effect? *Quarterly Review of Biology* 87:289–313.

Cobey, K. D., G. Stulp, F. Laan, A. Buunk, and T. V. Pollet. 2013. Sex differences in risk taking behavior among Dutch cyclists. *Evolutionary Psychology* 11:350–364.

Cohen, S., and D. Janicki-Deverts. 2012. Who's stressed? Distributions of psychological stress in the United Sates in probability samples from 1983, 2006, and 2009. *Journal of Applied Social Psychology* 42:1320–1334.

Collins, K. J., C. Dore, A. N. Exton-Smith, R. H. Fox, I. C. MacDonald, and P. M. Woodward. 1977. Accidental hypothermia and impaired temperature homeostasis in the elderly. *British Medical Journal* 1:353–356.

Cooke, P. St. G. 1859. *Scenes and Adventures in the Army; or, Romance of Military Life.* Lindsay and Blakiston, Philadelphia.

Cooper, A., and E. L. Smith. 2011. *Homicide Trends in the United States, 1980–2008: Annual Rates for 2009 and 2010.* NCJ 236018. Bureau of Justice Statistics, U.S. Department of Justice. Electronic document, http://www.bjs.gov/content/pub /pdf/htus8008.pdf.

Cowgill, L. W., C. D. Eleazer, B. M. Auerbach, D. H. Temple, and K. Okazaki. 2012. Developmental variation in ecogeographic body proportions. *American Journal of Physical Anthropology* 148:557–570.

Cypess, A. M., et al. (12 authors). 2009. Identification and importance of brown adipose tissue in adult humans. *New England Journal of Medicine* 360:1509–1517.

Dabbs, J. M., E.-L. Chang, R. A. Strong, and R. Milun. 1998. Spatial ability, navigation strategy, and geographic knowledge among men and women. *Evolution and Human Behavior* 19:89–98.

Daly, M., and M. Wilson. 1983. *Sex, Evolution, and Behavior.* 2nd ed. Willard Grant Press, Boston.

Daly, M., and M. Wilson. 1988. *Homicide.* Aldine de Gruyter, New York.

Davie, G. S., M. G. Baker, S. Hales, and J. B Carlin. 2007. Trends and determinants of excess winter mortality in New Zealand: 1980 to 2000. *BMC Public Health* 7:263, doi:10.1186/1471-2458-7-263.

Dayan, T., E. Tchernov, Y. Yom-Tov, and D. Simberloff. 1989. Ecological character displacement in Saharo-Arabian *Vulpes*: Outfoxing Bergman's Rule. *Oikos* 55:263–272.

DeBow, J. D. B. 1854. *Statistical View of the United States . . . Being a Compendium of the Seventh Census. . . .* Washington, DC.

DeLafosse, P. H. 1994. *Trailing the Pioneers: A Guide to Utah's Emigrant Trails, 1829–1869.* Utah State University Press, Logan.

DeMaster, D. P., and I. Stirling. 1981. *Ursus maritimus. Mammalian Species* 145:1–7.

Demerath, E. W., et al. (11 authors). 2007. Anatomical patterning of visceral adipose tissue: Race, sex, and age variation. *Obesity* 15:2984–2993.

Deschênes, O., and M. Greenstone. 2011. Climate change, mortality, and adaptation: Evidence from annual fluctuations in weather in the US. *American Economic Journal: Applied Economics* 3(4):152–185.

Deschênes, O., and E. Moretti. 2009. Extreme weather events, mortality, and migration. *Review of Economics and Statistics* 91:659–681.

Dewey, K. G. 1997. Energy and protein requirements during lactation. *Annual Review of Nutrition* 17:19–36.

Dirck, B. 2007. *Lincoln the Lawyer*. University of Illinois Press, Chicago.

Dixon, K. J. 2011. An archaeology of despair. In *An Archaeology of Desperation: Exploring the Donner Party's Alder Creek Camp*, edited by K. J. Dixon, J. M. Schablitsky, and S. A. Novak, pp. 101–131. University of Oklahoma Press, Norman.

Dixon, K. J., J. M. Schablitsky, and S. A. Novak, editors. 2011. *An Archaeology of Desperation: Exploring the Donner Party's Alder Creek Camp*. University of Oklahoma Press, Norman.

Dorius, G. L. 1997. Crossroads in the West: The intersections of the Donner Party and the Mormons. *Nauvoo Journal* 9:17–27.

Driver, H. E. 1969. *Indians of North America*. 2nd ed., revised. University of Chicago Press, Chicago.

Dupre, M. E., A. N. Beck, and S. O. Meadows. 2009. Marital trajectories and mortality among US adults. *American Journal of Epidemiology* 170:546–555.

Dyson, T., and C. Ó Gráda. 2002. Introduction. In *Famine Demography: Perspectives from the Past and Present*, edited by T. Dyson and C. Ó Gráda, pp. 1–18. Oxford University Press, Oxford.

Eagly, A. H., and W. Wood. 2009. Sexual selection does not provide an adequate theory of sex differences in aggression. *Behavioral and Brain Sciences* 32:276–277.

Edler von Eyben, F., C. Graugaard, and M. Vaeth. 2005. All-cause mortality and mortality of myocardial infarction for 989 legally castrated men. *European Journal of Epidemiology* 20:863–869.

Egan, F. 1985. *Frémont: Explorer for a Restless Nation*. University of Nevada Press, Reno.

Emslie, C., and K. Hunt. 2008. The weaker sex? Exploring lay understandings of gender differences in life expectancy: A qualitative study. *Social Science & Medicine* 67:808–816.

Eskes, T., and C. Haanen. 2007. Why do women live longer than men? *European Journal of Obstetrics & Gynecology and Reproductive Biology* 133:126–133.

Eveleth, P. B., and J. M. Tanner. 1990. *Worldwide Variation in Human Growth*. 2nd ed. Cambridge University Press, Cambridge.

Everitt, B. S. 1977. *The Analysis of Contingency Tables*. Wiley and Sons, New York.

Fausto-Sterling, A. 2012. *Sex/Gender: Biology in a Social World*. Routledge, New York.

Florez-Duquet, M., and R. B. McDonald. 1998. Cold-induced thermoregulation and biological aging. *Physiological Reviews* 78:339–358.

Florido, R., T. Tchkonia, and J. L. Kirkland. 2011. Aging and adipose tissue. In *Handbook of the Biology of Aging*, edited by E. J. Masoro and S. N. Austad, pp. 119–139. 7th ed. Academic Press, San Diego.

Foster, F., and M. Collard. 2013. A reassessment of Bergmann's rule in modern humans. *PLoS One* 8(8):e72269.

Frémont, J. C. 1845. *Report of the Exploring Expedition to the Rocky Mountains in the Year 1842, and to Oregon and North California in the Years 1843–'44.* Gales and Seaton, Washington, DC.

Frisancho, A. R. 1993. *Human Adaptation and Accommodation.* University of Michigan Press, Ann Arbor.

Galdas, P. M., F. Cheater, and P. Marshall. 2005. Men and health-seeking behavior: Literature review. *Journal of Advanced Nursing* 49:616–623.

Gilbert, B. 1983. *Westering Man: The Life of Joseph Walker.* University of Oklahoma Press, Norman.

Goldman, N. 1993. Marriage selection and mortality patterns: Inferences and fallacies. *Demography* 30:189–208.

Gove, W. R. 1973. Sex, marital status, and mortality. *American Journal of Sociology* 79:45–67.

Graham, T. E. 1988. Thermal, metabolic, and cardiovascular changes in men and women during cold stress. *Medicine & Science in Sports & Exercise* 20 (Supplement):S185–S192.

Graham, T. E., M. Viswanathan, J. P. Van Dijk, A. Bonen, and J. C. George. 1989. Thermal and metabolic responses to cold by men and eumenorrheic and amenorrheic women. *Journal of Applied Physiology* 67:282–290.

Grant, G. D. 1856. The Companies Yet on the Plains. *Deseret News*, November 19. Journal History, November 30, 1856. Electronic document, https://history.lds.org /overlandtravels/sources/8750/grant-george-d-the-companies-yet-on-the-plains -deseret-news-weekly-19-nov-1856-293.

Grayson, D. K. 1991. Donner Party deaths: A demographic assessment. *Journal of Anthropological Research* 46:223–242.

Grayson, D. K. 1994a. Differential mortality and the Donner Party disaster. *Evolutionary Anthropology* 2:151–159.

Grayson, D. K. 1994b. *Willie Handcart Company Membership List.* Manuscript on file at the History Department Library, Church of Jesus Christ of Latter-day Saints, Salt Lake City.

Grayson, D. K. 1996. Human mortality in a natural disaster: The Willie Handcart Company. *Journal of Anthropological Research* 52:185–205.

Grayson, D. K. 2011. *The Great Basin: A Natural Prehistory.* University of California Press, Berkeley.

Grayson, D. K. 2016. *Giant Sloths and Sabertooth Cats: Extinct Mammals and the Archaeology of the Ice Age Great Basin.* University of Utah Press, Salt Lake City.

Grebenkemper, J., K. Johnson, and A. Morris. 2012. Locating the grave of John Snyder: Field research on a Donner Party death. *Overland Journal* 30:92–108.

Greene, T. C., and P. A. Bell. 1987. Environmental stress. In *Sex Differences in Human Performance*, edited by M. A. Baker, pp. 81–106. Wiley and Sons, Chichester.

Grün, G., A. P. Wunderlich, M. Spitzer, R. Tomcak, and M. W. Riepe. 2000. Brain activation during human navigation: Gender-different neural networks as substrate of performance. *Nature Neuroscience* 3:404–408.

Gudde, E. G., and E. K. Gudde, editors. 1961. *From St. Louis to Sutter's Fort, 1846, by Heinrich Lienhard.* University of Oklahoma Press, Norman.

Hafen, L. R. 1973. *Broken Hand: The Life of Thomas Fitzpatrick; Mountain Man, Guide and Indian Agent.* Old West Publishing, Denver.

Hafen, L. R., and A. W. Hafen. 1992. *Handcarts to Zion: The Story of a Unique Western Migration, 1856–1860.* University of Nebraska Press, Lincoln.

Hallwas, J. E., and R. D. Launius. 1995. *Cultures in Conflict: A Documentary History of the Mormon War in Illinois.* Utah State University Press, Logan.

Hamilton, J. B., and G. E. Mestler. 1969. Mortality and survival: Comparison of eunuchs with intact men and women in a mentally retarded population. *Journal of Gerontology* 24:395–411.

Hammond, L. E., S. Cuttell, P. Nunley, and J. Meyler. 2014. Anthropometric characteristics and sex influence magnitude of skin cooling following exposure to whole body cryotherapy. *Biomedical Research International* 2014:628724.

Hanks, E. K. 1856. Ephraim K. Hanks' narrative. Journal History, November 30, 1856.

Hardesty, D. L. 1997. *The Archaeology of the Donner Party.* University of Nevada Press, Reno.

Harms, M., and P. Seale. 2013. Brown and beige fat: Development, function, and therapeutic potential. *Nature Medicine* 19:1252–1263.

Harrison, G. A., J. M. Tanner, D. R. Pilbeam, and P. T. Baker. 1988. *Human Biology.* 3rd ed. Oxford University Press, Oxford.

Hashiguchi, N., Y. Feng, and Y. Tochihara. 2010. Gender differences in thermal comfort and mental performance at different vertical air temperatures. *European Journal of Applied Physiology* 109:41–48.

Hasselstrom, L. M., editor. 1984. *Journal of a Mountain Man: James Clyman.* Mountain Press, Missoula.

Hastings, L. W. 1845. *The Emigrants' Guide to Oregon and California.* Conclin, Cincinnati.

Hattori, K., N. Numata, M. Ikoma, A. Matsuzaka, and R. R. Danielson. 1991. Sex differences in the distribution of subcutaneous and internal fat. *Human Biology* 63:53–63.

Hawkes, K. 1990. Why do men hunt? Benefits for risky choices. In *Risk and Uncertainty in Tribal and Peasant Economies*, edited by E. Cashdan, pp. 145–166. Westview Press, Boulder.

Hawkes, K. 1993. Why hunter-gatherers work: An ancient version of the problem of public goods. *Current Anthropology* 34:341–361.

Hawkes, K., and R. Bliege Bird. 2002. Showing off, handicap signaling, and the evolution of men's work. *Evolutionary Anthropology* 11:58–67.

Hawkins, B. R., and D. B. Madsen. 1990. *Excavation of the Donner-Reed Wagons: Historic Archaeology along the Hastings Cutoff.* University of Utah Press, Salt Lake City.

Haymes, E. M., and C. L. Wells. 1986. *Environment and Human Performance.* Human Kinetics Publishers, Champaign, IL.

Hazzard, W. R. 1986. Biological basis of the sex differential in longevity. *Journal of the American Geriatrics Society* 34:455–471.

Hill, K., and A. M. Hurtado. 1996. *Ache Life History: The Ecology and Demography of a Foraging People.* Aldine de Gruyter, New York.

Hionidou, V. 2002. "Send us either food or coffins": The 1941–2 famine on the Aegean Island of Syros. In *Famine Demography: Perspectives from the Past and Present,* edited by T. Dyson and C. Ó Gráda, pp. 181–203. Oxford University Press, Oxford.

Hodgson, K., L. Barton, M. Darling, V. Antao, F. A. Kim, and A. Monavvari. 2015. Pets' impact on your patients' health: Leveraging benefits and mitigating risk. *Journal of the American Board of Family Medicine* 28:526–534.

Holt-Lunstad, J., T. B. Smith, and J. B. Layton. 2010. Social relationships and mortality risk: A meta-analytic review. *PLoS Medicine* 7(7):e1000316.

Hopkins, S. W. 1969. *Life among the Paiutes: Their Wrongs and Claims*. Facsimile reprint of the 1883 edition. Chalfant Press, Bishop, CA.

Houghton, E. P. D. 1997. *The Expedition of the Donner Party and Its Tragic Fate*. Facsimile reprint of the 1911 edition. University of Nebraska Press, Lincoln.

House, J. S., K. R. Landis, and D. Umberson. 1988. Social relationships and health. *Science* 241:540–545.

House, J. S., C. Robbins, and H. L. Metzner. 1982. The association of social relationships and activities with mortality: Prospective evidence from the Tecumseh Community Health Study. *American Journal of Epidemiology* 116:123–140.

Hrdy, S. B. 1981. *The Woman That Never Evolved*. Harvard University Press, Cambridge.

Hu, Y., and N. Goldman. 1990. Mortality differentials by marital status: An international comparison. *Demography* 27:233–250.

Huang, J., J. Wang, and W. Yu. 2014. The lag effects and vulnerabilities of temperature effects on cardiovascular disease mortality in a subtropical climate zone in China. *International Journal of Environmental Research and Public Health* 11:3982–3994.

Hudders, L., C. De Backer, M. Fisher, and P. Vyncke. 2014. The rival wears Prada: Luxury consumption as a female competition strategy. *Evolutionary Psychology* 12:570–587.

Hummer, R. A., C. G. Ellison, R. G. Rogers, B. E. Moulton, and R. R. Romero. 2004. Religious involvement and adult mortality in the United States: Review and perspective. *Southern Medical Journal* 97:1223–1230.

Hummer, R. A., R. G. Rodgers, C. B. Nam, and C. G. Ellison. 1999. Religious involvement and U.S. adult mortality. *Demography* 36:273–285.

Hunt, K., J. Adamson, C. Hewitt, and I. Nazareth. 2011. Do women consult more than men? A review of gender and consultation for back pain and headache. *Journal of Health Services Research and Policy* 16:108–117.

Hyde, J. S. 2005. The gender similarities hypothesis. *American Psychologist* 60:581–592.

Ide, S. 1944. *The Conquest of California: A Biography of William B. Ide*. Biobooks, Oakland.

Jackson, D., and M. L. Spence, editors. 1970. *The Expeditions of John Charles Frémont*, Vol. 1: *Travels from 1838 to 1844*. University of Illinois Press, Urbana.

Jamal, A., I. T. Agaku, E. O'Connor, B. A. King, J. B. Kenemer, and L. Neff. 2014. Current cigarette smoking among adults—United States, 2005–2013. *Morbidity and Mortality Weekly Report* 63(47):1108–1112. Electronic document, http://www.cdc.gov/mmwr/preview/mmwrhtml/mm6347a4.htm?s_cid=mm6347a4_w#tab.

Jaques, J. 1853. Polygamy. *Millennial Star* 15(7):97–102, 15(9)133–136, 15(10):145–149, and 15(11):161–166.

Jaques, J. (as J. J.). 1878a. Some Reminiscences. *Salt Lake Daily Herald*, December 8, 1. Electronic document, https://history.lds.org/overlandtravels/sources/7743/j-aques-john-some-reminiscences-salt-lake-daily-herald-8-december-1878-1.

Jaques, J. (as J. J.). 1878b. Some Reminiscences. *Salt Lake Daily Herald*, December 15, 1. Electronic document, https://history.lds.org/overlandtravels/sources/7744/j-aques-john-some-reminiscences-salt-lake-daily-herald-15-december-1878-1.

Jaques, J. (as J. J.). 1878c. Some Reminiscences. *Salt Lake Daily Herald*, December 22, 1. Electronic document, https://history.lds.org/overlandtravels/sources/7745/j-aques-j -ohn-some-reminiscences-salt-lake-daily-herald-22-dec-1878-1.

Jensen, A., compiler. n.d. *Handcart companies biographical information.* Manuscript on file at the History Department Library, Church of Jesus Christ of Latter-day Saints, Salt Lake City.

Johnson, K. 1994. The Pioneer Palace car: Adventures in western mythmaking. *Crossroads Newsletter* (Summer):5–8.

Johnson, K., editor. 1996. *"Unfortunate Emigrants": Narratives of the Donner Party.* Utah State University Press, Logan.

Johnson, K. 2011a. Sufferers in the mountains: The Donner Party disaster. In *An Archaeology of Desperation: Exploring the Donner Party's Alder Creek Camp,* edited by K. J. Dixon, J. M. Schablitsky, and S. A. Novak, pp. 31–62. University of Oklahoma Press, Norman.

Johnson, K. 2011b. The aftermath of tragedy: The Donner camps in later years. In *An Archaeology of Desperation: Exploring the Donner Party's Alder Creek Camp,* edited by K. J. Dixon, J. M. Schablitsky, and S. A. Novak, pp. 63–86. University of Oklahoma Press, Norman.

Johnson, L., and J. Johnson. 1987. *Escape from Death Valley.* University of Nevada Press, Reno.

Jones, D. W. 1890. *Forty Years among the Indians.* Juvenile Instructor's Office, Salt Lake City.

Jones, J. H., R. Bliege Bird, and D. W. Bird. 2013. To kill a kangaroo: Understanding the decision to pursue high-risk/high-gain resources. *Proceedings of the Royal Society B* 280, doi:20131210.

Kaciuba-Uscilko, H., and R. Grucza. 2001. Gender differences in thermoregulation. *Current Opinion in Clinical Nutrition and Metabolic Care* 4:533–536.

Kane, T. 1851. The Mormons. *Millennial Star* 13(14):218–221.

Kaplan, R. M., and M. T. Toshima. 1990. The functional effects of social relationships on chronic illnesses and disability. In *Social Support: An Interactional View,* edited by B. R. Sarason, I. G. Sarason, and G. R. Pierce, pp. 427–453. Wiley, New York.

Karastergiou, K., S. R. Smith, A. S. Greenberg, and S. K. Fried. 2012. Sex differences in human adipose tissues—the biology of pear shape. *Biology of Sex Differences* 3(1):13, doi:10.1186/2042-6410-3-13.

Karjalainen, S. 2012. Thermal comfort and gender: A literature review. *Indoor Air* 22:96–109.

Keatinge, W. R. 1960. The effects of subcutaneous fat and of previous exposure to cold on the body temperature, peripheral blood flow and metabolic rate of men in cold water. *Journal of Physiology* 153:166–178.

Keatinge, W. R. 1978. Body fat and cooling rates in relation to age. In *Environmental Stress: Individual Human Adaptations,* edited by L. J. Folinsbee, J. A. Wagner, J. F. Borgia, B. L. Drinkwater, J. A. Gliner, and J. F. Bedi, pp. 299–302. Academic Press, New York.

Keatinge, W. R., M. Khartchenko, N. Lando, and V. Lioutov. 2001. Hypothermia during sports swimming in water below 11°C. *British Journal of Sports Medicine* 35:352–353.

Kellerman, A. L., and J. A. Mercy. 1992. Men, women, and murder: Gender-specific differences in rates of fatal violence and victimization. *Journal of Trauma* 33:1–5.

Kennedy, J. C. G. 1864. *Population of the United States in 1860*. Government Printing Office, Washington, DC.

Kennedy, S., J. K. Kiecolt-Glaser, and R. Glaser. 1990. Social support, stress, and the immune system. In *Social Support: An Interactional View*, edited by B. R. Sarason, I. G. Sarason, and G. R. Pierce, pp. 253–266. Wiley, New York.

Kenney, K. W., and T. A. Munce. 2003. Aging and human temperature regulation. *Journal of Applied Physiology* 95:2598–2603.

Keys, A., J. Brozek, A. Henschel, O. Mickelsen, and H. L. Taylor. 1950. *The Biology of Human Starvation*, Vol. 2. University of Minnesota Press, Minneapolis.

Kilbourne, E. M. 1997. Cold environments. In *The Public Health Consequences of Disasters*, edited by E. K. Noki, pp. 270–286. Oxford University Press, New York.

Kimball, H. C. 1856. Remarks by President Heber C. Kimball. Journal History, November 2, 1856.

King, J. A. 1992. *Winter of Entrapment: A New Look at the Donner Party*. P. D. Meany, Toronto.

King, J. A. 1994. *Winter of Entrapment: A New Look at the Donner Party*. Revised ed. K&K Publications, Lafayette, California.

King, J. A. 1998. *Winter of Entrapment: A New Look at the Donner Party*. 3rd ed. K&K Publications, Lafayette, California.

Kingma, B., A. Frijns, and W. van Marken Lichtenbelt. 2012. The thermoneutral zone: Implications for metabolic studies. *Frontiers in Bioscience* E4:1975–1985.

Kingwell, E., M. van der Kop, Y. Zhao, A. Shirani, F. Zhu, J. Oger, and H. Tremlett. 2012. Relative mortality and survival in multiple sclerosis: Findings from British Columbia, Canada. *Journal of Neurology, Neurosurgery, and Psychiatry* 83:61–66.

Kirkwood, T. B. L. 2005. Understanding the odd science of aging. *Cell* 120:437–447.

Kisker, E. E., and N. Goldman. 1987. Perils of single life and benefits of marriage. *Social Biology* 34:135–152.

Klentrou, P., M. Cunliffe, J. Slack, B. Wilk, O. Bar-Or, M. J. De Souza, and M. Plyley. 2004. Temperature regulation during rest and exercise in the cold in premenarcheal and menarcheal girls. *Journal of Applied Physiology* 96:1393–1398.

Kobrin, F. E., and G. E. Hendershot. 1977. Do family ties reduce mortality? Evidence from the United States, 1966–1968. *Journal of Marriage and the Family* 39:737–745.

Korns, J. R., and D. L. Morgan, editors. 1994. *West from Fort Bridger: The Pioneering of Immigrant Trails across Utah, 1846–1850*. Revised and updated by W. Bagley and H. Schindler. Utah State University Press, Logan.

Kruger, D., and R. M. Nesse. 2004. Sexual selection and the male:female mortality ratio. *Evolutionary Psychology* 2:66–85.

Kurtén, B. 1965. The Pleistocene Felidae of Florida. *Bulletin of the Florida State Museum* 9:215–273.

Lancaster, H. O. 1990. *Expectations of Life: A Study in the Demography, Statistics, and History of World Mortality*. Springer-Verlag, New York.

Langley, R. L. 2009. Human fatalities resulting from dog attacks in the United States, 1979–2005. *Wilderness & Environmental Medicine* 20:19–25.

Lassek, W. D., and S. J. C. Gaulin. 2006. Changes in body fat distribution in relation to parity in American women: A covert form of maternal depletion. *American Journal of Physical Anthropology* 131:295–302.

Lassek, W. D., and S. J. C. Gaulin. 2009. Costs and benefits of fat-free muscle mass in men: Relationship to mating success, dietary requirements, and native immunity. *Evolution and Human Behavior* 30:322–28.

Laughlin, G. A., E. Barrett-Connor, and J. Bergstrom. 2008. Low serum testosterone and mortality in older men. *Journal of Clinical Endocrinology & Metabolism* 93:68–75.

Lendrem, B. A. D., D. W. Lendrem, A. Gray, and J. D. Isaacs. 2014. The Darwin Awards: Sex differences in idiotic behavior. *British Medical Journal* 349:g7094, doi:10.1136/bmj.g7094.

Leonard, W. R., and P. T. Katzmarzyk. 2010. Body size and shape: Climatic and nutritional influences on human body morphology. In *Human Evolutionary Biology*, edited by M. P. Muehlenbein, pp. 157–169. Cambridge University Press, Cambridge.

Levine, G. N., K. Allen, L. T. Braun, H. E. Christian, E. Friedmann, K. A. Taubert, S. A. Thomas, D. L. Wells, and R. A. Lange. 2013. Pet ownership and cardiovascular risk: A scientific statement from the American Heart Association. *Circulation* 127, doi:10.1161/CIR.0b013e31829201e1.

Li, G., S. P. Baker, J. A. Langlois, and G. D. Kelen. 1998. Are female drivers safer? An application of the decomposition method. *Epidemiology* 9:379–384.

Li, K., M. Nakajima, I. Ibañez-Tallon, and N. Heintz. 2016. A cortical circuit for sexually dimorphic oxytocin-dependent anxiety behaviors. *Cell* 167:60–72.

Lillard, L. A., and C. W. A. Panis. 1996. Marital status and mortality: The role of health. *Demography* 33:313–327.

Lingenfelter, R. E. 1986. *Death Valley and the Amargosa: A Land of Illusion*. University of California Press, Berkeley.

Liu, H., and D. J. Umberson. 2008. The times they are a changin': Marital status and health differentials from 1972 to 2003. *Journal of Health and Social Behavior* 49:239–253.

Lockley, F. n.d. *Across the Plains by Prairie Schooner: Personal Narrative of B. F. Bonney of His Trip to Sutter's Fort, California, in 1846, and of his Pioneer Experiences in Oregon during the Days of Oregon's Provisional Government*. Koke-Tiffany, Eugene. Electronic document, https://archive.org/stream/acrossplainsbyproobonn/acrossplainsbyproobonn_djvu.txt.

Longmire, J. L., M. Maltbie, R. W. Pavelka, L. M. Smith, S. M. Witte, O. A. Ryder, D. L. Ellsworth, and R. J. Baker. 1993. Gender identification in birds using microsatellite DNA fingerprint analysis. *Auk* 110:378–381.

Low, B. S. 2000. *Why Sex Matters: A Darwinian Look at Human Behavior*. Princeton University Press, Princeton.

Luy, M. 2003. Causes of male excess mortality: Insights from cloistered populations. *Population and Development Review* 29:647–676.

Ma, W., C. Yang, C. Chu, T. Li, J. Tan, and H. Kan. 2013. The impact of the 2008 cold spell on mortality in Shanghai, China. *International Journal of Biometeorology* 57:179–184.

Maccoby, E. E. 1998. *The Two Sexes*. Belknap Press of Harvard University Press, Cambridge.

Macintyre, K. 2002. Famine and the female mortality advantage. In *Famine Demography: Perspectives from the Past and Present*, edited by T. Dyson and C. Ó Gráda, pp. 240–259. Oxford University Press, Oxford.

Macnab, A. J., and M. Bennett. 2005. Refrigerator blindness: Selective loss of visual acuity in association with a common foraging behavior. *Canadian Medical Association Journal* 173:1494–1495.

Madsen, S. A. 1998. *The Second Rescue: The Story of the Spiritual Rescue of the Willie and Martin Handcart Pioneers*. Deseret Book, Salt Lake City.

Maklakov, A. S., and V. Lummaa. 2013. Evolution of sex differences in lifespan and aging: Causes and constraints. *Bioessays* 35:717–724.

Malina, R. M. 2005. Variation in body composition associated with sex and ethnicity. In *Human Body Composition*, edited by S. B. Heymsfield, T. G. Lohman, Z. Wang, and S. B. Going, pp. 271–298. 2nd ed., Human Kinetics, Champaign, IL.

Manly, W. L. 1977. *Death Valley in '49*. Facsimile reprint of the 1894 edition. Chalfant Press, Bishop, CA.

Mataud, M. P. 2004. Gender differences in stress and coping style. *Personality and Individual Differences* 37:1401–1415.

Mayr, E. 1966. *Animal Species and Evolution*. Harvard University Press, Cambridge.

McArdle, W. D., F. I. Katch, and V. L. Katch. 2007. *Exercise Physiology: Energy, Nutrition, and Human Performance*. 6th ed. Lippincott Williams & Wilkins, Philadelphia.

McBurney, D. H., S. J. C. Gaulin, T. Devineni, and C. Adams. 1997. Superior spatial memory of women: Stronger evidence for the gathering hypothesis. *Evolution and Human Behavior* 18:165–174.

McClure, C. K., J. Catov, R. Ness, and E. B. Schwarz. 2012. Maternal visceral adiposity by consistency of lactation. *Maternal and Child Health Journal* 16:316–321.

McFarland, R. 1997. Female primates: Fat or fit? In *The Evolving Female: A Life History Perspective*, edited by M. E. Morbeck, A. Galloway, and A. L. Zihlman, pp. 163–175. Princeton University Press, Princeton.

McGlashan, C. F. 1947. *History of the Donner Party: A Tragedy of the Sierra*. Facsimile reproduction of the 1880 edition. Stanford University Press, Stanford.

McLaughlin, M. 2007. *The Donner Party: Weathering the Storm*. Mic Mac Publishing, Carnelian Bay, CA.

McLean, C. P., and E. R. Anderson. 2009. Brave men and timid women: A review of the gender differences in fear and anxiety. *Clinical Psychology Review* 29:496–505

McLean, C. P., A. Asnaani, B. T. Litz, and S. G. Hofmann. 2011. Gender differences in anxiety disorders: Prevalence, course of illness, comorbidity and burden of illness. *Journal of Psychiatric Research* 45:1027–1035.

McMillen, M. M. 1979. Differential mortality by sex in fetal and neonatal deaths. *Science* 204:89–91.

Meiri, S. 2011. Bergmann's rule—what's in a name? *Global Ecology and Biogeography* 20:203–207.

Meiri, S., and T. Dayan. 2003. On the validity of Bergmann's rule. *Journal of Biogeography* 30:331–351.

Meiri, S., Y. Yom-Tov, and E. Geffen. 2007. What determines conformity to Bergmann's rule? *Global Ecology and Biogeography* 16:788–794.

Miller, A. E. J., J. D. MacDougall, M. A. Tarnopolsky, and D. G. Sale. 1993. Gender differences in strength and muscle fiber characteristics. *European Journal of Applied Physiology and Occupational Physiology* 66:254–262.

Miller, S. C., C. C. Kennedy, D. C. DeVoe, M. Hickey, T. Nelson, and L. Kogan. 2015. An examination of changes in oxytocin levels in men and women before and after interaction with a bonded dog. *Anthrozoös* 22:31–42.

Min, K.-J., C.-K. Lee, and H.-N. Park. 2012. The lifespan of Korean eunuchs. *Current Biology* 22:R792–R793.

Moffat, S. D., E. Hampson, and M. Hatzipantelis. 1998. Navigation in a "virtual" maze: Sex differences and correlation with psychometric measures of spatial ability in humans. *Evolution and Human Behavior* 19:73–87.

Montesanto, A., V. Latorre, M. Giordano, C. Martino, F. Domma, and G. Passarino. 2011. The genetic component of human longevity: Analysis of the survival advantage of parents and siblings of Italian nonagenarians. *European Journal of Human Genetics* 19:882–886.

Morgan, D. L. 1963. *Overland in 1846: Diaries and Letters of the California–Oregon Trail.* University of Nebraska Press, Lincoln.

Morgan, D. L. 1964. *Jedediah Smith and the Opening of the West.* University of Nebraska Press, Lincoln.

Mullen, F., Jr. 1997. *The Donner Party Chronicles.* Nevada Humanities Committee, Reno.

Murphy, M., E. Grundy, and S. Kalogirou. 2007. The increase in marital status differences in mortality up to the oldest age in seven European countries, 1990–99. *Population Studies* 61:287–298.

Murphy, S. L., J. Xu, and K. D. Kochanek. 2013. Deaths: Final data for 2010. *National Vital Statistics Reports* 61(4):1–117.

Murphy, V. R. 1980. *Across the Plains in the Donner Party: A Personal Narrative of the Overland Trip to California 1846–1847.* Outbooks, Golden, CO.

Musick, M. A., J. S. House, and D. R. Williams. 2004. Attendance at religious services and mortality in a national sample. *Journal of Health and Social Behavior* 45:198–213.

Nagasawa, M., S. Mitsui, S. En, N. Ohtani, Y. Sakuma, T. Onaka, K. Mogi, and T. Kikusui. 2015. Oxytocin-gaze positive loop and the coevolution of human-dog bonds. *Science* 348:333–336.

National Center for Health Statistics. 2011. *Health, United States, 2010: With Special Feature on Death and Dying.* Publication 2011–1232. U.S. Department of Health and Human Services, Hyattsville, MD. Electronic document, http://www.cdc.gov/nchs/data/hus/hus10.pdf.

National Center for Health Statistics. 2012. *Health, United States, 2011: With Special Feature on Socioeconomic Status and Health.* Publication 2012–1232. U.S. Department of Health and Human Services. Hyattsville, MD. Electronic document, http://www.cdc.gov/nchs/data/hus/hus11.pdf.

National Highway Traffic Safety Administration. 2014. *Traffic Safety Facts 2012: A Compilation of Motor Vehicle Crash Data from the Fatality Analysis Reporting System and the General Estimates System.* DOT HS 812 032. U.S. Department of Transportation, Washington, DC.

National Highway Traffic Safety Administration. 2015. *Traffic Safety Facts: 2013 Data.* DOT HS 812 169. U.S. Department of Transportation, Washington, DC.

National Park Service. 2012. *National Historic Trails Auto Tour Interpretive Guide: Across Nevada.* National Trails Intermountain Region, National Park Service, Washington, DC.

Neal, D. M., J. B. Perry, Jr., K. Green, and R. Hawkins. 1988. Patterns of giving and receiving help during severe winter conditions: A research note. *Disasters* 12:366–374.

Neumayer, E. and T. Plümper. 2007. The gendered nature of natural disasters: The impact of catastrophic events on the gender gap in life expectancy, 1981–2002. *Annals of the Association of American Geographers* 97:551–566.

Ngun, T. C., N. Ghahramani, F. J. Sánchez, S. Bocklandt, and E. Vilain. 2011. The genetics of sex differences in brain and behavior. *Frontiers in Neuroendocrinology* 32:227–246.

Nieschlag, E., S. Nieschlag, and H. M. Behre. 1993. Lifespan and testosterone. *Nature* 366:215.

Northcutt, W. 2003. *The Darwin Awards III: Survival of the Fittest.* Dutton, New York.

Novak, S. A., and K. J. Dixon. 2011. Introduction. In *An Archaeology of Desperation: Exploring the Donner Party's Alder Creek Camp*, edited by K. J. Dixon, J. M. Schablitsky, and S. A. Novak, pp. 1–27. University of Oklahoma Press, Norman.

Nunis, D. B., Jr., editor. 1991. *The Bidwell-Bartleson Party: 1841 California Emigrant Adventure.* Western Tanager Press, Santa Cruz.

Nuzzo, R. 2014. Statistical errors. *Nature* 506:150–152.

Ó Gráda, C. 2009. *Famine: A Short History.* Princeton University Press, Princeton.

Olff, M., J. L. Frijling, L. D. Kubzansky, B. Bradley, M. A. Ellenbogen, C. Cardoso, J. A. Bartz, J. R. Yee, and M. van Zuiden. 2013. The role of oxytocin in social bonding, stress regulation and mental health: An update on the moderating effects of context and interindividual differences. *Psychoneuroendocrinology* 38:1883–1894.

Olsen, A. D. 2006. *The Price We Paid: The Extraordinary Story of the Willie and Martin Handcart Pioneers.* Deseret Book, Salt Lake City.

Olsen, A. D., and J. S. Allphin. 2013. *Follow Me to Zion.* Deseret Book, Salt Lake City.

O'Neill, M. S., A. Zanobetti, and J. Schwartz. 2003. Modifiers of the temperature and mortality association in seven US cities. *American Journal of Epidemiology* 157:1074–1082.

Orzack S. H., J. W. Stubblefield, V. R. Akmaev, P. Colls, S. Munné, T. Scholl, D. Steinsaltz, and J. E. Zuckerman. 2015. The human sex ratio from conception to birth. *Proceedings of the National Academy of Sciences* 112: E2102–E2111.

Ou, C. Q., Y. F. Song, J. Yang, P. Y. Chau, L. Yang, P. Y. Chen, and C. M. Wong. 2013. Excess winter mortality and cold temperatures in a subtropical city, Guangzhou, China. *PLoS One* 8(10):e77150

Palmer, J. 1906. Journal of travels over the Rocky Mountains, to the mouth of the Columbia River. In *Early Western Travels*, Vol. 30, edited by R. G. Thwaites, pp. 21–311. Arthur H. Clark, Cleveland.

Paternostro, G. 1994. Longevity and testosterone. *Nature* 368:408.

Paterson, J. D. 1990. Comment—Bergmann's rule is invalid: A reply to V. Geist. *Canadian Journal of Zoology* 68:1610–1612.

Pawlowski, B., R. Atwal, and R. I. M. Dunbar. 2008. Sex differences in everyday risk-taking behavior. *Evolutionary Psychology* 6:29–42.

Petree, S. A., editor. 2006. *Recollections of Past Days: The Autobiography of Patience Loader Rozsa Archer.* Utah State University Press, Logan.

Pike, I. L., and L. A. Milligan. 2010. Pregnancy and lactation. In *Human Evolutionary Biology*, edited by M. P. Muehlenbein, pp. 338–350. Cambridge University Press, Cambridge.

Pond, C. M. 1992. An evolutionary and functional view of mammalian adipose tissue. *Proceedings of the Nutrition Society* 51:367–377.

Pond, C. M. 1997. The biological origins of adipose tissue in humans. In *The Evolving Female: A Life History Perspective*, edited by M. E. Morbeck, A. Galloway, and A. L. Zihlman, pp. 147–162. Princeton University Press, Princeton.

Pond, C. M. 1998. *The Fats of Life*. Cambridge University Press, Cambridge.

Pond, C. M. 1999. Physiological specialisation of adipose tissue. *Progress in Lipid Research* 38:225–248.

Pond, C. M., and C. A. Mattacks. 1987. The anatomy of adipose tissue in captive *Macaca* monkeys and its implications for human biology. *Folia Primatologia* 48:164–185.

Pond, C. M., C. A. Mattacks, R. H. Colby, and M. A. Ramsay. 1992. The anatomy, chemical composition, and metabolism of adipose tissue in wild polar bears (*Ursus maritimus*). *Canadian Journal of Zoology* 70:326–341.

Pond, C. M., C. A. Mattacks, R. H. Colby, and N. J. C. Tyler. 1993. The anatomy, chemical composition and maximum glycolytic capacity of adipose tissue in wild Svalbard reindeer (*Rangifer tarandus platyrhynchus*) in winter. *Journal of Zoology* 229:17–40.

Pond, C. M., and M. A. Ramsay. 1992. Allometry of the distribution of adipose tissue in Carnivora. *Canadian Journal of Zoology* 70:342–347.

Pratt, P. P. 1840. Prospectus of the Latter-day Saints. *Millennial Star*. Electronic document, https://ia801403.us.archive.org/30/items/prospectusoflattooprat /prospectusoflattooprat.pdf.

Preston, S. H., N. Keyfitz, and R. Schoen. 1972. *Causes of Death: Life Tables for National Populations*. Seminar Press, New York.

Pugh, L. G. C. E. 1966. Accidental hypothermia in walkers, climbers, and campers: Report to the Medical Commission on Accident Prevention. *British Medical Journal* 1(5480):123–129.

Qureshi, A. I., M. Z. Memon, G. Vazquez, and M. F. K. Suri. 2009. Cat ownership and the risk of fatal cardiovascular diseases. Results from the second National Health and Nutrition Examination Study Mortality Follow-up Study. *Journal of Vascular and Interventional Neurology* 2:132–135.

Rarick, E. 2008. *Desperate Passage*. Oxford University Press, Oxford.

Rattarasarn, C., R. Leelawattana, S. Soonthornpun, W. Setasuban, and A. Thamprasit. 2004. Gender differences of regional abdominal fat distribution and their relationships with insulin sensitivity in healthy and glucose-intolerant Thais. *Journal of Clinical Endocrinology & Metabolism* 89:6266–6270.

Regan, J. C., and L. Partridge. 2013. Gender and longevity: Why do men die earlier than women? Comparative and experimental evidence. *Best Practice & Research Clinical Endocrinology & Metabolism* 27:467–479.

Rennie, D. W., B. G. Covino, B. J. Howell, S. H. Song, B. S. Kang, and S. K. Hong. 1962. Physical insulation of Korean diving women. *Journal of Applied Physiology* 17:961–966.

Richards, F. D., and D. Spencer. 1856. Journey from Florence to G. S. L. City. Journal History, October 4, 1856. Electronic document, https://history.lds.org /overlandtravels/sources/8762/journey-from-florence-to-g-s-l-city-deseret-news -weekly-22-october-1856-258.

Rivers, J. P. W. 1982. Women and children last: An essay on sex discrimination in disasters. *Disasters* 6:256–267.

Rivers, J. P. W. 1988. The nutritional biology of famine. In *Famine*, edited by G. A. Harrison, pp. 57–106. Oxford University Press, Oxford.

Riverton Wyoming Stake. n.d. *Second Rescue Mission Files*. Manuscript on file at the History Department Library, Church of Jesus Christ of Latter-day Saints, Salt Lake City.

Roberts, D. 2008. *Devil's Gate: Brigham Young and the Great Mormon Handcart Tragedy*. Simon & Schuster, New York.

Roberts, D. F. 1953. Body weight, race, and climate. *American Journal of Physical Anthropology* 11:533–558.

Roberts, D. F. 1978. *Climate and Human Variability*. 2nd ed. Cummings, Menlo Park, CA.

Rogers, R. G., B. G. Everett, J. M. Saint Onge, and P. M Krueger. 2010. Social, behavioral, and biological factors and sex differences in mortality. *Demography* 47:555–578.

Rogerson, J. 1879. Reminiscence [1879], 22–28. Electronic document, https://history.lds.org/overlandtravels/sources/18999/rogerson-josiah-reminiscence-1879-22-28.

Rogerson, J. 1907a. Captain J. G. Willie's or, the Fourth Handcart Company of 1856 [No. 1], *Salt Lake Herald*, December 15. Electronic document, https://history.lds.org/overlandtravels/sources/20905/rogerson-josiah-captain-j-g-willie-s-or-the-fourth-handcart-company-of-1856-no-1-salt-lake-herald-15-dec-1907.

Rogerson, J. 1907b. Martin's Handcart Company, 1856 [No. 3], *Salt Lake Herald*, October 27. Electronic document, https://history.lds.org/overlandtravels/sources/20888/rogerson-josiah-martin-s-handcart-company-1856-no-3-salt-lake-herald-27-october-1907.

Rogerson, J. 1907c. Martin's Handcart Company, 1856 [No. 4], *Salt Lake Herald*, November 3. Electronic document, https://history.lds.org/overlandtravels/sources/20889/rogerson-josiah-martin-s-handcart-company-1856-no-4-salt-lake-herald-3-november-1907.

Rogerson, J. 1907d. Martin's Handcart Company, 1856 [No. 5], *Salt Lake Herald*, November 10. Electronic document, https://history.lds.org/overlandtravels/sources/20890/rogerson-josiah-martin-s-handcart-company-1856-no-5-salt-lake-herald-10-november-1907.

Rogerson, J. 1907e. Martin's Handcart Company, 1856 [No. 6], *Salt Lake Herald*, November 17. Electronic document, https://history.lds.org/overlandtravels/sources/20891/rogerson-josiah-martin-s-handcart-company-1856-no-6-salt-lake-herald-17-november-1907.

Rogerson, J. 1907f. Martin's Handcart Company, 1856 [No. 9], *Salt Lake Herald*, December 1. https://history.lds.org/overlandtravels/sources/20893/rogerson-josiah-martin-s-handcart-company-1856-no-9-salt-lake-herald-1-december-1907.

Rogerson, J. 1913. Tells Story of Trials of the Handcart Pioneers. *Salt Lake Tribune*, November 30, 11. Electronic document, https://history.lds.org/overlandtravels/sources/7750/rogerson-josiah-tells-story-of-trials-of-the-handcart-pioneers-salt-lake-tribune-30-nov-1913-11.

Rogerson, J. 1914. Strong Men, Brave Women and Sturdy Children Crossed the Wilderness Afoot. *Salt Lake Tribune*, January 4. Electronic document, https://history.lds.org/overlandtravels/sources/9480/rogerson-josiah-sr-strong-men-brave-women-and-sturdy-children-crossed-the-wilderness-afoot-in-salt-lake-tribune-4-jan-1914.

Rohner, R. 1976. Sex differences in aggression: Phylogenetic and enculturation perspectives. *Ethos* 4:57–72.

Rolle, A. 1991. *John Charles Frémont: Character as Destiny.* University of Oklahoma Press, Norman.

Ronay, R., and W. von Hippel. 2010. The presence of an attractive woman elevates testosterone and physical risk taking in young men. *Social Psychological and Personality Science* 1:57–64.

Saely, C. H., K. Geiger, and H. Drexel. 2012. Brown versus white adipose tissue: A minireview. *Gerontology* 58:15–23.

Scalfari, A., V. Knappertz, G. Cutter, D. S. Goodin, R. Ashton, and G. C. Ebers. 2013. Mortality in patients with multiple sclerosis. *Neurology* 81:184–192.

Schaefer, O. 1977. Are Eskimos more or less obese than other Canadians? A comparison of skinfold thickness and ponderal index in Canadian Eskimos. *American Journal of Clinical Nutrition* 30:1623–1628.

Schoenbach, V. J., B. H. Kaplan, L. Fredman, and D. G. Kleinbaum. 1986. Social ties and mortality in Evans County, Georgia. *American Journal of Epidemiology* 123:577–591.

Schreiner, P. J., J. G. Terry, G. W. Evans, W. H. Hinson, J. R. Crouse III, and G. Heiss. 1996. Sex-specific associations of magnetic resonance imaging-derived intra-abdominal and subcutaneous fat areas with conventional anthropometric indices: The Atherosclerosis Risk in Communities Study. *American Journal of Epidemiology* 144:335–345.

Schwartz, J. 2005. Who is sensitive to extremes of temperature? A case-only analysis. *Epidemiology* 16:67–72.

Sebastiani, P., and T. T. Perls. 2012. The genetics of extreme longevity: Lessons from the New England Centenarian study. *Frontiers in Genetics* 3(277):1–7.

Sebastiani, P., et al. (16 authors). 2012. Genetic signatures of exceptional longevity in humans. *PLoS One* 7(1):e29848.

Seifarth, J. F., C. L. McGowan, and K. J. Milne. 2012. Sex and life expectancy. *Gender Medicine* 9:390–401.

Shephard, R. J., and A. Rode. 1976. On the body composition of the Eskimo. In *Circumpolar Health*, edited by R. J. Shephard and S. Itoh, pp. 91–97. University of Toronto Press, Toronto.

Shores, M. M., A. M. Matsumoto, K. L. Sloan, and D. R. Kivlahan. 2006. Low serum testosterone and mortality in male veterans. *Archives of Internal Medicine* 166:1660–1665.

Sidebottom, A. C., J. E. Brown, and D. R. Jacobs, Jr. 2001. Pregnancy-related changes in body fat. *European Journal of Obstetrics & Gynecology and Reproductive Biology* 94:216–223.

Silverman, I., J. Choi, and M. Peters. 2007. The hunter-gatherer theory of sex differences in spatial abilities: Data from 40 countries. *Archives of Sexual Behavior* 36:261–268.

Sjöström, L. 1988. Measurement of fat distribution. In *Fat Distribution during Growth and Later Health Outcomes*, edited by C. Bouchard and F. E. Johnston, pp. 43–61. Liss, New York.

Slagboom, P. E., et al. (14 authors). 2011. Genomics of human longevity. *Philosophical Transactions of the Royal Society B* 366:35–42.

Smith, D. C., K. M. Schrieber, A. Saltos, S. B. Lichenstein, and R. Lichenstein. 2013. Ambulatory cell phone injuries in the United States: An emerging national concern. *Journal of Safety Research* 47:19–23.

Smith, E. A., R. Bliege Bird, and D. W. Bird. 2003. The benefits of costly signaling: Meriam turtle hunters. *Behavioral Ecology* 14: 116–126.

Smith, J. 1850. Who Is the Liar? *Millennial Star* 12(2): 29–31.

Snow, W. 1852. Intelligence from Denmark, Norway, and Sweden. *Millennial Star* 14(35): 557–558.

Speakman, J. R. 2005. Body size, energy metabolism and lifespan. *Journal of Experimental Biology* 208:1717–1730.

Spence, M. L., and D. Jackson, editors. 1973. *The Expeditions of John Charles Frémont*, Vol. 2: *The Bear Flag Revolt and the Court-Martial*. University of Illinois Press, Urbana.

Stenhouse, F. 1875. *"Tell it All": The Story of a Life's Existence in Mormonism*. Worthington, Hartford.

Stenhouse, T. B. H. 1873. *The Rocky Mountain Saints: A Full and Complete History of the Mormons*. Appleton, New York.

Stephenson, L. A., and M. A. Kolka. 1993. Thermoregulation in women. *Exercise and Sport Sciences Reviews* 21:231–262.

Stewart, G. R. 1953. *The Opening of the California Trail*. University of California Press, Berkeley.

Stewart, G. R. 1960. *Ordeal by Hunger: The Story of the Donner Party*. Houghton Mifflin, Boston.

Stewart, G. R. 1962. *The California Trail: An Epic with Many Heroes*. University of Nebraska Press, Lincoln.

Stindl, R. 2004. Tying it all together: Telomeres, sexual size dimorphism and the gender gap in life expectancy. *Medical Hypotheses* 62:151–154.

Stine, S. 2015. *A Way across the Mountain: Joseph Walker's 1833 Trans-Sierran Passage and the Myth of Yosemite's Discover*. Arthur H. Clark, Norman.

Stini, W. A. 1981. Body composition and nutrient reserves in evolutionary perspective. *World Review of Nutrition and Dietetics* 37:55–83.

Stinson, S. 1985. Sex differences in environmental sensitivity during growth and development. *Yearbook of Physical Anthropology* 28:123–147.

Stirling, I. 1988. *Polar Bears*. University of Michigan Press, Ann Arbor.

Stocks, J. M., N. A. S. Taylor, M. J. Tipton, and J. E. Greenleaf. 2004. Human physiological responses to cold exposure. *Aviation, Space, and Environmental Medicine* 75:444–457.

Taniguchi, Y., R. Lenhardt, D. I. Sessler, and A. Kurz. 2011. The effect of altering skin-surface cooling speeds on vasoconstriction and shivering thresholds. *Anesthesia & Analgesia* 113:540–544.

Taylor, J. 1855. Hand carts for the Plains. *The Mormon*, December 1, 2. Electronic document, https://history.lds.org/overlandtravels/sources/7891/hand-carts-for-the-plains-the-mormon-1-dec-1855-2.

Taylor, N. A. S., I. B. Mekjavic, and M. J. Tipton. 2008. The physiology of acute cold exposure, with particular reference to human performance in the cold. In *Physiological Bases of Human Performance during Work and Exercise*, edited by N. A. S. Taylor and H. Groeller, pp. 359–377. Elsevier, Edinburgh.

Taylor, S. E., L. C. Klein, B. P. Lewis, T. L. Gruenewald, R. A. Gurung, and J. A. Upde-graff. 2000. Biobehavioral responses to stress in females: Tend-and-befriend, not fight-or-flight. *Psychological Review* 107:411–429.

The Church of Jesus Christ of Latter-day Saints. 2015a. Edward Martin Company (1856). Electronic document, https://history.lds.org/overlandtravels/companies/192.

The Church of Jesus Christ of Latter-day Saints. 2015b. James G. Willie Company (1856). Electronic document, https://history.lds.org/overlandtravels/companies/319 /james-g-willie-company.

Thornton, J. Q. 1986. *Camp of Death: The Donner Party Mountain Camp, 1846–1847.* Outbooks, Golden, CO.

Thorslund, M., J. W. Wastesson, N. Agahi, M. Lagergren, and M. G. Parker. 2013. The rise and fall of women's advantage: A comparison of national trends in life expectancy at age 65 years. *European Journal of Aging* 10:271–277.

Tikuisis, P., D. G. Bell, and I. Jacobs. 1991. Shivering onset, metabolic response, and convective heat transfer during cold air exposure. *Journal of Applied Physiology* 70:1996–2002.

Tilkens, M. J., C. Wall-Scheffler, T. D. Weaver, and K. Steudel-Numbers. 2007. The effects of body proportions on thermoregulation: An experimental assessment of Allen's rule. *Journal of Human Evolution* 53:286–291.

Treves, A., and A. Naughton-Treves. 1999. Risk and opportunity for humans coexisting with large carnivores. *Journal of Human Evolution* 36:275–282.

Trovato, F., and N. M. Lalu. 1996. Narrowing sex differentials in life expectancy in the industrialized world: Early 1970s to early 1990s. *Social Biology* 43:20–37.

Trussell, J. 1995. Women's longevity. *Science* 270:719–720.

Tuckel, P., W. Milczarski, and R. Maisel. 2014. Pedestrian injuries due to collisions with bicycles in New York and California. *Journal of Safety Research* 51:7–13.

Turner, J. G. 2012. *Brigham Young: Pioneer Prophet.* Harvard University Press, Cambridge.

Turner, L. S. 1996. *Emigrating Journals of the Willie and Martin Handcart Companies and the Hunt and Hodgett Wagon Trains.* Privately published.

Udry, J. R. 1994. The nature of gender. *Demography* 31:561–573.

United Nations. 2011. World Population Prospects: The 2010 Revision, Vol. II: *Demo-graphic Profiles.* United Nations, New York.

United Nations. 2013. *World Population Prospects: The 2012 Revision.* Department of Economic and Social Affairs, Population Division, United Nations. Files MORT/4-2 (Male deaths by five-year age group, major area, region, and country: POP/DB /WPP/Rev.2012/Mort/F04-2) and MORT/4-3 (Female deaths by five-year age group, major area, region, and country: POP/DB/WPP/Rev.2012/Mort/F04-3).

Unruh, J. D., Jr. 1979. *The Plains Across: The Overland Emigrants and the Trans-Mississippi West, 1840–1860.* University of Illinois Press, Urbana.

van der Lans, A. A., et al. (12 authors). 2013. Cold acclimation recruits human brown fat and increases nonshivering thermogenesis. *Journal of Clinical Investigations* 123:3395–3403.

van Marken Lichtenbelt, W. D., and P. Schrauwen. 2011. Implications of nonshivering thermogenesis for energy balance regulation in humans. *American Journal of Physi-ology—Regulatory, Integrative and Comparative Physiology* 301: R285–R296.

van Marken Lichtenbelt, W. D., J. W. Vanhommerig, N. M. Smulders, J. M. A. F. L. Drossaerts, G. J. Kemerink, N. D. Bouvy, P. Schrauwen, and G. J. J. Teule. 2009. Cold-activated brown adipose tissue in healthy men. *New England Journal of Medicine* 360:1500–1508.

Van Someren, E. J. W. 2011. Age-related changes in thermoreception and thermoregulation. In *Handbook of the Biology of Aging*, edited by E. J. Masoro and S. N. Austad, pp. 463–478. 7th ed. Academic Press, San Diego.

Vaupel, J. W. 2010. Biodemography of human aging. *Nature* 464:536–542.

Verbrugge, L. M. 1985. Gender and health: An update on hypotheses and evidence. *Journal of Health and Social Behavior* 26:156–182.

Verbrugge, L. M., and D. L. Wingard. 1987. Sex differentials in health and mortality. *Women & Health* 12:103–145.

Virtanen, K. A., et al. (11 authors). 2009. Functional brown adipose tissue in healthy adults. *New England Journal of Medicine* 360:1518–1525.

Wagner, J. A., and S. M. Horvath. 1985. Influences of age and gender on human thermoregulatory responses to cold exposures. *Journal of Applied Physiology* 58:180–186.

Waite, A. J., and E. L. Lehrer. 2003. The benefits from marriage and religion in the United States: A comparative analysis. *Population and Development Review* 29:255–276.

Waldron, I. 1983. Sex differences in human mortality: The role of genetic factors. *Social Science and Medicine* 17:321–333.

Waldron, I. 1986. What do we know about causes of sex differences in mortality? A review of the literature. *Population Bulletin of the United Nations* 18-1985:59–76.

Waldron, I. 1993. Recent trends in sex mortality ratios for adults in developed countries. *Social Science and Medicine* 36:451–462.

Waldron, I. 2009. Gender differences in mortality—Causes and variation in different societies. In *The Sociology of Health & Illness: Critical Perspectives*, edited by P. Conrad, pp. 38–55. 8th ed. Worth, New York.

Walker, R. W. 1974. The Stenhouses and the making of a Mormon image. *Journal of Mormon History* 1:51–72.

Wallace, J. E. 1996. Gender differences in beliefs of why women live longer than men. *Psychological Reports* 79:587–591.

Wang, Y., K. Hunt, I. Nazareth, N. Freemantle, and I. Petersen. 2013. Do men consult less than women? An analysis of routinely collected UK general practice data. *BMJ Open* 3: e003320, doi:10.1136/bmjopen-2013-003320.

Wardle, M. G., M. R. Gloss, and D. S. Gloss III. 1987. Response differences. In *Sex Differences in Human Performance*, edited by M. A. Baker, pp. 107–120. Wiley and Sons, Chichester.

Wasserstein, R. L., and N. A. Lazar. 2016. The ASA's statement on *p*-values: Context, process, and purpose. *American Statistician*, doi:10.1080/00031305.2016.1154108.

Wells, J. C. K. 2012. The evolution of human adiposity and obesity: Where did it all go wrong? *Disease Models & Mechanisms* 5:595–607.

Whitacre, C. C., et al. (15 authors). 1999. A gender gap in autoimmunity. *Science* 283:1277–1278.

White, D. A., compiler and annotator. 1997. *News of the Plains and Rockies: 1803–1865*, Vol. 3. Arthur H. Clark, Spokane.

Widdowson, E. M. 1976. The response of the sexes to nutritional stress. *Proceedings of the Nutrition Society* 35:175–180.

Willie, J. G. 1856. Synopsis of the 4th Handcart Company's trip from Liverpool, England, to Great Salt Lake City in the spring, summer and autumn of 1856. Journal History, November 9, 1856.

Wingard, D. L. 1984. The sex differential in morbidity, mortality, and lifestyle. *Annual Review of Public Health* 5:433–458.

Wisser, O., and J. W. Vaupel. 2014. *The Sex Differential in Mortality: A Historical Comparison of the Adult-Age Pattern of the Ratio and the Difference.* Max Planck Institute for Demographic Research Working Paper WP 2014-005.

Wood, W., and A. H. Eagly. 2002. A cross-cultural analysis of the behavior of women and men: Implications for the origins of sex differences. *Psychological Bulletin* 128:699–727.

Wood, W., and A. H. Eagly. 2012. Biosocial construction of sex differences and similarities in behavior. *Advances in Experimental Social Psychology* 46:55–123.

Woodruff, W. 1856. Letter to Geo. A. Smith. Journal History, October 31, 1856.

Woodruff, W. 1857. Letter to the Editor of the *Western Standard. Millennial Star* 19(12):188.

Woodward, W. 1856. James G. Willie Emigrating Company Journal, May–November, 16–53. Electronic document, https://history.lds.org/overlandtravels/sources/7439/james-g-willie-emigrating-company-journal-1856-may-nov-16-53.

Woodward, W. 1857. Additional information of Capt. Willie's handcart company. Journal History, November 9, 1856.

World Bank. 2015. World Development Indicators: Health Risk Factors and Future Challenges. Electronic document, http://wdi.worldbank.org/table/2.20.

World Health Organization. 2014. Global Health Estimates Summary Tables: Deaths by cause, age, and sex, 2000–2012. World Health Organization, Geneva.

Wyndham, C. H., et al. (10 authors). 1964. Physiological reactions to cold of Caucasian females. *Journal of Applied Physiology* 19:877–880.

Xuan, L. T. T., T. Egondi, L. T. Ngoan, D. T. T. Toan, and L. T. Huong. 2014. Seasonality in mortality and its relationship to temperature among the older population in Hanoi, Vietnam. *Global Health Action* 7:23115.

Yeap, B. B., H. Alfonso, S. A. Chubb, D. J. Handelsman, G. J. Hankey, O. P. Almeida, J. Golledge, P. E. Norman, and L. Flicker. 2014. In older men an optimal plasma testosterone is associated with reduced all-cause mortality and higher dihydrotestosterone with reduced ischemic heart disease mortality, while estradiol levels do not predict mortality. *Journal of Clinical Endocrinology & Metabolism* 99:E9–E18.

Young, B. 1856a. Remarks by President Brigham Young. Journal History, October 5, 1856.

Young, B. 1856b. Remarks by President Brigham Young. Journal History, November 2, 1856.

Young, B. 1856c. Remarks by President Brigham Young. Journal History, November 16, 1856.

Young, B. 1857. Letter to George Q. Cannon. *Millennial Star* 19(12):187–188.

Young, B., H. C. Kimball, W. Richards, and T. Bullock. 1849 [1997]. Second General Epistle of the Presidency of the Church of Jesus Christ of Latter-day Saints. . . .

In *News of the Plains and Rockies 1803–1865*, Vol. 3, compiled and annotated by D. A. White, pp. 212–225. Arthur H. Clark, Spokane.

Young, J. A. 1857. Remarks by Elder Joseph A. Young. *Millennial Star* 19(12):186.

Zhou, M. G., et al. (14 authors). 2014. Health impact of the 2008 cold spell on mortality in subtropical China: The climate and health impact national assessment study (CHINAs). *Environmental Health* 13:60, doi:10.1186/1476-069X-13-60.

Zick, C. D., and K. R. Smith. 1991. Marital transitions, poverty, and gender differences in mortality. *Journal of Marriage and Family* 53:327–336.

Zihlman, A. L. 1997. Women's bodies, women's lives: An evolutionary perspective. In *The Evolving Female: A Life History Perspective*, edited by M. E. Morbeck, A. Galloway, and A. L. Zihlman, pp. 185–197. Princeton University Press, Princeton.

Zihlman, A. L., and D. R. Bolter. 2015. Body composition in *Pan paniscus* compared with *Homo sapiens* has implications for changes during human evolution. *Proceedings of the National Academy of Sciences* 112:7466–7471.

INDEX

Page numbers in *italics* refer to illustrations or tables.

of, 67–68, *69*; sex and timing of in Donner Party, 108–10; total number of for Willie Handcart Company, 140, 141; Willie Handcart Company and Rocky Ridge episode, 139. *See also* mortality
Death Valley in '49 (Manly 1894), 3–4
Decker, Peter, 207
decontextualization, and relationship between gender and death in context of emigrant trail, 205–9
DeLafosse, P. H., 62n7
demography: and structure of Martin Handcart Company, 181–85; and structure of Willie Handcart Company, 142–46. *See also* age; family; sex
Denmark, and life expectancy, 70
Denton, John, 47, 55, 58, 103
Deseret News, 139–40
Devil's Gate (Wyoming), 175, 177, 178
Dirck, B., 63n71
Dixon, Kelly, 61, 205, 206, 207, 208
dogs, and health benefits of pets, 89, 94n136
Dolan, Patrick, 51
Donner, Eliza, 30, 57, 61
Donner, Elizabeth, 30, 56, 59, 109
Donner, George, 30, 33, 38, 45, 56, 59, 106, 110, 123n20
Donner, Isaac, 58
Donner, Jacob, 30, 49, 56, 106
Donner, Leanna, 47–48
Donner, Lewis, 59
Donner, Mary, 59
Donner, Samuel, 59
Donner, Solomon Hook, 58
Donner, Tamzene, 30, 32, 45, 47, 56–57, 59, 60, 103, 106, 109, 110, 113, 206
Donner, William Hook, 56, 65–66
Donner Creek (California), 17
Donner Lake (California), 17, 18, 45, 46
Donner Party: age and mortality rates for, 86, 170n121, 185, 188, 200n72, *210, 211,* 213n36; age and sex composition of, 96–98; and cannibalism, 1, 50–52, 60, 61 ; and causes of death, 65–66; chronology of deaths, 102–10, 200n72; Willie Handcart Company compared to, 143, 144, 146–49, 150, 151, 165; conclusions on relationship between gender and death for, 201–12; departure and early route of, 29–31; establishment of camps and snow in Sierra Nevada, 45–50; family structure and survivorship in, 90, 155, 200n72;

and final relief effort, 61; and First Relief, 52–54, 213n20; human biology and pattern of deaths in, 120–22; names of members of, *36–37*; planning of route for, 9–10; prediction of patterns of death in, 90–91; public awareness of story, 1–2, 95; route of from Independence (Missouri) to Sierra Nevada, 31–45; routes of emigrants prior to, 10–29; and salvage operation, 60–61; and Second Relief, 54–58; sex and mortality rates for, 101–2, 108–10, 152–54, 170n121, 188, 190, 200n72, *210, 211,* 213n36; sources on, 8n3; spelling of names, 62–63n69; and Third Relief, 58–60
Dudley, Mary Ann, 169n108

Eagly, Alice H., 6, 73, 203, 208
Eddy, Eleanor, 52, 109, 110, 113
Eddy, James, 56, 59
Eddy, Margaret, 110
Eddy, William, 44, 45, 49, 50–52, 53, 58–60, 103, 112, 207
Edmonds, Charles, 174–75
Egan, Ferol, 12
Elder, Joseph B., 137
elderly: and age structure of Martin Handcart Company, 181, 182–83; deaths in Martin Handcart Company and Willie Handcart Company compared, 190; and mortality rates from cold and/or famine, 86. *See also* age
Elliot, Milt, 52
Ellsworth, Edmund, 169–70n108
Emigrants' Guide to Oregon and California, The (Hastings 1845), 9, 21, 22, 27, 40
emigration. *See* California; Donner Party; handcart companies; Martin Handcart Company; Oregon; Oregon Trail; wagons; Willie Handcart Company
Emigration Canyon (Utah), 38
Emslie, C., 212n1
England. *See* Great Britain
Europe: emigration of Mormon converts from, 127; and life expectancy by sex, 66

Fallon, William, 60, 103
family: and composition of Willie Handcart Company, 144, *145*; and impact of social ties on mortality rates, 89–90; and mortality in Willie Handcart Company, 155–66; size of and days-to-death in Donner Party, 117–20, 123n41, 123–24n43, 200n72; and survivorship